"A Cosmos of My Own":
Faulkner and Yoknapatawpha
1980

"A Cosmos of My Own"

FAULKNER AND YOKNAPATAWPHA
1980

EDITED BY
DOREEN FOWLER
AND
ANN J. ABADIE

UNIVERSITY PRESS OF MISSISSIPPI
JACKSON • 1981

DEDICATED TO
Dorothy Crosby

Library of Congress Cataloging in Publication Data
Faulkner and Yoknapatawpha Conference (7th : 1980 :
  University of Mississippi)
  "A Cosmos of my own."

  Contents: "Saying no to death" / Robert W. Hamblin—
The cubist novel / Panthea Reid Broughton—Faulkner's
cubist novels / Panthea Reid Broughton—[etc.]
  1. Faulkner, William 1897–1962—Criticism and
interpretation—Congresses. I. Fowler, Doreen. II.
Abadie, Ann J. III. Title.
PS3511.A86Z489   1980   813'.52   81–7430
ISBN 0–87805–142–2   AACR2
ISBN 0–87805–143–0 (pbk.)

Contents

Contents

Introduction

Each year since 1974, The University of Mississippi has invited eminent Faulkner scholars to speak at a conference honoring the Mississippi author who has caught and held the admiration of the world. Considered together, the essays presented at the 1980 Faulkner and Yoknapatawpha Conference suggest that Faulkner criticism is taking a new tack. Critics seem no longer satisfied to look at a single work, but are instead surveying the whole corpus of Faulkner's fiction. In describing his oeuvre, Faulkner used the image of a cosmos, implying that his fictional world, like a cosmos, is composed of interrelated parts which together form a vast, unified, and harmonious system. It is this unity and interrelationship among Faulkner's seemingly diverse novels which critics now seem disposed to explore. Most of the essayists whose works constitute this volume focus attention not on the single part, but on the whole, the repeated image, the emerging design. With this approach to Faulkner's fiction, critics implicitly acknowledge that no single aspect of Faulkner's far-reaching cosmos can be fully understood or accurately assessed in isolation from the whole.

Among the critics represented here, two, Ellen Douglas, in "Faulkner in Time," and James Carothers, in "The Road to *The Reivers*," examine the entire range of Faulkner's work, searching for an overall design and meaning. Others seek to

Introduction

understand the meaning of one aspect of Faulkner's fiction—a theme, motif, or figure—by tracing its appearance throughout Faulkner's canon, looking for significant repetitions and differences. For example, Charles Nilon's first lecture measures Faulkner's aristocrats, while his second talk focuses on the black characters in Faulkner's fiction. Similarly, Ellen Douglas's other essay takes a comprehensive look at Faulkner's characterization of women, and James Carothers's second talk surveys Faulkner's heroes. In "'Saying No to Death,'" Robert Hamblin argues that Faulkner's subjects and techniques are shaped by a common motivation—an attempt to deny the realities of time and death; and Panthea Reid Broughton, in two closely related essays, discusses Faulkner's works in terms of modernist art, showing how Faulkner's narrative techniques can be interpreted as literary analogues for the visual devices of cubist painters. Two lectures, L. D. Brodsky's "The Collector as Sleuthsayer" and François Pitavy's "The Gothicism of *Absalom, Absalom!*," diverge from this attempt to analyze Faulkner's works in a comprehensive way, and look instead at specialized areas of Faulkner criticism. In "The Collector as Sleuthsayer," Brodsky shares with us the experience of collecting rare Faulkner texts; and in "The Gothicism of *Absalom, Absalom!*" Pitavy examines the unusual uses to which Faulkner puts Gothic techniques in *Absalom, Absalom!*

In "Faulkner in Time," Ellen Douglas offers her assessment of Faulkner's cosmos. Douglas begins by describing her experience of reading Faulkner's works over the years. She first read Faulkner as a high school student and was mesmerized by his heroic treatment of moral issues and also by "that rolling, hypnotic, irresistible language." Reading Faulkner in college, Douglas saw that he was "obssessed with what it was at that moment essential for me to be obsessed with—what does it all mean?" As a young writer, Douglas learned, almost unconsciously, from Faulkner—about specific detail, imagery, and dialect. But, later, Douglas writes, she "fell out of love with Faulkner." Something happened, not only to her perception of Faulkner but to the work itself. The novels changed, and Douglas characterizes this evolution as a shift from "the glorious" to "the overblown," from "austerity and clarity" to "self-indulgence and confusion." Faulkner's later works, according to Douglas, are glosses written on the earlier novels, glosses meant to transform his earlier tragic vision, but which only succeed in confusing Faulkner's reader.

Like Douglas, James Carothers takes a long look at all of Faulkner's novels, paying particular attention to the puzzling later works. But whereas Douglas is critical of these works, Carothers finds reasons for their alleged shortcomings. In "The Road to *The Reivers*," Carothers shows how *The Reivers* represents the culmination of themes and techniques Faulkner had employed throughout his developing career. In *The Reivers*, Faulkner calls up incidents and situations from earlier novels and presents them from an altered perspective, leaving himself open to the dual charge of repeating himself and of changing his mind. Carothers argues that Faulkner is deliberately repeating himself to stress his changed vantage point. In other words, Faulkner is invoking the situations and incidents from earlier novels so that he can, in essence, rewrite these early novels expunging from them tragic alienation and substituting comic affirmation. To the charge that Faulkner repeated himself, Carothers replies that Faulkner "always repeated himself with a difference and to a purpose."

Charles Nilon, in two essays, also takes a sweeping look at Faulkner's canon, searching for significant patterns and repetitions in Faulkner's treatment of two groups of people: aristocrats and blacks. In "Cooper, Faulkner, and the American Venture," Nilon surveys Faulkner's aristocrats and compares them with the landed gentry in the works of James Fenimore

Introduction

Cooper. According to Nilon, both authors believe that man's innate rapacity is a threat to the American venture, but whereas Cooper idealizes the aristocratic class and confidently predicts that America will thrive as long as aristocrats control the nation's destiny, Faulkner's portrayal of the aristocracy leads to a somewhat less sanguine conclusion. In Faulkner's novels, upper-class characters are heir to the same infirmities as other characters and are as helpless as any other class to guarantee the survival of the American dream of freedom. Nilon's subsequent lecture, "Blacks in Motion," traces the theme of the black pilgrimage throughout Faulkner's novels. The blacks in Faulkner's fiction are "going to cross Jordan," or, in other words, are searching for freedom and identity. In examining this quest, Nilon finds that it involves "picture-breaking," i.e., a popular stereotype about black behavior is exposed as unfounded. For example, Nilon shows how a number of Faulkner's black characters, among them Lucas Beauchamp in *Go Down, Moses* and Rider in "Pantaloon in Black," contradict the stereotype of "the amorous black man," who is supposedly incapable of love.

While Nilon focuses on blacks and aristocrats in Faulkner's fiction, Ellen Douglas, in "Faulkner's Women," analyzes Faulkner's portrayal of female characters. Reading the whole of Faulkner's corpus from beginning to end, Ellen Douglas uncovers an "intensity of rage" toward women that startles her largely because this rage is so "disproportionate to the miserable creature who evokes it." In trying to understand this fury, Douglas posits this conclusion—that Faulkner idealizes women, expects from them perfection, and is therefore outraged by their shortcomings. Douglas sums up: "In this sense woman is wilderness is South is lost innocence is failed and sinful humanity. Of course Faulkner hates women."

Another essay which surveys the full scope of Faulkner's

fiction looking for patterns of interrelationship is James Carothers's "The Myriad Heart: The Evolution of the Faulkner
Hero." In this essay, Carothers focuses on the hero figure in
successive Faulkner novels and finds that in the course of
Faulkner's literary career his presentation of heroic action
changes gradually. Defining the hero as one who acts decisively at personal risk to restore community order, Carothers
notes that in Faulkner's early fiction, *Soldiers' Pay* through
Sanctuary, only the vicious are capable of decisive action; in
what Carothers terms the second stage of Faulkner's literary
career, *Light in August* through *Go Down, Moses*, individuals
are capable of at least occasionally making a heroic attempt
for the community; and in the last novels, *Intruder in the
Dust* through *The Reivers*, the protagonists work effectively
to oppose evil.

The essential unity of Faulkner's fictional world is also
stressed by Robert Hamblin. In "'Saying No to Death': Toward William Faulkner's Theory of Fiction," Hamblin asserts
that all of Faulkner's work is a denial of mortality. In other
words, the overriding ethic of Faulkner's fiction is an attempt
to repudiate time and death—the limitations of human existence. Hamblin contends that Faulkner's subjects and his
style work to achieve this same end. For example, relics or
art-surrogates in Faulkner's fiction, like Charles Bon's letter
or Cecilia Farmer's signature on the jailhouse window, resist
time by making the past live again. Faulkner's tendency to
romanticism and extravagance, to the grotesque and the marvelous, and to mythologizing are all attempts to improve on
reality, to reject the real world and substitute a better world.
Faulkner's characteristic long sentences, which string together successions of clauses, strain against time in an effort,
in Faulkner's own words, "to say everything in one sentence
because you may not live long enough to have two sen-

Introduction

tences." Hamblin concludes with an affirmation of Faulkner's faith in art. If, says Hamblin, Faulkner's assessment of man was perhaps pessimistic, Faulkner's estimation of art and its potential was never despairing, because art struggles nobly with time to create something that, as Faulkner expressed it, lasts "longer than anything."

Like the preceding lecturers, Panthea Reid Broughton, in two essays, takes for her subject the entire range of Faulkner's fictional world. But Broughton's stated goal differs somewhat from that of the other essayists. Whereas the other authors seek to uncover thematic patterns and interrelationships among Faulkner's novels, Broughton attempts to relate Faulkner's art to pictorial art and, in particular, to cubism. Broughton begins by arguing that literary criticism does not possess the terminology needed to describe modern fiction. Literary criticism, which traces its roots to the Renaissance, upholds classical values: coherence and unity; while the modern novel is deliberately discontinuous, refusing to trace the linear development of a single plot line. In its rejection of conventional notions about form, Broughton contends, modern fiction closely resembles cubist art. Whereas the classical artist tried to disguise all signs of artificiality in his work, the cubist artist makes form, rather than subject, the primary vehicle of meaning, and calls attention to the flat canvas, the geometrical shapes and the techniques which constitute his painting. Faulkner's novels, Broughton concludes, are cubist, because, like the cubist painter, Faulkner calls attention to form, exploring the ways form can create meaning and engaging the reader in the fiction-making process. In her subsequent lecture, "Faulkner's Cubist Novels," Broughton expands on the theme of Faulkner's cubism, showing how specific Faulkner novels embody cubist techniques. She contends that Faulkner's personal artistic development presents a microcosm of the past one hundred years of literary history. According to Broughton, during his literary career, Faulkner passed through three stages of evolution, which correspond to the three major literary movements of the last century—romanticism, realism, and modernism. Before 1925, Faulkner wrote romantic poetry, poetry which expresses discontent and longing. In the next phase of development, the early novels, beginning with *Soldiers' Pay* and ending with *Sartoris*, Faulkner takes romanticism for his theme but appraises romantic yearnings with a detached and realistic eye. Finally, in the great novels, *The Sound and the Fury* inclusive of *Go Down, Moses*, Faulkner adapts the techniques of the cubist artist—the dismantling of forms to engage the reader in the creative process. In closing, Broughton speculates that "though cubist techniques are not sufficient conditions for greatness, they do seem to be necessary conditions in Faulkner's works."

In "The Gothicism of *Absalom, Absalom!*: Rosa Coldfield Revisited," François Pitavy fixes on one aspect of Faulkner's cosmos: Faulkner's manipulation of the techniques of the Gothic novel. Claiming that *Absalom, Absalom!* is a dream novel, made up of narratives more dreamed than real, Pitavy shows how aspects of the novel's story (the content of the novel), narration (the narrative act) and narrative (the discourse of the narrators) forward the end of Gothic fiction—to explore the dark side of consciousness and to assert the transcendence of the imagined and irrational over the actual and rational. Central to this purpose, Pitavy maintains, is the novel's nocturnality, which pervades not only the story but also the narration. The three places of narration—Miss Coldfield's shuttered office, Mr. Compson's gallery at twilight, and Quentin's and Shreve's "tomb-like" dormitory room at Harvard—are all dark or darkening. This encompassing darkness, intrinsic to the generation of the story, connotes the preeminence of irrational forces and the absence of the light of reason or objective fact. Focusing on Miss Coldfield's discourse, Pitavy notes that her insistent use of oxymorons, negative accretions, and incremental repetitions—essentially logically contradictory rhetorical devices—gives free rein to the unconscious. Pitavy concludes that the Gothicism of *Absalom, Absalom!* engages the reader in an exploration of the creative imagination—the power responsible for the work of art.

Finally, in "The Collector as Sleuthsayer," Louis Daniel Brodsky describes the evolution of his massive and unique Faulkner collection. The acquisition of this collection, according to Brodsky, can be divided into two phases. In the first phase, Brodsky purchased Faulkner books and ephemerae directly from dealers or from catalogues. But later, Brodsky explains, in the second phase, he pursued acquisitions more aggressively, seeking out and initiating contacts with Faulkner's friends and relations who possessed Faulkner books, manuscripts, and miscellany. After almost twenty years of such unflagging effort, Brodsky has amassed a collection which is "a record, a documentary" of Faulkner's literary career. Among the over six hundred items of interest to Faulkner scholars, the Brodsky collection includes holograph and typescript versions of early unpublished Faulkner poems; typescripts of *The Hamlet* and *The Wishing Tree*; cartoon drawings Faulkner produced as a high school student; legal documents, including four Faulkner wills, and Malcolm Cowley's Faulkner books, complete with marginal notes entered when Cowley was compiling *The Portable Faulkner*. Items from this collection were on display at the University's John Davis Williams Library during the conference.

The first day of this week-long meeting was designated as Dorothy Crosby Appreciation Day in honor of a generous contributor to the preservation of Rowan Oak, the antebellum home where William Faulkner lived from 1930 until his death in 1962. After being closed for nearly a year of restoration work, Rowan Oak was reopened to the public on this day with ceremonies that included speeches by Porter L. Fortune, Jr., Chancellor of The University of Mississippi; Frank D. Montague, an attorney from Hattiesburg, Mississippi; and Dorothy Crosby. On the third day of the conference Howard Bahr, Frank Childrey, William C. Connell, Jr., Evans Harrington, Hubert McAlexander, and James W. Webb conducted tours of Oxford, Lafayette County, and other locations in North Mississippi. On Thursday a musical program entitled "Black Music and Culture in the Works of William Faulkner" was presented by Thea Bowman, a Trinitarian nun who directs a program of intercultural awareness for the Catholic Diocese of Jackson, Mississippi, and who has lectured on black literature and given concerts at universities throughout the United States. Accompanying her were Norman Seawright and the Black Student Union Choir. Other conference events included an exhibition of watercolors and gallery lectures by William C. Baggett, Jr.; a slide presentation by J. M. Faulkner and Jo Marshall; the showing of three films, *William Faulkner: A Life on Paper*, *Faulkner's Mississippi: Land into Legend*, and *The Bear*; a display of Faulkner books submitted by twenty-five university presses and hosted by the University Press of Mississippi; and discussion sessions on topics such as "Faulkner in Oxford," "Faulkner in France," "Faulkner's Theory and Practice," and "Faulkner's Use of Folklore." Leaders of these discussions included conference lecturers and George W. Boswell, William Ferris, Aston Holley, John Pilkington, William McNeil Reed, William J. Roane, and James W. Webb. The editors wish to express their gratitude to all persons and organizations that contributed to

Introduction

the Seventh Annual Faulkner and Yoknapatawpha Conference. Special thanks are offered to the Oxford-Lafayette
County Chamber of Commerce, which gave financial support
to the conference, and to Dorothy Crosby, to whom this book
is dedicated.

Doreen Fowler
UNIVERSITY OF MISSISSIPPI
OXFORD, MISSISSIPPI

"A Cosmos of My Own":
Faulkner and Yoknapatawpha
1980

"Saying No to Death": Toward William Faulkner's Theory of Fiction

ROBERT W. HAMBLIN

Undoubtedly many critics even today agree with Henry Nash Smith's contention in 1932 that William Faulkner "has no theory of fiction."[1] Other readers, surveying the multitude of books and articles which analyze Faulkner's fictional techniques, may conclude that the Nobel laureate held many different, even contradictory theories. The truth, of course, lies in neither of these extremes. Faulkner, as he acknowledged many times, was not "a literary man," that is, one formally schooled in aesthetics and criticism; and he never developed, in the manner of Henry James or William Dean Howells, an elaborate definition of his aims and practices as a writer. Nevertheless, as revealed by even a cursory examination of his letters, essays, speeches, interviews, and fiction, Faulkner was more than mildly interested in literary theory throughout his career. Moreover, although he went through several phases as an author, producing poetry as well as prose and embracing varying combinations of realism, naturalism, and romanticism, and although he never offered an underlying premise for his art until the 1950s, that basic premise had been operative, though perhaps subconsciously, from the

---

1. James B. Meriwether and Michael Millgate, eds., *Lion in the Garden: Interviews with William Faulkner 1926–1962* (New York: Random House, 1968), 32. For each source utilized in this study all citations after the first appear (whenever feasible) parenthetically within the text.

3

very beginning of his career. At the risk of appearing to adopt a reductionist approach, I suggest that the key to Faulkner's theory of fiction is to be found in his statement, repeated many times after 1951 but implicit in even his earliest work, that writing was his way of "saying No to death."[2] This impulse, I believe, accounts not only for the origin of Faulkner's art but also for the principal features in the design of that art.

An initial demonstration of my thesis is provided by section five of "The Bear," one of those remarkable passages which communicate the very essence of Faulkner's views on life and death, and, by implication, on art. In this section Isaac McCaslin returns for one last time to the big woods in which he has served his hunting novitiate under Sam Fathers. Though Ike identifies with the "baseless and illusory hope"[3] that Major de Spain will revoke his agreement to sell the property to a Memphis lumber company, the youth knows that the wilderness is doomed. That doom, already foreshadowed by the deaths of Old Ben, Lion, and Sam, is now confirmed beyond doubt by the construction of the planing-mill at Hoke's Junction. As Ike rides the logging train into the wilderness, he perceives that even his clothes convey an awareness of death, "as garments carry back into the clean edgeless blowing of air the lingering effluvium of a sick-room or of death" (321).

Submerged once more in the deep woods, however, Ike is able to convince himself, at least momentarily, that nothing has changed or will change, that the woods are timeless and "death [does] not even exist" (327). Revisiting the grave sites of Lion and Sam Fathers, Ike observes

2. The earliest use of this phrase which I find in Faulkner's work occurs in *Requiem for a Nun* (New York: Random House, 1951), 215; but a virtually synonymous term, "saying No to time," appears in the unfinished manuscript of "Elmer" (unpublished typescript, Faulkner Collection at the University of Virginia, 60), written in 1925.
3. William Faulkner, *Go Down, Moses* (New York: Modern Library, 1955), 315.

the knoll which was no abode of the dead because there was no death, not Lion and not Sam: not held fast in earth but free in earth and not in earth but of earth, myriad yet undiffused of every myriad part, leaf and twig and particle, air and sun and rain and dew and night, acorn oak and leaf and acorn again, dark and dawn and dark and dawn again in their immutable progression and, being myriad, one: and Old Ben too, Old Ben too; they would give him his paw back even, certainly they would give him his paw back: then the long challenge and the long chase, no heart to be driven and outraged, no flesh to be mauled and bled. (328–29)

This vision of immortality, though, at least insofar as it relates to personal immortality, seems merely wishful thinking, an illusion, as the following incident suggests. Ike's hopeful reflections are interrupted by a "sharp shocking inrush" (329) of fear caused by the intrusion of a rattlesnake into the idyllic scene. Faulkner leaves no doubt as to the identity and the significance of this invader: the snake is "the old one, the ancient and accursed about the earth, fatal and solitary and [Ike] could smell it now: the thin sick smell of rotting cucumbers and something else which had no name, evocative of all knowledge and an old weariness and of pariah-hood and of death" (329). That "all knowledge" equates with death, not immortality, is further emphasized when Ike assigns to the serpent those titles of respect he learned from Sam Fathers: "Chief . . . , Grandfather" (330).

If the concluding segment of "The Bear" dramatizes Ike's initiation into the tragic realities of mutability and death, the section also demonstrates Ike's reluctance, even refusal, to accept these realities. Against his dual enemies, time and annihilation, Ike aligns the creative powers of memory and imagination. Ike's entry into the heart of the now-doomed wilderness is paralleled by a three-page flashback in which the youth recalls the killing of his first buck and Uncle Ash's subsequent demand for equal rights. The comic element in this episode (desirable since the humorous tone enables Faulkner to avoid sentimentality) in no way lessens the point that the recollection of the past provides Ike with one means of negating time and death. The same intent may be identified with the wistful dream-passage, cited previously, in which Ike envisions an ideal realm in which Old Ben will once again participate in the chase. Ike's imaginative leaps in this section, both backward and outward, seem obvious (though probably unconscious) attempts to deny or at least compensate for the inadequate present which is tyrannized by death. That this initiation in the wilderness is intended as a paradigm of all of Ike's subsequent experiences is indicated by the conjecture about his future marriage: "he would marry someday and they too would own for their brief while that brief unsubstanced glory which inherently of itself cannot last and hence why glory: and they would, might, carry even the remembrance of it into the time when flesh no longer talks to flesh because memory at least does last . . . " (326). Ike has learned from the wilderness experience the age-old truth that happiness and joy are fleeting, transient qualities, that "glory . . . cannot last"; but he protests such loss, and he registers his opposition through the exercise of both memory and imagination.

Faulkner could write movingly about Ike McCaslin's initiation in part because Ike's realizations were Faulkner's own. In fact, in Ike's confrontation with the harsh and inescapable reality of death, in his refusal to accept willingly this brutal fact, and in his employment of memory and imagination to deny death, one finds an almost exact corollary to Faulkner's theory of fiction.

Like Isaac McCaslin, Faulkner was extremely apprehensive concerning death.[4] This fear, even obsession, probably

4. See Jerold Howard Stock, "Suggestions of Death-Anxiety in the Life of William Faulkner," unpublished dissertation (West Virginia, 1977). A few of Stock's

originated in early childhood and may have derived from
what Faulkner later recalled as "those spells of loneliness and
nameless sorrow that children suffer,"[5] or from his close brush
with death from scarlet fever at age four, or from the successive deaths of his beloved grandmothers when he was nine
years old. Whatever the basis for his anxiety, it seems clear
that Faulkner's childhood was marked by a heightened awareness concerning death. One may be fairly certain that the
reaction of the four-year-old boy to the hearse in "Sepulture
South: Gaslight" is in some measure autobiographical:

> "What?" I said. "A deader? What's a deader?" And they told
> me. I had seen dead things before—birds, toads, the puppies the
> one before Simon (his wife was Sarah) had drowned in a croker-
> sack in the water-trough . . . , and I had watched him and Sarah
> both beat to bloody shapeless strings the snakes which I now
> know were harmless. But that this, this ignominy, should happen
> to people too, it seemed to me that God Himself would not per-
> mit, condone. So they in the hearse could not be dead: it must
> be something like sleep: a trick played on people by those same
> inimical forces and powers for evil which made Sarah and her
> husband have to beat the harmless snakes to bloody and shape-
> less pulp or drown the puppies—tricked into that helpless coma
> for some dreadful and inscrutable joke until the dirt was packed
> down, to strain and thrash and cry in the airless dark, to no es-
> cape forever. So that night I had something very like hysterics,
> clinging to Sarah's legs and panting: "I won't die! I won't!
> Never!"[6]

This boyhood abhorrence of death seems to have been intensified in the mature Faulkner by a corresponding disbelief, or
at least a serious doubt, concerning immortality. There are
many evidences of Faulkner's skepticism on this point, nota-

arguments seem somewhat strained, but his work represents an important contribution to Faulkner scholarship.

5. Joseph Blotner, ed., *Selected Letters of William Faulkner* (New York: Random House, 1977), 20.

6. Joseph Blotner, ed., *Uncollected Stories of William Faulkner* (New York:
Random House, 1979), 452. Cf. Vardaman's boring holes in his mother's coffin in
As I Lay Dying.

bly the early identification with the poetry of Swinburne and Housman, the dust-to-dust imagery of such apprenticeship works as "Mississippi Hills: My Epitaph" and "The Artist," the dramatic situation in the short story "Beyond," the handling of the Christ story in *A Fable*, and Faulkner's general preference for the word "oblivion" as a substitute for "death." Perhaps the most explicit statement of disbelief in an afterlife in all of Faulkner's writing is Harry Wilbourne's reflection upon rejecting suicide at the end of *The Wild Palms*: "*Between grief and nothing I will take grief.*"[7] In any event, it seems safe to conclude that it was not merely death which Faulkner feared, but death as obliteration.[8]

Faulkner's attitude toward death, and toward the time-ridden world which eventuates in death, is crucial to an understanding of his perception of himself as an artist. Confronted with death as possible annihilation, Faulkner was inclined to view art as the principal means by which man might defy time and death and achieve at least a measure of immortality. This belief accounts for the elevated, even religious tone of many of Faulkner's pronouncements on art. "Since man is mortal," Faulkner told Jean Stein, "the only immortality possible for him is to leave something behind him that is immortal since it will always move. This is the artist's way of scribbling 'Kilroy was here' on the wall of the final and irrevocable oblivion through which he must someday pass" (*LIG*, 253). Following the death of Albert Camus, Faulkner wrote: "When the door shut for him, he had already written on this side of it that which every artist who also carries through life with him that one same foreknowledge and hatred of death, is hoping to do:

7. (New York: Random House, 1939), 324. Similar statements appear in *Go Down, Moses*, 186, and *A Fable* (New York: Random House, 1954), 399.

8. Faulkner's anxiety about an afterlife is reflected in his remark to his brother Jack during their mother's final illness: "Maybe each of us will become some sort of radio wave." Murry C. Falkner, *The Falkners of Mississippi: A Memoir* (Baton Rouge: Louisiana State University Press, 1967), 189.

I was here.[9] In a letter to Joan Williams, Faulkner observed: "That's the answer, the reason for it all, the one and only way on earth you can say No to death: the best, the strongest, the finest, the most enduring: to make something."[10] Faulkner's most extended, and most sublime, commentary on the relationship of the artist and his art to death is the "Foreword" to *The Faulkner Reader.* Here Faulkner explains that the author's purpose is "to uplift man's heart" by "saying No to death," and he goes on to identify this purpose with the "completely selfish, completely personal" desire of the writer to achieve a natural immortality through his work. Faulkner concludes:

> So he who, from the isolation of cold impersonal print, can engender this excitement, himself partakes of the immortality which he has engendered. Some day he will be no more, which will not matter then, because isolated and itself invulnerable in the cold print remains that which is capable of engendering still the old deathless excitement in hearts and glands whose owners and custodians are generations from even the air he breathed and anguished in; if it was capable once, he knows that it will be capable and potent still long after there remains of him only a dead and fading name.

Given such views on art and time, one can easily understand Faulkner's attraction to Keats's "Ode on a Grecian Urn," which celebrates in both its content and its continuing acceptance the enduring power of all great art.[11]

If Faulkner's observations on art reflect an anxiety toward death and a corresponding desire for immortality, his comments also demonstrate the degree to which art, in his view, is interrelated with memory and imagination. Faulkner fre-

9. James B. Meriwether, ed., *Essays, Speeches, and Public Letters by William Faulkner* (New York: Random House, 1965), 114.
10. Quoted in Joseph Blotner, *Faulkner: A Biography* (New York: Random House, 1974), 1461.
11. For an excellent discussion of the Keatsian influence see Blanche H. Gelfant, "Faulkner and Keats: The Ideality of Art in 'The Bear,'" *Southern Literary Journal*, 2 (Fall, 1969), 43–65.

9

quently identified the sources of his fiction as "observation, experience, and imagination."[12] The first two of these equate with memory. According to Faulkner, all that a writer has seen, heard, read, and done is unconsciously stored in his memory, from which he can draw forth images and details to suit his needs. "Memory believes before knowing remembers,"[13] Faulkner observes in *Light in August*; and he told the cadets at West Point: "I think that every experience of the author affects his writing. . . .He has a sort of a lumber room in his subconscious that all this goes into, and none of it is ever lost. Some day he may need some experience that he experienced or saw, observed or read about, and so he digs it out and uses it. . . . Everything that happens to him he remembers. And it will be grist to his mill."[14] Since art derives partly from memory, it functions for the reader as a record of past experience. In his Nobel Prize acceptance speech Faulkner declares that the poet's privilege is "to help man endure by lifting his heart, by reminding him of the courage and honor and hope and pride and compassion and pity and sacrifice which have been the glory of his past" (*ESPL*, 120). In Japan Faulkner commented: "The reason that the books last longer than the bridges and the skyscrapers is that that is the best thing man has discovered yet to record the fact that he does endure, that he is capable of hope, even in darkness, that he does move, he doesn't give up, and that is not only a record of his past, where he has shown that he endures and hopes in spite of darkness, but it is a promise of the validity of that hope" (*LIG*, 177–78). At West Point Faulkner observed that the writer's purpose is "to uplift man's heart by

12. See, for example, Frederick L. Gwynn and Joseph L. Blotner, eds., *Faulkner in the University: Class Conferences at the University of Virginia 1957–1958* (Charlottesville: University of Virginia Press, 1959), 103, 123, 147, 181.

13. (New York: Modern Library, 1950), 104.

14. Joseph L. Fant III and Robert Ashley, eds., *Faulkner at West Point* (New York: Random House, 1964), 96.

showing man the record of the experiences of the human heart" (*FWP*, 48). As Faulkner demonstrates with the account of the race of the locomotives in *The Unvanquished*, the past is "not gone or vanished either," as long as succeeding generations continue "to tell it or listen to the telling."[15]

In stressing the link between his art and memory of his own and man's past, Faulkner was not endorsing a mimetic theory of fiction. Though he has often been called both a "realist" and a "naturalist," Faulkner has little in common with the photographic realism of Howells or the scientific documentation of Zola and Dreiser. For reasons which will be discussed later, Faulkner always stressed "imagination" as the principal ingredient in his fiction. Indeed, as evidenced by the handling of the past in *Absalom, Absalom!*, even memory frequently becomes for Faulkner and his characters imaginative reconstruction rather than simple recall. "I dont care much for facts," Faulkner once noted;[16] and he criticized John Steinbeck (mistakenly, one might add) for being "just a reporter, a newspaperman, not really a writer"(*LIG*, 91). At Charlottesville Faulkner observed, "The artist's prerogative . . . is to emphasize, to underline, to blow up facts, distort facts in order to state a truth" (*FIU*, 282). Yoknapatawpha, as Faulkner told Jean Stein, may have evolved from his "little postage stamp of native soil," but it was produced "by sublimating the actual into apocryphal"(*LIG*, 255). The Nobel Prize speech defines art not only as "the record of man" but also as "something which did not exist before," an artifact "create[d] out of the materials of the human spirit"(*ESPL*, 120, 119). In other words, art, according to Faulkner, results from both memory and invention, fact and imagination.

Close examination of Faulkner's belief that literature pro-

---

15. (New York: Random House, 1938), 112.
16. Malcolm Cowley, *The Faulkner-Cowley File: Letters and Memories 1944–1962* (New York: Viking Press, 1968), 89.

11

vides the writer with a means of saying No to death, of recording the heroic struggle of man, and of exercising the power of invention reveals that the three ideas are actually interdependent. Denial of death, in Faulkner's view, is the end of art; memory and imagination are the means. As was noted in Ike McCaslin's response to the loss of the wilderness, both the reconstruction of the past and the imagining of an ideal "other" world are ways of counteracting death, of keeping the beloved lost object alive. It remains to demonstrate how these notions worked to influence Faulkner's fictional techniques, particularly his handling of subject matter and his style.

One can hardly overstate the degree to which Faulkner's fiction is intertwined with memory. Like a host of other American writers, for example, Cooper, Hawthorne, Twain, Anderson, Wolfe, and especially Cather, Faulkner indulges in more than a modicum of nostalgia. As Henry Nash Smith inferred from his conversation with Faulkner in 1932, the author "loved [Oxford] as it was in his boyhood, before billboards and electric signs invaded the quiet, when a two-story gallery had surrounded the square" (*LIG*, 29). Faulkner himself was inclined to link his discovery of his true subject, the people and places and events of Yoknapatawpha, with the act of preservation through recollection. After producing scores of mediocre poems and two unsuccessful novels (both of which are significantly rooted in the present rather than the past), Faulkner wrote *Sartoris* (*Flags in the Dust*), the first of the Yoknapatawpha novels and the work which he said contains "the germ of my apocrypha" (*FIU*, 285). In explaining the genesis of this work, Faulkner observed that he had been "speculating idly upon time and death" and had concluded that "nothing served but that I try by main strength to recreate between the covers of a book the world as I was already preparing to lose and regret, feeling, with the morbidity of the young, that I was not only on the verge of decrepitude, but that growing old was to be an experience peculiar to myself alone out of all the teeming world, and desiring, if not the capture of that world and the feeling of it as you'd preserve a kernel [or] a leaf to indicate the lost forest, at least to keep the evocative skeleton of the dessicated [sic] leaf."[17] Faulkner further noted his concern that this world, his world, "should not pass utterly out of the memory of man," as well as his need to "reaffirm the impulses of my own ego in this actual world without stability" (124). Thus Sartoris derived from a protest against time and death and a consequent desire to preserve in print a passing scene. In fact, so strong was this impulse to oppose death through creativity that Faulkner could not be sure whether "I had invented the [fictional] world to which I should give life or if it had invented me, giving me an illusion of greatness" (124).

As these remarks on the composition of Sartoris suggest, the dramatic turnabout in Faulkner's career marked by the creation of Yoknapatawpha may be due as much to the discovery of art as a means of asserting the artist's ego in the face of death as to the discovery of native materials. In fact, the two discoveries can scarcely be distinguished. What better way, one perceives in retrospect, could Faulkner have dramatized the passing of his own world than by paralleling it with a previous generation which had already succumbed to time and death. Thus, one supposes, evolved the double time-frame and the dominant motif in Sartoris. All of the elements of this work conjoin to produce one single refrain: memento mori. The plot involves two generations of Sartorises, one past and the other passing. The protagonist, young Bayard Sartoris, seems old beyond his years, having already accepted the grim reality of death and unable to escape that reality, as his coun-

17. Joseph Blotner, "William Faulkner's Essay on the Composition of Sartoris," Yale University Library Gazette, 47 (January, 1973), 122–23.

terpart Horace Benbow does, through fancied wanderings "beyond the moon, about meadows nailed with firmamented stars to the ultimate roof of things, where unicorns filled the neighing air with galloping, or grazed or lay supine in golden-hoofed repose."[18] The action unfolds against the relentless progression of the seasons, from spring, to summer, to autumn, to winter, culminating in the cold December rain which "drop by drop . . . wore the night away, wore time away" (324). Even the occasional humor and the joyous descriptions of nature seem designed to accentuate, not relieve, the melancholy. Appropriately, the family's name, Sartoris, is associated with the tragic theme: "For there is death in the sound of it, and a glamorous fatality, like silver pennons downrushing at sunset, or a dying fall of horns along the road to Roncevaux" (380). Not surprisingly, one of the last scenes in the novel takes place in the cemetery, among the family's tombstones, the most prominent of which carries the inscription, "Pause here, son of sorrow; remember death" (375).

But the course of history, as symbolized by the tragic fate of the Sartoris clan, is just one pole, the negative one, in this novel. The other, the positive pole, is art, not the subject matter of the book but the book itself, which, as Faulkner said, was written to capture and preserve between its covers his passing world. It is not quite accurate to say, as many critics do, that Faulkner's major theme is time; more precisely, his principal concern is resistance to time. In *Sartoris* this positive, even heroic emphasis is symbolized by the marble statue of Colonel John Sartoris:

> He stood on a stone pedestal, in his frock coat and bareheaded, one leg slightly advanced and one hand resting lightly on the stone pylon beside him. His head was lifted a little in that gesture of haughty pride which repeated itself generation after generation with a fateful fidelity, his back to the world and his carven

18. William Faulkner, *Sartoris* (New York: Random House, 1961), 179.

eyes gazing out across the valley where his railroad ran, and the blue changeless hills beyond, and beyond that, the ramparts of infinity itself. The pedestal and effigy were mottled with seasons of rain and sun and with drippings from the cedar branches, and the bold carving of the letters was bleared with mold, yet still decipherable. . . . (375)

This monument, seemingly impervious to time and capable of evoking memories of the bygone past, symbolizes the relationship Faulkner perceives between art and memory. Another monument to this concept is *Sartoris* and the rest of the Yoknapatawpha novels and stories.[19]

The statue of John Sartoris is only one of many objects in Faulkner's fiction which are noteworthy for having survived the passing of time and which serve to evoke thoughts of persons and events from earlier years.[20] These "relics," or "art-surrogates" as they may be termed, take many forms. There is, for example, the pipe which old man Falls gives to aging Bayard Sartoris and which revives for Bayard memories of his father. Indeed, old man Falls is himself a relic, his sole purpose in *Sartoris* being to convey to Bayard and the reader the "far more palpable presence" of John Sartoris from "a dead period" (1). One thinks also of the hunting horn cherished over the years by Ike McCaslin and of the slipper and the pasture which recall the past, however dimly, to Benjy Compson's retarded mind. Sometimes the relic assumes a communal rather than a personal significance, as with the Jef-

19. Memory also plays an important role in the non-Yoknapatawpha works. For example, *The Wild Palms*, based in part on Faulkner's relationships with Helen Baird and Meta Carpenter, was originally entitled "If I Forget Thee, O Jerusalem." See Blotner, *Faulkner: A Biography*, 978, 989–91.

20. Cf. Faulkner's tendency, as reported by his brother John, to "squirrel away" toys and other items. "All of us had special storage places for our possessions. Jack's and mine were never very interesting. We broke our toys or forgot them. But Bill's was always neat and seemed to have everything in it he had ever owned. He was still that way about saving curious mementos up until he died. His study had more objects stashed about in it and most of us wondered why in the world he kept them." John Faulkner, *My Brother Bill: An Affectionate Reminiscence* (New York: Trident Press, 1963), 76.

ferson courthouse and jail in *Requiem for a Nun*. And occasionally the relic takes a written form, as with the old family
ledger which Ike McCaslin discovers in the plantation commissary, or the letter from Charles Bon to Judith Sutpen, pre-
served and passed on three generations later to Quentin
Compson. Significantly, Mr. Compson's explanation as to why
Judith gave Bon's letter to Quentin's grandmother echoes
Faulkner's own observations about the artist and death:

> Because you make so little impression, you see. You get born
> . . . and then all of a sudden it's all over and all you have left is a
> block of stone with scratches on it. . . . And so maybe if you
> could go to someone, the stranger the better, and give them
> something—a scrap of paper—something, anything . . . , at least
> it would be something just because it would have happened, be
> remembered even if only from passing from one hand to another,
> one mind to another, and it would be at least a scratch, some-
> thing. . . .[21]

Judith, according to Mr. Compson, is obsessed with the desire to communicate to others that she has existed, that she
was; and this compulsion leads her, in Mr. Compson's words,
"to make that scratch, that undying mark on the blank face of
the oblivion to which we are all doomed" (*AA*, 129). In this
instance, if not in others, there can be no doubt that Mr.
Compson speaks for his creator.

Another art-surrogate, Cecilia Farmer's signature scratched
on the jailhouse window in *Requiem for a Nun*, bears even
greater resemblance to Faulkner's definition of art and the
artist.[22] This signature, "a few faint scratches apparently no
more durable than the thin dried slime left by the passage of
a snail, yet which has endured a hundred years"(253), sur-

21. William Faulkner, *Absalom, Absalom!* (New York: Modern Library, 1951), 127.
22. Michael Millgate (*The Achievement of William Faulkner* [New York: Random House, 1966], 225) similarly links Cecilia's legacy with Faulkner's comments on art.

16

vives to evoke in the twentieth-century stranger to Jefferson a vicarious participation in Cecilia's life and time. The way Cecilia's story "comes alive" as the stranger gazes at her signature parallels Faulkner's observations on art in the "Foreword" to *The Faulkner Reader* and elsewhere:

> . . . suddenly . . . something has already happened: the faint frail illegible meaningless even inferenceless scratching on the ancient poor-quality glass you stare at, has moved, under your eyes, even while you stared at it, coalesced, seeming actually to have entered into another sense than vision: a scent, a whisper, filling that hot cramped strange room . . . : the two of them in conjunction—the old milky obsolete glass, and the scratches on it: that tender ownerless obsolete girl's name and the old dead date in April almost a century ago—speaking, murmuring, back from, out of, across from, a time as old as lavender, older than album or stereopticon, as old as daguerreotype itself. (*RFN* 254)

The capacity of Cecilia's signature to survive into the future and inspire imaginative, emotional responses in strangers reminds one of Faulkner's statement to Jean Stein: "The aim of every artist is to arrest motion, which is life, by artificial means and hold it fixed so that 100 years later when a stranger looks at it, it moves again since it is life" (*LIG*, 253). Critics have paid considerable attention to the first half of this statement, the notion that art is arrested motion, but Faulkner may have been more concerned with the second part of his definition. Only when art "moves again" has the creator successfully said No to death and thus achieved immortality.

An interesting parallel to Faulkner's fondness for "relics" and "art-surrogates" is his compulsion to return time and again to the same characters, incidents, and scenes in Yoknapatawpha. The resurrection of the Compson family in the "Appendix" to *The Sound and the Fury* and the continuation of the Snopes narrative over a period of thirty years are only the most prominent of the countless instances in which Faulkner retells and reworks previous stories. While such

17

repetitions and extensions serve various narrative purposes—
for example, suspenseful unfolding of plot, fuller characterization, and multiple viewpoint—one suspects that Faulkner's
practice in this regard is dictated as much by psychological as
by literary needs. Given his anxiety concerning time and
death, and given his concern about (initially) the acceptance
and (ultimately) the survival of his art, it seems reasonable to
suggest that Faulkner's return to his earlier stories was at least
partly motivated, though probably unconsciously, by his need
to be assured of the vitality of his art. Faulkner's reluctance
to reread his published work seems related to the same point.
A completed work (for the artist, that is) belongs to the past,
to (in one sense) death, a fact strongly to be resisted. One
form of resistance is to depend upon sympathetic readers to
respond vicariously to the work and thus cause it to "move
again." Another approach is for the creator to ensure that his
creation "move again" by the addition of appendices and extended chapters. Predictably, Faulkner's tendency to retell
old stories increased with his advancing years. Most critics
insist that Faulkner's late years are marked by a flagging creativity, but another possibility is that as Faulkner grew older,
as he became more and more conscious of his own mortality,
he felt more and more compelled (again subconsciously) to
inject new life into his earlier creations. In any case, the fact
remains that memory functions, within the confines of Yoknapatawpha as well as in the relation of Yoknapatawpha to
actuality, to resist time and say No to death.

If such reasoning is correct, then *The Reivers* becomes a
most significant work in the Faulkner canon. Indeed, this last
novel seems precisely the kind of book an artist who views
memory as an antidote to death would produce during the
late stage of his career. As the subtitle indicates, *The Reivers*
is "a reminiscence," a nostalgic recounting by Lucius Priest,
a grandfather bearing close resemblance to William Faulkner,

of events which occurred more than a half-century previously. In producing this novel Faulkner not only returned to the actual livery stable days of his own boyhood, but he also ranged freely throughout the fictional world of Yoknapatawpha. Elizabeth Kerr may be wrong in identifying *The Reivers* with "the Doomsday Book, the Golden Book, of Yoknapatawpha County" (*LIG*, 255) which Faulkner predicted he would someday write, but she is certainly correct in calling attention to the extent to which the novel draws upon Faulkner's previous works.[23] The use of the Memphis setting from *Sanctuary*, the manipulation of the initiation motif prevalent in Faulkner's works, references to key events in the history of Jefferson and Yoknapatawpha County, and the mention of numerous characters from earlier books—all such features demonstrate that *The Reivers* stands as a valediction in which Faulkner celebrates, through memory, the total achievement of Yoknapatawpha.

The use of memory as a means of opposing time and death affected not only Faulkner's subject matter but also his style. As Robert Penn Warren has explained, "The style of a writer represents his stance toward experience";[24] thus it is to be expected that Faulkner's style mirrors a strong resistance to death through the desire to preserve the past. One suspects that Marcel Proust served as an important model in this regard. "After I had read *A la Recherche du Temps Perdu*," Faulkner once observed, "I said 'This is it!'—and I wished I had written it myself" (*LIG*, 72). In any event, one finds in Faulkner's stream-of-consciousness prose the same obsession with the past, the same compulsion to preserve and restate it

---

23. See Elizabeth M. Kerr, "*The Reivers*: The Golden Book of Yoknapatawpha County," *Modern Fiction Studies*, 13 (Spring, 1967), 95–113. For a rejoinder see James B. Meriwether, "The Novel Faulkner Never Wrote: His Golden Book or Doomsday Book," *American Literature*, 42 (March 1970), 93–96.

24. "Why Do We Read Fiction?" *Saturday Evening Post*, 235 (October 20, 1962), 84.

in terms of the present.[25] Various critics have noted how Faulkner's style functions to unite past and present time. Alfred Kazin, for instance, describes Faulkner's prose as "an attempt to realize continuity with all our genesis, our 'progenitors'. . . with all we have touched, known, loved. This is why he needs those long successive parentheses, and parentheses within parentheses. They exemplify the chain of human succession."[26] Faulkner said as much himself. He told Cowley, "My ambition is to put everything into one sentence—not only the present but the whole past on which it depends and which keeps overtaking the present, second by second" (*FCF*, 112). At the University of Virginia, Faulkner stated: "To me, no man is himself, he is the sum of his past. There is no such thing really as was because the past is. . . . And so a man, a character in a story at any moment of action is not just himself as he is then, he is all that made him, and the long sentence is an attempt to get his past and possibly his future into the instant in which he does something . . ." (*FIU*, 84). In a letter to Cowley, Faulkner wrote, "I'm still trying to put all mankind's history in one sentence" (*FCF*, 17).

Readers will find this principle at work on almost any page of Faulkner's stream-of-consciousness prose, but the following passage from the opening of *Absalom, Absalom!* will serve as a case in point.

> It seems that this demon—his name was Sutpen—(Colonel Sutpen)—Colonel Sutpen. Who came out of nowhere and without warning upon the land with a band of strange niggers and built a plantation—(Tore violently a plantation, Miss Rosa Coldfield says)—tore violently. And married her sister Ellen and begot a

25. As Jean-Paul Sartre has written, "Proust really *should have* employed a technique like Faulkner's; that was the logical outcome of his metaphysic." "Time in Faulkner: *The Sound and the Fury*," *William Faulkner: Three Decades of Criticism*, ed. Frederick J. Hoffman and Olga W. Vickery (New York: Harbinger Books, 1963), 229–30.
26. "Faulkner's Vision of Human Integrity," *Harvard Advocate*, 135 (November, 1951), 33.

son and a daughter which—(Without gentleness begot, Miss Rosa Coldfield says)—without gentleness. Which should have been the jewels of his pride and the shield and comfort of his old age, only—(Only they destroyed him or something or he destroyed them or something. And died)—and died. Without regret, Miss Rosa Coldfield says—(Save by her) Yes, save by her. (And by Quentin Compson) Yes. And by Quentin Compson. (9)

In this passage Quentin's rumination over the public legend of Thomas Sutpen's career a half-century earlier is intermixed with the recall of Miss Rosa's recent interpretations and with Quentin's own present-tense emotional response. Throughout the passage Faulkner employs parenthetical interpolations and repetition of key phrases to dramatize the interrelationship of remote past, near past, and present time. The whole of *Absalom, Absalom!* is constructed on this principle, as are also the interior monologues of Benjy and Quentin Compson, Addie Bundren's death-bed reflections, Gail Hightower's reconstruction of his family's history, and Ike McCaslin's thoughts in "The Bear." The three prologues in *Requiem for a Nun,* the third of which is comprised of a single sentence extending to fifty pages, are only the most extreme forms of what is a common practice in Faulkner's fiction. That in certain instances, perhaps most, the past is brought forward as burden rather than delight matters little. In Faulkner's metaphysic the question of existence is seldom one of suffering versus joy; it is rather a question of being versus non-being. And Faulkner's heroes more often than not are those individuals who, like the artist, say No to death, who choose life even when that choice entails a considerable amount of anxiety, guilt, or pain.[27]

27. Cf. Louise's statement in "Dr. Martino" (*Collected Stories of William Faulkner* [New York: Random House, 1950], 577): "Then he told me one day, when I was big enough to understand, how there is nothing in the world but living, being alive, knowing you are alive. And to be afraid is to know you are alive, but to do what you are afraid of, then you *live.* He says it's better even to be afraid than to be dead."

"Saying No to Death"

As important as memory was for Faulkner, it could not, for demonstrable reasons, become the sole basis for his poetics. Merely to recall experience and to record it in stenographic fashion would be to duplicate, and thus to accept, the fallen world despoiled by time and death. And it is precisely this fallen world against which Faulkner rebels. To say No to death is ultimately to say No to life, since death is the essence of the life process. Faulkner's uneasy relationship to actuality is evidenced in his sense of Southern history, his disillusionment with his father, his rejection by Estelle Oldham and later by Helen Baird, his disappointment as an aviator during World War I, his struggle as a fledgling author, and even his misgivings about his smallish stature.[28] All of these disenchantments, however, these "little deaths," were mere earnest for what Faulkner had already accepted as the ultimate payment required by life. Whatever the effect on Faulkner's personality of his various frustrations, it is clear, as *The Marble Faun*, "Nympholepsy," and *Mayday* reveal, that Faulkner early on came to view the world through the jaundiced eye of the disillusioned romantic. And Faulkner never altogether recovered from his youthful disappointments. His oft-quoted comment about the reasons for the twentieth-century renaissance among Southern writers is quite revealing of his own personal outlook: "I myself am inclined to think it was because of the bareness of the Southerner's life, that he had to resort to his own imagination, to create his own Carcassonne"

This is not to suggest that Faulkner honors life at any price. As Cass Edmonds observes in *Go Down, Moses* (186): "There is only one thing worse than not being alive, and that's shame." Flem Snopes, Jason Compson, and Popeye Vitelli are examples of Faulkner characters who choose shameful lives, while Eula Varner Snopes demonstrates (at least in the opinion of Charles Mallison) that not every suicide is dishonorable. Concerning the last point, see *The Town* (New York: Vintage Books, 1961), 337.

28. One suspects that Faulkner's comments about Sherwood Anderson's size (*FIU*, 259–60) reflect Faulkner's own feelings of insecurity. See also Murry Falkner's observation in *Falkners of Mississippi*, 191–92.

(*FIU*, 136).[29] Similarly, in commenting on the origin of "The Bear," Faulkner remarked, "There's a case of the sorry, shabby world that don't quite please you, so you create one of your own, so you make Lion a little braver than he was, and you make the bear a little more of a bear than he actually was" (*FIU*, 59). As these quotations suggest, Faulkner has definite links with the Freudian definition of the artist as one who sublimates his frustrations and neuroses in symbolic projections and fantasies.[30] Art, in this view, serves as one form of compensation for the inadequacies of life; and imagination, the means of transcendence, becomes the principal ingredient in that art.

Here, as is so often the case in the study of Faulkner, one is confronted with a curious paradox. One impulse in Faulkner, his desire to say No to death, moved him to celebrate life and experience, even tragic experience, and to seek to preserve the world through an aesthetic of memory. But a stronger impulse, deriving from the ultimate recognition that life is ever subject to death, led Faulkner to oppose life as it is given and to transform it through an aesthetic of imagination.[31] This second impulse accounts for all those remarks in

29. Faulkner dramatizes this point, as well as other ideas he held concerning art and the artist, in the short story "Carcassonne." See my article, "'Carcassonne': Faulkner's Allegory of Art and the Artist," *Southern Review*, 15 (Spring, 1979), 355–65.
30. Much of the conversation in Faulkner's second novel, *Mosquitoes* (New York: Liveright Publishing Corporation, 1951), centers around a Freudian approach to literature. Consider, for example, Dawson Fairchild's statement, "That's about all the virtue there is in art: it's a kind of Battle Creek, Michigan [site of a renowned sanitarium], for the spirit" (319), and Julius's reflection, "Dante invented Beatrice, creating himself a maid that life had not had time to create, and laid upon her frail and unbowed shoulders the whole burden of man's history of his impossible heart's desire" (339). Bayard Sartoris (*U*, 262) and General Gragnon's aide (*F*, 44–45) also offer Freudian explanations for the creation of literature.
31. Strictly speaking, memory may be identified with realism and imagination with romance. Significantly, Faulkner produces neither a literature which copies life nor a literature of escapism but "a living literature" which draws from both extremes. See Faulkner's prefatory note to *The Mansion*.

which Faulkner claimed to have "improved on God."[32] As he told the students at Charlottesville, "No writer is satisfied with the folks that God creates. He's convinced that he can do much better than that" (*FIU*, 131–32). Such comments express not so much the attitude of an arrogant, egotistical artist as the felt need to embellish the "bareness" of "the sorry, shabby world" with imaginative fictions.

How deep-seated was Faulkner's compulsion to remake the actual world in his own image is demonstrated by the various personae Faulkner adopted throughout his lifetime. The most celebrated example, of course, is his pose as a returning war hero following World War I. Wearing his military uniform about Oxford and to nearby towns, posing for photographers with his Royal Flying Corps badge and wings displayed on his tunic, walking with a noticeable limp, Faulkner gave every appearance of being an experienced, war-wounded pilot. Other poses followed: bohemian poet, town character, simple farmer, Hollywood eccentric, romantic lover, English squire. While an innocent playfulness infuses much of Faulkner's role-playing (as when he told one interviewer, "I was born of a Negro slave and an alligator, both named Gladys Rock" [*LIG*, 9]), one must acknowledge a degree of neuroticism in such behavior. In extreme cases the necessity to embroider actuality becomes a pathological mythomania; in Faulkner's case the tendency seems to have been limited to a mild form of what Jules de Gaultier has termed "the Madame Bovary complex," defined as "the power given man to see himself other than what he is."[33] Such a complex is hardly surprising in an individual who, like Faulkner, expresses, both in words and in his dependence upon alcohol, a deep aversion to the

32. Blotner, "William Faulkner's Essay on the Composition of *Sartoris*," 123.
33. Jules de Gaultier, *Bovarysm*, trans. Gerald M. Spring (New York: Philosophical Library, 1970), 4. According to de Gaultier, the will-to-illusion is an essential faculty of man and becomes destructive, as in the case of Emma Bovary, only when it is sentimentalized.

24

real world. Writing and drinking, as Faulkner's poses illustrate, are not the only ways "to invent a world a little different from the shabby one" (*FIU*, 43) which man inhabits.

Faulkner's antipathy to the actual world is also reflected in such "non-fiction" pieces as the essay "Mississippi," which purports to be an autobiographical reminiscence tracing the formative influences upon Faulkner's mind and art. The first sentence establishes the interfusion of fancy and fact which characterizes the whole essay: "Mississippi begins in the lobby of a Memphis, Tennessee hotel and extends south to the Gulf of Mexico" (*ESPL*, 11). The piece goes on to summarize Mississippi history from the time of the Mound Builders to the mid-twentieth century. As in his Yoknapatawpha Saga, Faulkner oversimplifies a complex historical process to make it conform to his own particular version of *Paradise Lost*. Thus the virgin wilderness and the numerous Indian tribes are assigned to a prelapsarian but doomed era, slaveholding cotton planters and carpetbagging lumbermen are portrayed as destroyers of Eden, and twentieth-century rednecks who support demagogues and join the Ku Klux Klan are depicted as symbols of the ultimate degradation which is the inevitable consequence of man's inhumanity and folly. Judgment and retribution periodically come to this fallen world, as with the Civil War in the nineteenth century and the raging Mississippi River flood in the twentieth. But Faulkner's narrative, like Milton's great epic, is not without its *felix culpa*. The tragedies, whether man-made or natural, serve "merely to give man another chance to prove . . . just how much the human body could bear, stand, endure" (25–26).

Into this highly stereotyped and mythologized frame of history, Faulkner inserts both actual and fictional personages. Murrell, Mason, Hare, the two Harpes, Forrest, Bilbo, Vardaman, and Caroline Barr are mentioned; but so are the Sartorises and De Spains and Compsons, the McCaslins and Ewells and Hogganbecks, "and now and then a Snopes too because by the beginning of the twentieth century Snopeses were everywhere" (12). "Mississippi" contains fact and fiction, and fact made fiction. An actual millionaire sportsman, Paul Rainey, is transformed into the fictional Sales Wells; and the Faulkner of the essay becomes "in his hierarchial turn Master of the [hunting] camp" (13), though the real Faulkner never did. Oxford does not appear, but Jefferson does. In its blending of historical fact, memory, and imaginative constructs, "Mississippi" epitomizes Faulkner's art. It is Yoknapatawpha in miniature, a cosmos of Faulkner's own making, in part suggested by and modeled upon actuality, but created "by sublimating the actual into apocryphal." In such a cosmos not the mirrored world but the invented one is paramount: in this realm the imaginative artist, not God, is "Sole Owner & Proprietor."

There are several features of Faulkner's technique which may be linked to his aesthetic of imagination. One such feature is the propensity toward the grotesque and the marvelous. Readers are quick to notice how Faulkner's characters often tend to be distortions of typical human beings, extremes rather than well-rounded, "realistic" figures. Walter Slatoff describes the Compson family—with its alcoholic failure for a father, a hopeless hypochondriac for a mother, and an idiot, a neurotic suicide, a nymphomaniac, and a ruthless materialist for children—as "utterly monstrous"; and he reaches a similar conclusion about the murderer, the suicide, the two schizophrenics, the bigot, and the madman who appear in the cast of *Light in August*.[34] In some cases Faulkner's grotesquerie approaches caricature: the loquaciousness of Gavin Stevens, the stubbornness of Lucas Beauchamp, the animal-

34. *Quest for Failure: A Study of William Faulkner* (Ithaca, New York: Cornell University Press, 1960), 80.

ity of the Snopeses, the greed of Jason Compson, the sexuality of Eula Varner. Faulkner's comment about Eula, "she was larger than life, she was too big for this world" (*FIU*, 31), applies to many—indeed, most—of his characters. Like the figures with elongated bodies and noseless faces in Faulkner's early drawings, Faulkner's characters are grotesques drawn less from life than from the artist's creative vision. Apparently only such characters could provide their creator with a sense of control and even superiority over the deficient world of time and death.[35]

A tendency toward extravagance, even sensationalism, is also a marked characteristic of Faulkner's handling of incident and plot. Examples spring readily to mind: the macabre journey of the Bundrens, the rape of Temple Drake, the obsessive actions of Thomas Sutpen, the love affair of Ike Snopes and the cow, the gravedigging scenes in *Intruder in the Dust*, the insane behavior of Emily Grierson, the murderous act of Nancy Mannigoe, the escapades of the convict in *The Wild Palms*. Faulkner's comic incidents, like the horse-swapping antics of Pat Stamper or the deviltry of Byron Snopes's half-Indian children, have much in common with the "tall tale" tradition of the Southwestern yarnspinners; but the use of exaggeration and willful distortion is not restricted to Faulkner's comedy. Nor is it limited to individual scenes. Faulkner's overall plot designs, marked as they are by violent disruptions of chronology, radical shifts of viewpoint, and startling innovations of form (as in *The Wild Palms* and *Requiem for a Nun*), likewise tend toward extravagance and sensationalism. Here, too, as in Faulkner's grotesque characterizations and

---

35. The same point might be made in relation to Faulkner's cavalier handling of dates and other details from one novel to another. As Faulkner explained at Charlottesville, "When you go to the trouble to invent a private domain of your own, then you're the master of time, too. I have the right, I think, to shift these things around wherever it sounds best, and I can move them about in time and, if necessary, change their names" (*FIU*, 29).

shocking incidents, one perceives a need to escape the ordinary and the conventional and enter a realm of the ego's own
making.

Faulkner's rejection of the actual world of time and death
is likewise evidenced in his inclination toward mythologizing.
Thomas Sutpen is not merely a nineteenth-century Southern
planter: he is (depending upon the viewpoint) a god-like creator bringing order out of chaos, "creating the Sutpen's
Hundred, the *Be Sutpen's Hundred* like the oldentime *Be
Light*," or a satanic being, "this Faustus, this demon, this
Beelzebub . . . who hid horns and tail beneath human rai-
ment and a beaver hat" (*AA*, 9, 178). Or, as the title *Absalom,
Absalom!* implies, Sutpen is a kingly David undone by his
tragic flaw. Flem Snopes is more than a conniving, amoral
businessman: he is, as a key scene in *The Hamlet* reveals, an
archfiend capable of usurping the throne from the Prince of
Hell. Eula Varner (possibly the only character in Faulkner's
works for whom source critics, understandably, have not located a prototype) is alternately Helen, Lilith, Semiramis,
Eve, Venus—in short, the primal female whose "entire appearance suggested some symbology out of the old Dionysic
times."[36] In *Go Down, Moses* the wilderness is Eden, the
New South is Canaan, and Ike McCaslin is a Christ figure
seeking to atone for the sins of his race. The idealistic Gavin
Stevens is Don Quixote, frustrated and befuddled by the real
world. And so on throughout the fiction. Indeed, almost
every Faulkner character and event has a parallel in ancient
myth, the heroic epic, or the chivalric romance.[37] While such
correspondences serve to elevate Faulkner's fiction above its
local and regional setting and give the work a universal

36. William Faulkner, *The Hamlet* (New York: Vintage Books, 1956), 95.
37. For an extended treatment of this matter see Lynn Gartrell Levins, *Faulkner's Heroic Design: The Yoknapatawpha Novels* (Athens: University of Georgia
Press, 1976).

quality, the mythic elements also evidence Faulkner's compulsion to envelop drab, commonplace reality with an aura of romance and greatness. Through such conversions Faulkner could give meaning and significance to "the sorry, shabby world" of experience.

As in the case of his aesthetic of memory, Faulkner's aesthetic of imagination finds clear expression in his style. And the function is likewise the same: to protest and hopefully escape the tragic world of time and death. Recognizing, as Wallace Stevens does, that man "cannot look at the past or the future except by means of the imagination,"[38] Faulkner utilizes the stream-of-consciousness method as a tool of transcendence. On one occasion, in noting his agreement with Henri Bergson's idea of "the fluidity of time," Faulkner observed, "There is only the present moment, in which I include both the past and the future, and that is eternity" (*LIG*, 70). In other words, immortality, "eternity," equates with the imaginative leap from the present moment into either the past or the future. Conversely, to be trapped in any one of these dimensions—the dead past, the dying present, or the nonexistent future—is to be defeated by time and death. In the same interview statement Faulkner went on to say that "time can be shaped quite a bit by the artist; after all, man is never time's slave" (*LIG*, 70). In a physical sense, of course, as Faulkner well knew, man *is* time's slave; but through the exercise of his imagination man can reshape time to his own purposes. In so doing he transcends the limitations of the physical world and makes contact with "eternity."

Readers will find in almost any stream-of-consciousness passage in Faulkner's books an application of this principle. One was cited at the beginning of this paper, Ike McCaslin's thoughts upon returning to the big woods at the end of "The

38. "Imagination as Value," *The Necessary Angel: Essays on Reality and the Imagination* (New York: Alfred A. Knopf, 1951), 144.

Bear." Another good example is a seven-page passage in *Intruder in the Dust*.[39] The time is Monday night shortly after ten o'clock, and Chick Mallison and his Uncle Gavin Stevens are "standing beside the sheriff's car in the alley beside the jail watching Lucas and the sheriff emerge from the jail's side door and cross the dark yard toward them" (211). As the sheriff and Lucas move toward the car, Chick turns and walks the short block to the edge of the town square, now empty after the frenzied excitement of the day. Feeling like an actor waiting in the wings to complete the last act of a drama, Chick notes "the square which was more than dead: abandoned" (211), illuminated only by the lights in an all-night cafe and Stevens's second-story law office. As he looks over "the whole dark lifeless rectangle" (211), Chick contrasts this Monday night with "the other the normal Monday nights when no loud fury of blood and revenge and racial and family solidarity had come roaring in from Beat Four" (212–13). These other Monday nights are characterized by the various activities of movie-goers and livestock buyers. Next Chick's thoughts turn to the appearance of the square on the previous night, Sunday, when the citizens of Jefferson sat quietly behind their doors anticipating the lynching of Lucas Beauchamp. As the narrative continues, the focus shifts back to the present scene, then briefly to Chick's projections of the coming week: "tomorrow it would be over, tomorrow of course the Square would wake and stir, another day and it would fling off hangover, another and it would even fling off shame . . . " (214). The reflection concludes with a two-page italicized section which repeats Gavin's words to Chick—expressed presumably many times but most recently only thirty minutes earlier—about the future of black and white Southerners. Following this recollection, Chick leaves the square and returns

39. (New York: Random House, 1948), 211–17.

to the alley to observe again "the sheriff and Lucas cross[ing] the dark yard" (217).

The reader is surprised to learn that this entire seven-page narrative has occupied only a minute or two, perhaps only seconds, in actual time. Obviously Faulkner's intent here is to capture in the slow-motion process of linear prose the rapid and kaleidoscopic thought patterns which can perhaps be rendered convincingly (if at all in art) only by the motion picture film. But one senses in such passages more than an attempt to capture what Faulkner once defined as "the whole complete nuance of the moment's experience" (*LIG*, 107). One perceives also an urgency, even a desperation, a straining against the limits of time through the creative power of the imagination. All of Faulkner's characteristic stylistic devices— his penchant for stringing together a succession of coordinate, often synonymous terms; the extensive use of lengthy series of subordinate and parenthetical phrases and clauses; the pervasive reliance upon analogy, simile, and metaphor; and the attempt to utilize (and sometimes misapply) the whole range and scope of the English vocabulary—derive from this same urgency. Faulkner well understood his purpose in this regard, even if some of his readers have not. As he stated in Japan, "I would say that that style is a result of a need, of a necessity. This is what I mean, man knows that he cannot live forever, he has only a short time to live, there could be in a man's mind, in his heart, a desire to express some universal truth and he knows he has only a certain number of years to express that truth in, and so in my own case anyway, it's the compulsion to say everything in one sentence because you may not live long enough to have two sentences" (*LIG*, 141). Thus Faulkner's idiosyncratic style not only mirrors the interaction of man with time but also records his protest against its tyranny.

In considering Faulkner's style as a means of denying time

and death, one should pay particular attention to one aspect of that style, the extensive use of figurative language. Faulkner readers are quite familiar with his proclivity to describe characters, actions, and objects not as isolated, independent entities but almost always in relation to other persons and things. Indeed, one might conclude that nothing in Faulkner's work has significance in and of itself, but only as it is transformed metaphorically by the creative imagination. The pattern is exemplified by *Intruder in the Dust*, not generally considered one of Faulkner's best novels but one of the most conspicuous in its use of figurative language. This work contains, by quick count, more than three hundred figures of speech, including similes, metaphors, personifications, and analogies.[40] It seems inadequate to account for such a preponderance of figures as merely a holdover from Faulkner's practice as a poet. To perceive the ultimate significance of this characteristic of Faulkner's style, one must look beyond such facile labels as "Faulkner's poetic prose" and consider the psychological basis for metaphoric language. As almost all theorists agree, man resorts to metaphor when ordinary language proves inadequate for his needs, when he desires to capture, through suggestion, an intensity or a significance which cannot be conveyed by direct treatment. In this regard, the inclination toward metaphor readily serves Faulkner's aesthetic of memory. As René Wellek and Austin Warren explain, "We metaphorize . . . what we love, what we want to linger over and contemplate, to see from every angle and under every lighting, mirrored in specialized focus by all kinds of like things."[41] But metaphor is not only a way of enhancing an object as object; it is also a reaching beyond, an attempt at

40. Roughly one-half of the figures in *Intruder in the Dust* are similes; about one-third are metaphors or personifications. Strangely, Edwin R. Hunter (*William Faulkner: Narrative Practice and Prose Style* [Washington: Windhover Press, 1973], 215) finds only twenty-eight similes and four metaphors in the novel.
41. *Theory of Literature*, 3rd ed. (New York: Harvest Book, 1963), 197.

metamorphosis. The root meaning of the word "trope," the generic term for all figures of speech, is "turning away"; thus metaphoric language is basically an attempt to transcend the commonplace and the conventional. As Philip Wheelwright insists, "What really matters in a metaphor is the psychic depth at which the things of the world, whether actual or fancied, are transmuted by the cool heat of the imagination."[42] And so it is with Faulkner. Like his use of mythic correspondence for character and incident, the employment of figurative language evidences a need to transcend "the sorry, shabby world" through the creative force of the imagination. Metaphor, then, in Faulkner's method becomes just one more means of "saying No to death."

I have sought to demonstrate that a desire, not always conscious, to protest the tragic realities of time and death provided both the impetus and the pattern for Faulkner's fictional creation. I have noted that Faulkner's twin aesthetics of memory and imagination, both clearly exhibited in his subject matter and style, are logical derivations of the compulsion to "say No to death." Now, in conclusion, I wish to identify one major inference to be drawn from this approach to Faulkner's work.

Critics have debated at length whether Faulkner's fiction, on balance, makes a positive or negative statement regarding the human condition. Some readers find in Faulkner's books an unrelieved pessimism; others find a strong assertion of humanistic values; still others find that Faulkner began in cynicism but ended in hope. These various judgments explain the conflicting reactions to Faulkner's Nobel Prize acceptance speech: one reader interprets the address as nothing more than empty rhetoric, while another insists that it is a statement of genuine belief and promise.

42. *Metaphor and Reality* (Bloomington: Indiana University Press, 1962), 71.

"Saying No to Death"

The disagreement about Faulkner's definition of man is bound to continue, but even the most emphatic nay-sayer concerning Faulkner's view of man's behavior and potential must concede that the writer's feelings for art and the artist are extremely positive. In considering the crass materialism of the Snopeses, the pathetic fates of Quentin Compson, Addie Bundren, Joe Christmas, and Thomas Sutpen, and the noble but largely ironic deeds of Dilsey Gibson, Ike McCaslin, and the French corporal, one should remember that he is viewing the world through the refraction of art. The world that Faulkner mirrors may be one of tragedy and grief, but the art which images that world is a magnificent triumph, a thing of beauty. While Faulkner as historian, or politician, or psychologist, or philosopher, or theologian may despair, Faulkner as artist has supreme faith in the value of creativity and the nature of art. One suspects that the Nobel Prize address is only secondarily a statement about mankind and its destiny: it is first and foremost a declaration of faith in the creative act of the poet. Perhaps Faulkner was mistaken (though one hopes not) in viewing his own artistic struggle and triumph as emblematic of the fate of man,[43] but this question should not be allowed to obscure his characterization, in the Nobel Prize speech and elsewhere, of the poet's role as heroic. The poet is heroic because he is totally dedicated to his craft and will allow neither hardship nor success to distract him from his task. The poet is heroic because he risks the impossible and because he refuses to accept defeat, even though it is inevitable.[44] The poet is heroic because he matches his imagination against "the sorry, shabby world." Above all, the poet is heroic because through his creativity he "says No to death." In these ways, in its processes and not

43. I agree with Blotner's contention that "there was . . . probably an intensely personal component in the words of the speech" (*Faulkner: A Biography*, 1367).
44. See, for example, *Lion in the Garden*, 81, 88, 138, 221, 238.

necessarily its content or message, art may be said to be "the salvation of mankind" (*LIG*, 71). "The most important thing," Faulkner said, "is that man continues to create, just as woman continues to give birth. Man will keep writing on pieces of paper, on scraps, on stones, as long as he lives" (*LIG*, 73). All men, of course, strive in their own ways to overcome time and death, but the artist, according to Faulkner, comes closest to success. As he observed at Nagano, "[Man] can't live forever. He knows that. But when he's gone somebody will know he was here for his short time. He can build a bridge and will be remembered for a day or two, a monument, for a day or two, but somehow the picture, the poem—that lasts a long time, a very long time, longer than anything" (*LIG*, 103).

The Cubist Novel:
Toward Defining the Genre

PANTHEA REID BROUGHTON

Throughout the years William Faulkner made numbers of statements about the novel itself, its relationship to poetry, and its challenges for him. As Hugh Kenner reminded this conference two years ago, Faulkner said that writing a novel was like "trying to nail together a henhouse in a hurricane."[1] Any number of his other statements suggest that Faulkner thought of the novel as an especially challenging form, but I would like to point to one simple, little-noticed reference which has, I think, very large implications. In the biography, Joseph Blotner quotes from a letter Faulkner wrote to Hal Smith in the fall of 1932. Explaining how he put together the poems which were to form *A Green Bough*, Faulkner wrote "I chose the best manuscripts and built a volume just like a novel."[2] Clearly, Faulkner thought of a novel as something to be *built*, like a wall or a house, from separate parts. The image of a whole built out of separate parts which have been arranged in space is, I think, a crucial one for understanding Faulkner's novels; for the novels are spatial not linear constructions.

Obviously, the metaphor of building a work of literature is

1. Quoted by Hugh Kenner, "Faulkner and Joyce," in *Faulkner, Modernism, and Film: Faulkner and Yoknapatawpha 1978*, Evans Harrington and Ann J. Abadie, eds. (Jackson: University Press of Mississippi, 1979), 20.
2. Joseph Blotner, *Faulkner: A Biography* (New York: Random House, 1974), 790.

not new. Probably most notably, George Herbert reified the metaphor in the collection of verse called *The Temple* (1623). But Herbert thought of the order he built as substantial—a replication of divine order.[3] Faulkner saw his order, on the other hand, as insubstantial—like a henhouse in a hurricane. However insubstantial it might prove, Faulkner's order was self-created, autonomous. It was not achieved by reflecting divine order nor by tracing a plot line. He *chose* to use disparate, improbable fragments and to build from them a new sort of novel.

I am afraid that we really have not fully appreciated that fact and instead have been too often influenced by the misconceived notion that Faulkner just could not write a proper novel. Of course, that misconception is not the only one that has affected our understanding of Faulkner. But it seems to me that the notion that Faulkner could not handle the novel form has been finally more damaging than the two more absurd misconceptions that plagued Faulkner during the early years of his career.

One notion that seems absurd to us now was that because he lived in the "backward South," Faulkner was incapable of working with the complicated concepts and high values that characterize great writing. As John Chamberlain wrote in a 1931 review of *Sanctuary*: "Very possibly the material which is presented to Mr. Faulkner's sensibility by his environment is not of an order to make of him a Joyce or a Dostoevsky."[4] That attitude survived at least until 1950 when the *New York Times* greeted the news that Faulkner had won the Nobel Prize for Literature with the following comments:

His [Faulkner's] field of vision is concentrated on a society that

3. See, for example, Louis L. Martz on the unity of *The Temple*, in *The Poetry of Meditation: A Study in English Religious Literature of the Seventeenth Century* (New Haven: Yale University Press, 1954).

4. John Chamberlain, "Dostoevsky's Shadow in the Deep South," *New York Herald-Tribune Book Review* (15 February 1931), 9.

The Cubist Novel

is too often vicious, depraved, decadent, corrupt. Americans must feverently hope that the award by a Swedish jury and the enormous vogue of Faulkner's works in Latin America and on the European Continent, especially in France, does not mean that foreigners admire him because he gives them the picture of American life they believe to be typical and true. There has been too much of that feeling lately, again especially in France. Incest and rape may be common pastimes in Faulkner's "Jefferson, Miss." but they are not elsewhere in the United States.[5]

A second misconception was that it was not Faulkner's limited background so much as sordid imagination that forever should relegate his works to the trash bins. Henry Seidel Canby first used the phrase "The School of Cruelty" in 1931,[6] and the label was slow to die. A 1941 review, for instance, describes *The Hamlet* as "Faulkner's latest explosion in a cesspool."[7] The assumptions that something was wrong with either Faulkner's material or his mind persisted for at least twenty years. But such failures of sensitivity and understanding have long since been exposed as mere provincial prejudices. No one talks that way about Faulkner any more.

The third misconception exhibited an aesthetic prejudice. It was the unfortunate assumption, to which I have already referred, that Faulkner had not mastered the novel form. In 1926 Faulkner's New Orleans friend John McClure, reviewing *Soldiers' Pay*, objected to the novel's "random method of assemblage [which] is a technical deficiency."[8] Similarly, a 1930 review of *As I Lay Dying* regrets that Faulkner will not

5. Quoted by Robert Penn Warren, Introduction to *Faulkner: A Collection of Critical Essays*, Robert Penn Warren, ed. (Englewood Cliffs, N.J.: Prentice–Hall, Inc., 1966), 9.
6. Henry Seidel Canby, "The School of Cruelty," *Saturday Review* (21 March 1931), 673–74.
7. Donald Stanford, "*The Beloved Returns* and Other Recent Fiction," *The Southern Review*, 6 (Winter, 1941), 619.
8. John McClure, "Literature and Less," *New Orleans Times-Picayune* (11 April 1926), Magazine Section, 4.

use more traditional forms.[9] Then the assumption that Faulkner could not write novels was validated and ensconced by Malcolm Cowley. In the 1942 review of *Go Down, Moses* that declared Faulkner to be "the most considerable novelist of this generation," Cowley also wrote that *Go Down, Moses* "as a whole is a little too formless and repetitive to make a satisfactory novel."[10] Similarly, Cowley's otherwise valuable introduction to *The Portable Faulkner* directed attention towards Faulkner's "mythical kingdom" and the Yoknapatawpha saga and away from the individual novels. In fact, Cowley said that Faulkner is "not primarily a novelist."[11]

We are all deeply grateful to Malcolm Cowley for the judgment and bravery he showed in bringing out *The Portable Faulkner* and reviving interest in one of the greatest writers of our time. But his emphasis upon the canon as a whole and his conviction that Faulkner did not really write novels have directed critical attention away from the form of Faulkner's individual novels. And so the notion that Faulkner really did not master the novel form, though hardly as prejudiced and imbalanced as the other misconceptions about Faulkner, has had a longer life, and I believe that it has done a comparable amount of harm.

Of course, a number of critics over the years have known better. Important essays by Conrad Aiken in 1939 and Warren Beck in 1941 took Faulkner's style seriously. And through the years we have seen and are seeing more and more attention paid to the style and structure of Faulkner's work. At last we

9. Margaret Cheney Dawson, "Beside Addie's Coffin," *New York Herald-Tribune Book Review* (5 October 1930), 6.
10. Malcolm Cowley, "Go Down to Faulkner's Land," *The New Republic* (29 June 1942), 900.
11. Malcolm Cowley, Introduction to *The Portable Faulkner*, Malcolm Cowley, ed. (New York: The Viking Press, 1946), 18. In his introduction for the 1967 revised edition Cowley alters the statement to say "It had better be admitted that almost all his novels have some obvious weakness in structure" (xxiv).

have several full-length studies which have addressed themselves to the question of form in Faulkner's fiction. Joseph
Reed in *Faulkner's Narrative*, Albert J. Guerard in *The
Triumph of the Novel*, Arthur F. Kinney in *Faulkner's Narrative Poetics*, and most recently Donald M. Kartiganer in
*The Fragile Thread: The Meaning of Form in Faulkner's Nov-
els* all insist that we must come to terms with Faulkner's radical experiments with form itself. Kartiganer is perhaps most
explicit about the problem; he says:

> This fragmentary structure is the core of Faulkner's novelistic
> vision, describing a world of broken orders, a world in which the
> meetings of men and words need to be imagined again.
> The general critical response to this fragmentation has been to
> see it as a flaw, and either to dismiss the work accordingly or to
> discover in it some principle of unity. The assumption has been
> that if Faulkner is to have major status, his structural idiosyncra-
> cies must be clarified: that is to say, drained of their power and
> made consistent with conventional notions of literary order.[12]

Kartiganer has named the very problem with which I want to
deal. Each of these critics—Reed, Guerard, Kinney, and Kartiganer—says that a major blind spot in Faulkner criticism
has been its failure to appreciate Faulkner's technical innovations. Together these critics have done much to shrink that
blind spot. It seems to me, however, that the work they set
out to do is only partially complete; for until we have a working definition of the genre in which Faulkner wrote, a myopic
view of his formal failures and a blindness to his technical
successes will persist.

Our problem of defining and analyzing the form in which
Faulkner wrote is actually part of a larger problem which I
see as a critical failure to define the modern novel. Of course,
we cannot define this form if we are still debating the question of whether the novel is dead or alive. In *The Nature of*

12. Donald M. Kartiganer, *The Fragile Thread: The Meaning of Form in Faulkner's Novels* (Amherst: The University of Massachusetts Press, 1979), xiii-xiv.

Narrative Robert Scholes and Robert Kellogg insist that "something must be done about our veneration of the novel as a literary form."[13] Thus they set out, in their words, "to put the novel in its place."[14] Scholes and Kellogg consider the novel as representative of "only a couple of centuries in the continuous narrative tradition of the Western world which can be traced back five thousand years."[15] Thus the novel is not the end-product of a teleological process, but merely a stage in a continuous evolutionary process. If the epic is "as dead as the dinosaur,"[16] Scholes and Kellogg imply that the novel too is becoming similarly extinct. Clearly, when they speak of the novel, these critics mean the realistic novel as written by Turgenev, Tolstoy, Balzac, George Eliot, or Theodore Dreiser. They say that narratives written by Joyce, Proust, Mann, Lawrence, and Faulkner have already broken away from that tradition. Thus, from Scholes and Kellogg's point of view, whatever he did write, William Faulkner did not write novels.

In *The Triumph of the Novel* Albert J. Guerard sets forth an apparently antithetical thesis. He feels that the novel is an inherently open form which has from its beginning incorporated playfulness, fantasy, excess, and distortion. Guerard insists that the novel is as much anti-realist as realist. "Great fiction," he says, "is art and invention, not reduplicated reality."[17] He admits that he has been "irritated by F. R. Leavis's priggish and essentially artless view of fiction, and by the stubbornness with which many reviewers and editors (but also eminent academic critics . . .) [have] clung decade after

---

13. Robert Scholes and Robert Kellogg, *The Nature of Narrative* (London: Oxford University Press, 1966; rpt. 1976), 5.
14. *Ibid.*, 3.
15. *Ibid.*, 9.
16. *Ibid.*, 11.
17. Albert J. Guerard, *The Triumph of the Novel: Dickens, Dostoevsky, Faulkner* (New York: Oxford University Press, 1976), 12.

decade to nineteenth-century and 1930ish assumptions concerning 'the novel' and its mimetic obligations."[18]

Apparently, Scholes and Kellogg on the one hand and Guerard on the other represent radically opposed views; it seems that they would not venerate the novel, while he would. Actually though, this is mainly a disagreement about whether or not the novel is inherently realistic. Scholes and Kellogg think it is, Guerard that it is not. If they disagree about the definition of the novel though, the three do not disagree at all about realism. Each sees realism as a convention of nineteenth-century fiction which has little relevance to modern fiction. And the three critics alike regret that modern literary criticism tenaciously clings to and tries to impose standards better suited to the literature of another age.

Perhaps modern literary criticism is not as recalcitrant as Scholes, Kellogg, and Guerard claim. And perhaps those critics are setting up a false dichotomy between realist and anti-realist traditions. But they are correct in insisting that literary criticism has been notably derelict in defining, explaining, and establishing standards for those modern long prose narratives (whether or not we call them novels) which are significantly different from their nineteenth century predecessors. In other words, criticism has been tardy in acknowledging that the novel is not what it used to be. If we look, for example, for a definition of the novel in any literary handbook, we will find discussions which emphasize character development, cause and effect plotting, a coherent view of character and society, and the resolution of conflict. Such definitions suggest that novels be valued by standards of plausibility, continuity, and unity.[19] Though applicable to such a novel as

18. *Ibid.*, 11–12.
19. David Madden, for instance, distinguishes a novel from a short story: the novel "usually subjects the reader to an experience in more detail and depicts a greater variety of characters who are involved in a plot constituted of a multiplicity of episodes, with greater scope in time and space," *A Primer of the Novel: For*

Sister Carrie, those standards bear only the most tangential relationship to such a novel as *The Sound and the Fury*. Judged by them, Faulkner's great work either is not a novel or is a very inept one.

Of course, we all know that *The Sound and the Fury* is one of the great books of the modern age, even if it does not conform to our textbook definition of the novel. There are several possible explanations for this disparity between fact and theory. One is simply that such a time lag is inevitable between a constantly evolving genre and the theory that must see it before it can describe it; but that explanation ignores the fact that we have had sixty years for theory to catch up with fact. Another explanation is that textbook writers are using a fixed and superannuated theory to prescribe rather than describe; that seems to be a more plausible but still incomplete theory. But finally I suspect that we simply lack the terminology for describing accurately what the modern novel does and how it does it. To be sure, literary theory and especially theory of narrative are now very popular, even faddish, concerns. One would assume that out of all this writing on the topic a clear and workable definition of the modern novel will evolve, but I do not believe that thus far it has. In fact, much of contemporary theorizing seems to replicate the old

Readers and Writers (Metuchen, N.J.: The Scarecrow Press, 1980), 8. *The Dictionary of World Literature*, Joseph Shipley, ed. (New York: Philosophical Library, 1953), says that "with respect to structure it is helpful to distinguish between two overlapping but recognizable types of fiction—the panoramic (or epic) and the dramatic (scenic or well-made)" (286), but neither of these types includes the sort of fragmented novel Faulkner writes. In *A Reader's Guide to Literary Terms* (New York: The Noonday Press, 1960), Karl Beckson and Arthur Gany write vaguely and none-too-helpfully, "In the late nineteenth and the twentieth centuries the novel, as an art form, has reached its fullest development. Concerned with their craft, novelists such as Flaubert, Henry James, Virginia Woolf, James Joyce, E. M. Forster, and Thomas Mann have utilized various devices to achieve new aesthetic forms within the genre" (138). *A Handbook to Literature* (New York: The Odyssey Press, 1960), by William Flint Thrall and Addison Hibbard, revised and enlarged by C. Hugh Holman, devotes six pages to the novel, but it relates new techniques in fiction only with stream-of-consciousness novel (322).

problem in more modish terms. For instance, in *Narrative Suspense*, Eric S. Rabkin borrows from psychology for visual models of Gestalt perceptual patterns analogous to those found in the modern novel. But Rabkin uses phrases like "anticontextual bisociation with a residue"[20] which obfuscate rather than clarify. Again we seem to have theory with no obvious commonsensical connection with practice. In my terms, the abstract and the actual are split; in Addie Bundren's "words [literary theory, in this case] go straight up in a thin line, quick and harmless, [while] terribly doing [the novel] goes along the earth, clinging to it, so that after a while the two lines are too far apart for the same person to straddle from one to the other."[21]

Obviously, if our theory continues to float up into the air with little connection to fact, we critics and teachers are not in control of our trade. Also, we do a disservice to the literature we profess to teach: we fault these modern novels for not being something else and fail to appreciate what they are. But literary theory and literary fact should not be so far apart that only an academic acrobat can straddle them. We need a definition whose theory is congruent with fact.

My point is that, in the early twentieth century, modern novels developed a new shape which literary criticism to date has not adequately described. I think that Faulkner's point about building a collection of poems as he built a novel suggests not only the way that he put together novels but the way Joyce, Stein, Dos Passos, Woolf, and others also built novels. That is, they made novels not by tracing the linear development of a single plot line, but rather by building and arranging blocks of narrative with an eye for the sorts of patterns they were creating.

20. Eric Rabkin, *Narrative Suspense* (Ann Arbor: The University of Michigan Press, 1973), 127.
21. William Faulkner, *As I Lay Dying*, corrected and reset under the direction of James B. Meriwether (New York: Random House, 1964), 165.

I think that "cubist" is the most appropriate term for describing that arranging and patterning of narrative shapes which typifies the modern novel. Obviously, I believe that the novel is not dead; it is just different. Incidentally, as you may have noticed, of the four recent books on form in Faulkner which I mentioned earlier, two authors (Reed and Kinney) follow Scholes and Kellogg by preferring the term "narrative" to "novel," at least in their titles, while Kartiganer follows Guerard in preferring the term "novel." Perhaps I am only evening the score—making it three to three—by continuing to use the term "novel." But I do believe with Guerard that the novel has always been an open form. My use of the term "cubist" simply distinguishes one major direction that form took in the early modern period. I happen to think that it was the major direction and that most of our contemporary novelists also write cubist novels, but that is an argument which I will not begin to broach today.

My claim that the term "cubist" can be used with some precision to describe the modern novel needs explanation. "Cubiste" and "cubique" were terms first used in derision by the art critic Louis Vauxcelles in 1908 and 1909. The reference was to Braque's L'Estaque landscapes which seemed also to Matisse to be composed of "petits cubes."[22] Of course, neither Braque's landscapes nor the works that followed were merely made of cubes; but however abusively the term was intended and however inaccurate the designation remained, "cubism" became the only appropriate word to describe a new movement founded upon radically new assumptions about the nature of art, about its relationship with what is commonly called reality, and about the demands it might legitimately make upon the viewer.

As conceptual artists, the cubists did not paint or sculpt

22. Nicholas Wadley, *Cubism* (London: The Hambyn Publishing Group Limited, 1970), 12.

from the motif or on location; without a model they were freed from referential obligations. Cubist art (especially in the analytic state) took objects, shapes, even persons from nature and disassembled, juxtaposed, and arranged those parts with (rather than in) space. Often cubist art presented several sides of a single object at once on a flat plane. Forms were geometrized or reduced to elemental shapes. Sometimes shapes were outlined sharply to emphasize their separateness; sometimes planes merged in startling ways (as when a roof and a wall were not distinguished). Either way, commonplace assumptions about form were undermined. In fact, the effect of cubist art upon the viewer was part of its strategy. At the same time that the viewer perceived the aesthetic order of the art work (usually achieved from arranging disassembled objects), the viewer longed to reassemble the original subject. Engaged by that tension between the two orders, the viewer became incorporated into the art work. Thus, in such autonomous art, meaning derived less from subject matter than from the formal arrangement of the work and the viewer's relation to it.

In Paris during the early years of the century, cubist painters were associated with musicians, architects, and even one amateur mathematician. But their closest ties were with the literary avant-garde: Alfred Jarry, Guillaume Appolinaire, Max Jacob, and of course Gertrude Stein. During the half decade or so before the outbreak of World War I these artists and writers set out to renew the arts of their times. The patterns of cross fertilization between the artists and the various arts were complex and involuted, much too complicated to trace here today. But clearly the sort of excited borrowing and influencing that characterized the relationships between Braque, Picasso, and later Gris also characterized the relationships between them and their literary friends. Jarry, Apollinaire, Jacob, and Stein all consciously tried to do with words what their colleagues did with paint, and the painters in turn imitated some of the strategies of literature. Thus this group initiated a pattern of cross-fertilization between the visual and verbal arts which continued at least through the 1930s.

In the case of Gertrude Stein, John Dos Passos, E. E. Cummings, and Hemingway, the influence is direct and easily demonstrable. Upon James Joyce and Virginia Woolf too the impact of cubist art, though less direct, is traceable. With Faulkner the question may seem more problematic, but Ilse Dusoir Lind's paper on the influence of painting on Faulkner, given at this conference two years ago, does establish how much Faulkner cared about the visual arts and how pervasive was their influence on his fiction.[23] Also a more restricted study by Watson G. Branch entitled "Darl Bundren's 'Cubistic' Vision" explores in considerable detail Faulkner's knowledge of and interest in modern art, especially cubism.[24] Both of these critics have laid very impressive groundwork for the sorts of things I want to suggest. But I am not making an argument for direct influence. Even if Faulkner had never heard of cubism, I believe that his novels could appropriately be described as cubist.

After all cubism as a movement was never really revived after World War I. But cubism itself epitomized the beginning of the twentieth century. It signalled the end of a harmonious, ordered world and the emergence of a fragmented, discontinuous world. In *The Banquet Years: The Arts in France 1885–1918*, Roger Shattuck explains:

> The twentieth century has addressed itself to arts of juxtaposition as opposed to earlier arts of transition. Transition refers to those

23. Ilse Dusoir Lind, "The Effect of Painting on Faulkner's Poetic Form," in *Faulkner, Modernism, and Film*, 127–48.
24. Watson G. Branch, "Darl Bundren's 'Cubistic' Vision," *Texas Studies in Literature and Language*, 19 (Spring, 1977), 42–59.

The Cubist Novel

works that rely upon clear articulation of the relations between parts of the places they join. . . . The whole "classic" idea of style in art arose from the undisputed supremacy of transition. It ruled that in any artistic experience each part must follow from the last; witness the logical sequence of a tragedy or the massive symmetry of classic architecture. In great part its reward lies in the steadiness with which it carries the spectator along from beginning to end.[25]

Shattuck's point is that such steadiness is antithetical to our age. Two years ago at the Faulkner and Yoknapatawpha Conference, Bruce Kawin made a similar point about our age and its art: "The central anxiety of modernism—that the old, harmonious world lay busted into fragments—was central to its triumph. That triumph consisted in acknowledging fragmentation and then butting the fragments up against each other; this juxtaposition itself did not so much provide the longed-for connective tissue as it pointed beyond itself to a conceptual space in which the fragments might cohere."[26] From Kawin's point of view, juxtaposition and montage are virtually synonymous terms; thus he finds that the montage device in film epitomizes all the arts of our time.

Shattuck too sees the modern as an art of juxtaposition or "setting one thing beside the other without connective."[27] But "juxtaposition, through its fusion of subject and object, achieves not so much a new style, as an absence of style in the old sense of expressed transitions."[28] Thus "the arts of juxtaposition offer difficult, disconcerting, fragmented works whose disjunct sequence has neither beginning nor end."[29] But Shattuck is dissatisfied with his own terminology; for "juxtaposition implies succession . . . and ultimately it be-

25. Roger Shattuck, *The Banquet Years: The Arts in France 1885–1918* (New York: Harcourt, Brace and Company, 1958), 256–57.
26. Bruce Kawin, "The Montage Element in Faulkner's Fiction," in *Faulkner, Modernism, and Film*, 106.
27. Shattuck, 256.
28. *Ibid.*, 265.
29. *Ibid.*, 257.

comes apparent that the mutually conflicting elements of montage—be it movie or poem or painting—are to be conceived not successively but simultaneously, to converge in our minds as contemporaneous events."[30]

Thus Shattuck echoes the major point in Joseph Frank's seminal essay "Spatial Form in Modern Literature." Frank's thesis is that "modern literature, as exemplified by such writers as T. S. Eliot, Ezra Pound, Marcel Proust, and James Joyce, is moving in the direction of spatial form. . . . All these writers ideally intended the reader to apprehend their work spatially, in a moment of time, rather than as sequence."[31] In other words, the reader is to see the parts of even a long narrative arranged together as on a canvas. The terminology Shattuck and Frank use has been enormously helpful in characterizing the modern, but it needs further refining. As Shattuck himself realizes, "juxtaposition" is a less than precise term for naming a single technique; it does not serve adequately as a generic term for all the modern arts. I feel that the term "montage" has similar limitations. And Frank's "spatial form" is a crucially important theory but, after all, a rather vague generic term. "Cubist," on the other hand, is a generic term which subsumes the phenomena Shattuck, Kawin, and Frank describe while encompassing other characteristics also essential to modern art.

Christopher Gray begins his *Cubist Aesthetic Theories* by insisting upon the centrality of cubism for our time. He explains:

> In the art of the twentieth century, Cubism occupies a position as important as that of Romanticism in the nineteenth. The Cubist movement, gradually forming in the second half of the first decade of the twentieth century and developing up to the end of the second decade, marks a major turning point in the history of

30. *Ibid.*, 266.
31. Joseph Frank, *The Widening Gyre: Crisis and Mastery in Modern Literature* (New Brunswick, N.J.: Rutgers University Press, 1963), 9.

art. Ideas first formulated and given a concrete and unified expression by the Cubists have played a major role in determining the course of the development of modern art during the first half of this century, and give every indication of a vital and determining influence on the art of the second half of the century. As time passes it becomes more and more evident that a thorough understanding of the major developments of Cubism is a sine qua non for the intelligent criticism of all later artistic developments.

Cubism was more than another artistic "ism." It was something much deeper. Cubism was a vital force which found expression in music and literature as well as in the visual arts of painting and sculpture. It embodied a whole new outlook on the world and reality—a new Weltanschauung, an attitude sometimes ill formulated, full of inconsistencies in logic, even at times unconscious, but nevertheless powerful in its effect on artistic creation.[32]

In other words, cubism was not merely a movement lasting from 1909 to 1914, but rather a radical exploration of form and of the relationships between artist, art object, world, and viewer. Consequently, its influence has altered the shape and meaning of art in our time. Cubism then is the quintessential modern movement.

Because of the direct influence of cubism upon some modern literature and of the centrality of cubism to all that is modern, we do well to consider the modern novel as cubist. But I think that there is a third practical reason which is perhaps the best justification for seeing the modern through the frame of cubist art. This final reason is simply a matter of appropriate terminology.

As we all know, modern literary criticism dates from the Renaissance, but its roots are classical. Thus it tends to value linearity, coherence, and unity; and since the romantic period it has sought organic wholeness in literature. Thus literary criticism's own history has ill-equipped it to come to terms

32. Christopher Gray, *Cubist Aesthetic Theories* (Baltimore: The Johns Hopkins Press, 1953), 3.

with modern narratives that are intentionally discontinuous. Art criticism, on the other hand, has a relatively short history which in at least one way is a real advantage. Because art criticism first emerged in its own right during the early modern period, it is naturally attuned to modernist aims. Thus it explains discontinuity in painting and sculpture much more effectively than literary criticism to date has explained discontinuity in a narrative. Perhaps then if we literary critics simply borrowed some of the terminology our colleagues use to describe cubist art we would have very useful tools for describing the modern novel.

I hope that by looking at a few slides I can show you something of how this terminology works with regard to painting, and then in my second paper I want to suggest how it will work with Faulkner's fiction. I must begin this demonstration with advance apologies, for I am not an art historian, and I will not even attempt to do full justice to the works I will show you. I am using these paintings today merely as visual illustrations of the techniques I find also at work in the fiction of William Faulkner. I will cover them hastily and no doubt superficially and will not exhaust my topic today—though I may exhaust my audience. You will notice that the comparisons I make between cubistic and novelistic techniques rarely include reference to Faulkner. I have split what might have been one almost interminable talk in half. Thus this treatment of cubism and the modern novel has become a sort of preamble for my talk on Faulkner's cubistic novels.

First, I want to show you several aspects of the technique called flattening that the cubists learned from Cézanne and that Matisse, who was on the fringes of the cubist group, then thoroughly explored. Cézanne's *Bibemus Quarry* (c. 1898) is a landscape without depth. In fact it looks as if rocks and trees simply are stacked on top of each other. Matisse's *Harmony in Red* (1908–9) flattens the tablecloth into the wall paper and

51

his *Studio with "La Danse"* (1909) further flattens the foreground into the background so that neither is more important
than the other. Similarly Matisse's *The Blue Window* (1911)
flattens the objects inside the window into the scenery outside. With Picasso's *Still Life with Violin and Fruit* (1913),
flattening is absolute. Here there is no depth, not even an
illusion of space that one could live in. Such flattening of foreground into background was a reaction against illusionist art.
The vanishing perspective of illusionist art was designed to
make the flat painting seem to contain virtually infinite
depth. Cubist painting, on the other hand, acknowledged the
flat surface of the canvas as a way of proclaiming art's independence of nature. In literature, a similar flattening of foreground into background, so that the former has no special
status, occurs in Gertrude Stein's *The Making of Americans*
and in E. E. Cummings's *The Enormous Room*. With Faulkner, we might think of the stories of Joe Christmas and Lena
Grove in terms of figure and field; seeing either as figure
shifts the other to the status of field.

Flattening also meant that space, even empty space, could
be as important as objects. In the first of these three
Cézannes, *Chateau Noir* (1900–04), the sky is a focal point,
while in *Mont Sainte-Victoire* (1904–06) the sky is darker and
more clearly accentuated than the mountain. And in *Morning
in Provence* (1900–06) a nearly blank foreground dominates
the painting. Analogously, Virginia Woolf devotes the "Time
Passes" section of *To the Lighthouse* to "blank" or non-human
activities. In Faulkner the quality of life, even volition, given
to the wilderness in "The Bear" is comparable.

When planes were flattened, distinctions between them
broke down. We see this phenomenon best in the paintings
which triggered the beginning of the cubist movement. First
a Cézanne, *Quarry at Bibemus* (1898–1900): note how the
rocks here blur into each other. We can see the influence of

Cézanne upon Braque; his *House at L'Estaque* (1908) exhibits a similar blurring of houses and roofs. And his *Le Chateau de la Roche-Guyon* (1909) merges shapes until they are virtually indistinguishable. That breaking down of conventional distinctions between planes is called "passage of planes." The phrase also applies to the merging of characters in *In Our Time* and *The Autobiography of Alice B. Toklas*; of chronologies in *Goodbye to Berlin*; and of the fictive and real world in *Les Faux-monnayeurs*. Faulkner, of course, is always breaking down distinctions, most unforgettably in his presentation of Joe Christmas who "passes" as either black or white.

Also flattening in painting invited the merging of inside with outside phenomenon, as we see in DeLaunay's *The City of Paris* (1910–12) and Picasso's *Seated Woman* (1927). In literature the stream-of-consciousness technique, especially with Joyce, Woolf, and Faulkner, accomplished a similar merging.

If on the one hand the cubists accepted the limits of the flat canvas, ·on the other they devised new ways to challenge those limits. This early Cézanne, *Still Life: Basket of Apples* (1890–94), exemplifies the beginnings of both experiments; that is, it flattens objects, table, and background but it does so by presenting different perspectives at once. Later cubists began presenting an apparently unrestricted number of vantage points—inside, outside, left, right—all at once as if several different paintings had been combined. Picasso's *Les Demoiselles d'Avignon* (1907), placing five female figures together, makes a single plane into five planes. A later Picasso, *Oil on Canvas* (1936), further suggests how one plane could become many; for this "profile" shows both eyes and both breasts. Writers who present different perspectives upon the same person or event, as Joyce does in *Ulysses* and Faulkner does in *As I Lay Dying*, adapt a similar technique.

Cubists also challenged the limits of their medium by cre-

53

ating motion on a flat canvas. Marcel Duchamp's *Nude Descending the Staircase* (1912) is the most famous example. But Jacques Villon's *Soldiers on the March* (1913) is another important example of, in Faulkner's terms, arresting motion. Virginia Wolfe's writings, especially *Mrs. Dalloway, To the Lighthouse*, and *The Waves* offer a comparable accomplishment.

The collage was at once a way to point out the difference between artifice and reality, and a way to collapse that difference. It also blurred the distinction between painting and sculpture. The addition of a newspaper into Braque's *Still Life on the Table* (1912) asks us to realize that any material is suitable for art. Similarly, Schwitter's *Cherry Picture* (1921) collapses distinctions between the "real" and the invented. John Dos Passos's camera eye technique offers a related juxtaposition of the "real" and the fictive. And the newspaper clippings which appear throughout John Hawkes's *The Lime Twig* also blur the distinction between apparent reporting and invention.

If cubists broke down conventional assumptions about what a painting was made of and how it differed from other arts, they also broke down conventional assumptions about organic unity. In their paintings they carefully created tensions between parts and wholes. The "petites sensations" of interest in these two Cézannes are tiny focal points which pull our eyes away from the larger subject matter of the paintings *Chateau Noir* (1904–6) and *Bend in Forest Road* (1902–6). Individual narratives work in similar ways in *Winesburg, Ohio* or in *The Hamlet* where the Snopes/Stamper trade, or the spotted horses sequence, or the Labove/Eula romance are at once separate narratives and parts of the whole.

Cubism developed tensions between the whole and the part within the painting and within the object being painted. 1907 saw the publication, one year after his death, of

Artist as a Young Man, the patterns of encounter and retreat

Absalom, Absalom!

Portrait of Ambrose Voillard (1909–10) as an interesting ar-

seum of Modern Art, 1977), 155.

Cézanne's now famous letter which spoke of treating nature
"in terms of the cylinder, the sphere, the cone."[33] That notion
inspired Braque to reduce the landscape _La Roche-Guyon: Le
Chateau_ (1909) to geometric shapes. Picasso further abstracted a landscape _The Reservoir, Horta de Ebro_ (1909) into
geometric patterns. He worked similarly with two female figures: _Nude in the Forest_ (1908) and _Seated Woman_ (1909).
Fernand Léger's later painting _The Women_ (1921) is not so
much a study of women as it is of circles and cylinders among
straight lines.

In cubist paintings forms were not only reduced to basic
geometric shapes, they were faceted into repeating geometrical planes. We see such faceting in Léger's _Nudes in the
Forest_ (1910), Juan Gris's _Portrait of Picasso_ (1912), and Gris's
Guitar and Flowers (1912).

Such geometrizing soon moved toward synthetic cubism by
distancing itself further and further from the motif. Braque's
Still Life with Violin and Pitch (1909–10), for instance, shows
more interest in geometric arrangements than in its putative
subjects. Similarly, mostly by its title and the minimal suggestion of windows do we know what Braque's _The Roofs_
(1911) has as its subject. A comparable structuring by geometric patterns is basic to the five sections of _Portrait of the
Artist as a Young Man_, the patterns of encounter and retreat
in _In Our Time_, and the repeating patterns of rejection in
Absalom, Absalom!

As I have already suggested, cubism intentionally engaged
its viewers by coercing them to see the painting in two ways
at once. With Delaunay's _Eiffel Tower in Trees_ (1909) we may
choose to see the figure or the field. We may view Picasso's
Portrait of Ambrose Voillard (1909–10) as an interesting ar-

33. Paul Cézanne, quoted by William Rubin, "Cézannisme and the Beginnings
of Cubism" in _Cézanne: The Late Work_, William Rubin, ed. (New York: The Museum of Modern Art, 1977), 155.

55

rangement of lines and shapes or we may hunt for the resemblance to Voillard. With Braque's *Man with a Guitar* (1911) we enjoy the arrangement of broken shapes and we also seek to reassemble them so that they form a man with a guitar. Similarly, this Duchamp would seem to be an abstract arrangement of shapes pleasing in their own right, but when we learn that its title is *The Passage of the Virgin to the Bride* (1912) we search for referential clues. In literature such tension between the surface of the work of art and the subject that lies behind it is nowhere better illustrated than in *Absalom, Absalom!*

The last slides I want to show are a series of pairs illustrating art from earlier years alongside cubist art. Each comparison, I think, illustrates the essence of cubism: that cubist art creates meaning from form alone. Take these two breakfast scenes. To Chardin's *Remains of Breakfast* (1763) our aesthetic response is infused with our pleasure in the plenty the scene illustrates. But Gris's *Breakfast* (1914) disallows any such associations with an actual meal. Corot's *Village Church of Rosny-Sur-Seine* (1844) pleases us first because of the pastoral associations its tidy husbandry carries, while Cézanne's *Le Cabanon de Jourdan* (1906) carries no such associations. David's *Sappho and Phaon* (1809) asks us to respond to the story as much as to the painting, while Picasso rigorously suppressed any story element from *Les Demoiselles d'Avignon*. He eliminated, for example, clothed male figures that he had used in earlier versions of the painting; the men suggested a story while the final arrangement of female forms does not. Ingres's *Grande Odalisque* (1914) is lovely and seductive. She calls forth, as Stephen Daedelus would say, our kinetic responses. Braque's *The Bather* (1907) is not only unlovely, she is abstracted from individuality and presented as one among several similar block-shapes. Clearly, our response to her is static, that is, unemotional and therefore purely aesthetic.

Similarly, it is difficult not to respond first to the opulent fleshiness of Rubens's *Three Graces* (1639) and then to the artistry of the painting; but we see Picasso's *Three Women* (1908) merely as interesting, interrelated abstract shapes. Cubism then subverted our response to the subject matter itself and asked us instead to respond to form alone. Obviously form has always carried meaning, but not until cubism did form become the primary vehicle of meaning.

Picasso said, "Through art we express our conception of what nature is not."[34] That 1923 statement has been taken as a validation for abstract or non-referential art, but the context of the statement reveals that Picasso meant all art, in all times. Certainly the classical art we have seen today, however "representational" it may be, presents an orderly perfection and beauty. We yearn for that perfection and beauty but realize that they cannot be found in nature but can be found in art. On the other hand, the cubists set out to create an order in art that did not appeal to our yearning for beauty or perfection. Viewing these sets of slides today, you may conclude that we have lost more than we have gained. To me at least it does seem that experiments with mere form, or "pure" form, become finally both boring and reductionist. But I do feel that in elevating form to a level of meaning in its own right, the cubists opened all sorts of possibilities for using tensions between subject and form to create new meanings.

This "show and tell" session has been designed to illustrate a number of cubist techniques which have analogues in the modern novel. It has also been designed to show how useful a number of terms from art criticism—such as flattening, passage of planes, collage, petites sensations, and faceting—can be in describing the modern novel. And it was intended to establish that the essence of cubism was a radical exploration

34. Pablo Picasso, quoted by Alfred H. Barr, Jr., *Picasso: Fifty Years of His Art* (New York: Museum of Modern Art, 1946), 270.

of the meaning of form itself. Of course, the novel is made of words which are referential; thus it cannot become a pure form like abstract art. (Gertrude Stein's attempts to so purify the novel were abysmal failures.) But nevertheless the modern novelist, like the cubist painter, has explored ways in which form can create meaning. In the simplest terms, then, the cubist novel is one in which a linear narrative is broken so that the structure or arrangement of its parts itself forms a level of meaning. In *The Sound and the Fury*, for example, meaning results as much from the patterning of the four sections as from the "story" of the decline of the Compson family.

I have talked a great deal and still have not said much about the subject you came to this conference to hear about. Perhaps I need to end this address by saying simply "To be continued." And if today I've spent a lot of our time on cubism, a good bit on the modern novel, and very little on Faulkner's novels, I plan later to reverse the proportions.

Faulkner's Cubist Novels

PANTHEA REID BROUGHTON

Faulkner's career is usually seen in stages: the rather gawky and derivative early verse; the magnificent novels published between 1929 and 1942; and the rather windy prose fiction of the late forties and the fifties. Such a division of all Faulkner's career into three parts is convenient but inaccurate. It is unfair to the late and wholly neglectful of the early fiction. And it fails to acknowledge that there were two, rather than one, major transformations in the 1920s. One occurred in 1928 when Faulkner wrote *The Sound and the Fury*, but the other occurred three years earlier when he began writing prose and stopped writing poetry.

Those two remarkable transformations almost defy explanation. Here was a young Mississippian who until around 1925 had been drawing highly artificial illustrations while writing overly stylized third-rate poetry; then about 1925 he gave up both drawing and poetry and made an abrupt shift to fiction writing. He then produced three not quite satisfactory novels. These novels—*Soldiers' Pay*, *Mosquitoes*, and *Flags in the Dust*—do show considerable artistry and increasing control; certainly his third book, *Flags in the Dust* (published as *Sartoris* in 1929), is vastly superior to anything that preceded it. But we cannot describe Faulkner's career in terms of a gradual pattern of ever-increasing accomplishment. For when he wrote *The Sound and the Fury* he seems to have taken a quantum leap from apprenticeship to mastery, from fiction that did little more than temporarily engage readers to fiction that permanently altered the genre of fiction and our understandings of ourselves.

Both Cleanth Brooks and Gary Lee Stonum have examined the complex significance of Faulkner's transition from poetry to prose.[1] But too many of us have simply assumed the appropriateness of a "failed"[2] poet's giving up poetry; thus we have not asked enough questions about why Faulkner suddenly became almost excusively a prose writer. But if we have not been sufficiently curious about that first transformation, we have been almost obsessed by the second. Often the power and skill of *The Sound and the Fury* are explained in terms of Faulkner's return (both literally and metaphorically) to Mississippi. There is no doubt, as we all are learning more fully this week, that Faulkner's discovery of his "own little postage stamp of native soil"[3] was crucial to his art. But *Sartoris*, not *The Sound and the Fury*, was the first published work set here. The return home then, as Mr. Compson would say, "just does not explain"[4] the break between those two novels.

That break between the apprenticeship of *Flags in the Dust/Sartoris* and *The Sound and the Fury* apparently perplexed Faulkner as much as it does us. It is the single issue he addressed in 1933 in two versions of an introduction to the novel. (Faulkner was writing an introduction for what was to be a new edition of the novel; the edition was never pub-

1. See Cleanth Brooks, *William Faulkner: Toward Yoknapatawpha and Beyond* (New Haven: Yale University Press, 1978), especially the first four chapters. And Gary Lee Stonum, *Faulkner's Career: An Internal Literary History* (Ithaca: Cornell University Press, 1979), especially the first two chapters.
2. In Japan in 1955 Faulkner said "I look at myself as a failed poet." *Lion in the Garden: Interviews with William Faulkner 1926–1962*, James B. Meriwether and Michael Millgate, eds. (New York: Random House, 1968), 119. Similar statements recur throughout his published interviews and classroom sessions.
3. *Ibid.*, 255.
4. William Faulkner, *Absalom, Absalom!* (New York: The Modern Library facsimile of the First Edition, 1964), 100.

lished, the introductions almost forgotten, until a missing page of one and all of the other were found in the Rowanoak papers in 1970; the two introductions were published by James B. Meriwether in 1972 and 1973.)[5] In these introductions Faulkner looks back over his then seven-year career as a novelist in order to explain for himself what happened when he wrote *The Sound and the Fury*. In what may be the first introduction[6] he partially attributes the transformation to a new disregard for the marketplace: he writes, "I seemed to shut a door between me and all publishers' addresses and book lists. I said to myself, Now I can write."[7] But Faulkner also says that his intention was to make something perfect which would serve as a substitute for certain deficiencies in

5. "An Introduction for *The Sound and the Fury*," James B. Meriwether, ed., *The Southern Review*, n. s. VIII (Autumn, 1972). And "An Introduction to *The Sound and the Fury*," James B. Meriwether, ed., *The Mississippi Quarterly*, 26 (Summer, 1973), rpt. *A Faulkner Miscellany* (Jackson: University Press of Mississippi, 1974).

6. Meriwether describes the version he published in *The Southern Review* as "apparently the last," but he also says of the *Mississippi Quarterly* version that "it is at least possible that it was written later, rather than earlier" (*A Faulkner Miscellany*, 156). I would date the *MQ* version last for two reasons. First, the *SoR* version speaks of losing "my daughter in infancy" (710) while the *MQ* version more accurately states "[I] was destined to lose my first daughter in infancy" (*A Faulkner Miscellany*, 159). The Faulkners' first daughter Alabama was born January 11 and died January 20, 1931 (see Joseph Blotner, *Faulkner: A Biography* [New York: Random House, 1975], 681–82). Bennett Cerf introduced the idea of a new edition of *The Sound and the Fury* to Faulkner around Christmas in 1932 (see *Selected Letters of William Faulkner*, Joseph Blotner, ed. [New York: Random House, 1977], 69). The Faulkners' daughter Jill was born June 24, 1933 (Blotner, 803). Faulkner refers to the introduction in letters written to Ben Wasson in June and August of 1933, mailing one version to Wasson—we do not know which one—in mid-August of 1933 (*Letters*, 71 and 74). It seems feasible to me that the introduction which speaks of losing his daughter was being written or at least formulated during early 1933 when Faulkner was still grieving over the loss of one child and apprehensive about the birth of another. That version may not have been written down until after Jill's birth (see *Letters*, 71), but Faulkner must have been fearful then that this child too might die. That poignant, romantic introduction seems then best dated in this period, while the more matter-of-fact version which refers to a "first" daughter and thus implies a second daughter seems a more appropriate expression of the period when he wrote to Wasson "Jill getting fatter and fatter." Secondly, since the *MQ* version is dated August 19, 1933, and Wasson mailed one version to Random House on August 24, 1933 (*Letters*, 74), the *MQ* version must have been the last version.

7. *The Southern Review*, n. s. 8 (Autumn, 1972), 710.

his own life; he determined, "Now I can make myself a vase like that which the old Roman kept at his bedside and wore the rim slowly away with kissing it. So I, who never had a sister and was fated to lose my daughter in infancy, set out to make myself a beautiful and tragic little girl."[8] This explanation is puzzling, not only because of the ambiguous vase metaphor, but because Caddy, the beautiful and tragic little girl, is conspicuously absent from most of *The Sound and the Fury*. Faulkner's theory suggests, though, the importance of absence rather than presence and of discovering a reservoir of profound psychic desire. But Faulkner's theory still does not explain; for he did not first tap that reservoir with *The Sound and the Fury*. Everything he had written before 1925 does express a profound desire for something or someone lost or missing, but *The Sound and the Fury* itself does not.

Faulkner's theory is deceiving, then, not because Caddy is absent from *The Sound and the Fury*, but because the book is not a romantic lament for her parting. In fact, though Benjy, Quentin, and Jason cannot cope with Caddy's absence, the book itself does. The brothers may be hapless romantics, but *The Sound and the Fury* is not a romantic book. Faulkner may have theorized like a romantic in one introduction written in 1933, but he quit writing like one partially in 1925 and completely in 1928.

8. *Ibid.* I am grateful to James B. Meriwether for providing me with the following explanations of the allusion to the old Roman and his vase: "Faulkner's allusion to Sienkiewicz's *Pan Michael* in the foreword to the *Faulkner Reader* is well known. But another Sienkiewicz novel probably provides the source for an allusion in the 1933 introduction to *The Sound and the Fury*. . . . In the first chapter of *Quo Vadis*, translated by Jeremiah Curtin, Boston: Little Brown, 1897, p. 6, Petronius is talking to his young friend Marcus Vinicius about the variety of man's pleasures— some prefer war to love; 'Bronzebeard loves song, especially his own; and old Scaurus his Corinthian vase, which stands near his bed at night, and which he kisses when he cannot sleep. He has kissed the edge off already.'" However ironically Sienkiewicz's anecdote may be presented, Faulkner's retelling of it is romantic; for him, the vase or work of art is so beautiful it compensates for life's inadequacies and substitutes for a lost love.

It seems to me that the transformations in Faulkner's work which took place in 1925 and 1928 were significant precisely because they were rejections of a destructive romanticism. These transformations cannot be explained as discoveries of desire or even of place, but rather as passages through literary stages in search of a form appropriate to the times in which Faulkner lived. It took him about ten years to discover that form. But before he could make that discovery he had to pass through about one hundred years of literary evolution.

Let me explain the sort of literary evolution to which I refer. As we know, art never duplicates nature; in Picasso's terms it always shows us what nature is not. But the ways in which it does so can express a variety of understandings about art and its relation to this world and to a transcendent other realm. In the eighteenth century the visual arts showed us people, landscapes, still lifes which were recognizable as such; but at the same time the arts presented those subjects in a harmony, order, and beauty which allied them with eternity and made them fit objects of our admiration. In his memorably ambiguous advice to poets, Pope captures the spirit of such art:

> First follow Nature, and your Judgment frame
> By her just Standard, which is still the same:
> *Unerring Nature*, still divinely bright,
> One *clear*, *unchang'd*, and *Universal* Light,
> Life, Force, and Beauty, must to all impart,
> At once the *Source*, and *End*, and *Test* of *Art*.[9]

The romantics held a less sanguine view of the interrelatedness of art, nature, the universal, and the divine. They assumed that perfection, like Keats's nightingale, had flown beyond this realm. Lost to a community with shared values, it could be apprehended only through the individual imagina-

---

9. Alexander Pope, "An Essay on Criticism," in *Poetry and Prose of Alexander Pope*, Aubrey Williams, ed. (Boston: Houghton Mifflin Company, 1969), 40.

tion of the artist. Its imprint remained in the perfection and beauty of the art form.

With the advent of realism, belief in a perfect order, even one elsewhere, waned. Beauty, perfection, and the orderly distinction between right and wrong all seemed illusions designed to distract people from the problems of the here and now. The realistic artist saw his principal responsibility as depicting the local, the familiar, the *real*, with accuracy. Of course, as Picasso suggests, "real" art is an oxymoron, a contradiction in terms. And there were other contradictions in realism. The naturalists, for example, wanted to expose wrongs so that conditions might be bettered; but their theory allowed no place for the concepts of wrong or of improvement.

The modern period was ushered in by an awareness of the contradictions and limitations of so-called realism. Also modern art began to embody that loss of faith in transcendent values which realistic art had mouthed. Einstein's theory of relativity and Bergson's of fluidity were each expressions of and symbols of a time when absolutes were lost. In Quentin Compson's words, "all stable things had become shadowy[,] paradoxical."[10] In this situation psychology, philosophy, art, and even, to some degree, religion turned to the human mind as the last remaining location for meaning. If the romantics had believed in the ontological status of perfect forms—the ode or the sonnet or the beautiful landscape painting—the moderns no longer saw inherent beauty or meaning in such forms. Instead, meaning might only be found in the consciousnesses of individual men and women. The moderns adapted the strategy of dismantling forms in order to coerce the viewer or reader to reassemble them and thereby prevent

10. William Faulkner, *The Sound and the Fury* (New York: Random House, Vintage Books, 1954), 211. Hereafter references to this edition will be abbreviated *SF* and included in the text.

him from remaining a passive bystander or consumer of art. In that engagement of the audience with the creative process the moderns located meaning. And it seems to me that postmodern art continues to do so.

It may be an admission of spiritual and aesthetic bankruptcy that we can no longer believe, as the eighteenth century could, that literature might live because truth can be immanent in it; or that we cannot believe, as the romantics could, that literature lives in emulation of and aspiration toward a world elsewhere; but that, instead, our literature lives only by compelling us to participate in it. Such compulsion is indeed a desperate strategy for achieving meaning, for it assumes no community of shared values beyond the one the writer and reader create together. But it does assume meaning, not better than, but different from, the art of other ages. Thus, though desperate, it is not bankrupt. And finally, even such a desperate strategy confirms Faulkner's belief that literature can be one of the props of civilization, one of the means, as Robert Hamblin reminds us, of saying *no* to death. It can do so because, if rightly made, it will, in Faulkner's terms, live or move again whenever it is read.

That notion of literature as living, moving art predominates in what I believe to be Faulkner's second version of the introduction to *The Sound and the Fury.* As I have suggested (see footnote 6), the first version was decidedly romantic. But the second version is more modernist. It suggests that Faulkner had a sense of his passage through the sort of evolutionary process I have been describing. This version is longer, less poetic, and slightly less ambiguous. Faulkner begins it by saying that "art is no part of Southern life";[11] and yet art "is almost the sum total of the Southern artist. It is his breath, blood, flesh, all. [In the South he is] forced to choose, lady

11. *A Faulkner Miscellany*, 156.

65

and tiger fashion, between being an artist and being a man."[12] Seeing life, or Southern life, and art in mutually exclusive terms, Faulkner also sees the Southerner's art as intensely personal: "Because it is himself that the Southerner is writing about, not about his environment."[13] Apparently, though, by "himself" Faulkner means his reactions to his environment; for he sees only two alternatives for the Southern writer— either escaping or indicting the South. He says, "I seem to have tried both of the courses. I have tried to escape and I have tried to indict. After five years I look back at *The Sound and the Fury* and see that that was the turning point: in this book I did both at one time."[14]

Here Faulkner acknowledges something of the evolutionary process he has passed through. In his early romantic stage he did try to escape not only the South but this world altogether. In his second realistic stage, he returned to this world and the South principally to indict it for its foibles. Faulkner is right in saying that he combined both approaches in *The Sound and the Fury*. But he also says that he did something else which is, I think, the real clue to the breakthrough this novel represents. He speaks of removing himself from the novel and says that after finishing the first three sections, "I saw that I was merely temporising; That I should have to get completely out of the book."[15] That remark is peculiar because Faulkner seems to enter the book as the omniscient narrator in the fourth section, not to exit from it as he says he does. But Faulkner seems to be acknowledging that the first three sections were intensely subjective and more personal for him than is apparent, while the fourth section is objective.

At some deeper level, though, getting "completely out of the book" does not mean just being objective. It means

12. *Ibid.*, 157.
13. *Ibid.*, 158.
14. *Ibid.*
15. *Ibid.*, 161.

achieving enough distance to "extract some ultimate distillation"[16] from his materials. Faulkner does not explain the sort of distillation he has in mind; but he seems to mean refining out of his art both a romantic yearning for escape and a realistic urge to indict, and leaving a structure which lives independent of the author's personal feelings. Faulkner ends the introduction by rejecting the metaphor of *The Sound and the Fury* as a perfect vase:

> There is a story somewhere about an old Roman who kept at his bedside a Tyrrhenian vase which he loved and the rim of which he wore slowly away with kissing it. I had made myself a vase, but I suppose I knew all the time that I could not live forever inside of it, that perhaps to have it so that I too could lie in bed and look at it would be better; surely so when that day should come when not only the ecstacy of writing would be gone, but the unreluctance and the something worth saying too. It's fine to think that you will leave something behind you when you die, but it's better to have made something you can die with. Much better the muddy bottom of a little doomed girl climbing a blooming pear tree in April to look in the window at the funeral. Oxford.
> 19 August, 1933.[17]

Knowing that he "could not live forever inside of it," Faulkner seems to acknowledge that he could not create a beautiful work of art as substitute for or retreat from life; in other words, he could not use art as a romantic escape. The next to the last sentence seems also to reject the romantic notion of art as perfect form and to substitute a faith in art as a part of life. The implication is that *The Sound and the Fury* is neither a cold pastoral, nor a depiction of "marbles in a glade"[18] or any other state of arrested motion; rather it is art which lives and moves. Faulkner knows he can die with it because he and others can live with it.

16. *Ibid*.
17. *Ibid*.
18. William Faulkner, *The Marble Faun* (Boston: Four Seas Co., 1924), 31.

Faulkner did not begin his career, however, either writing or thinking in those terms. He began as a romantic, rejecting this world, yearning for another, and writing poetry which aimed not at motion and life but rather at a state of arrested motion[19] which was perfect precisely because it would be lifeless. This poetry did not seek to transform the sorry shabby world; it sought to escape it. Faulkner yearned to escape this world because it seemed to offer him nothing but unhappiness. He may never have been a very happy man, but his young manhood was an exceedingly unhappy time. His childhood sweetheart married another man and he was refused for flight training on the humiliating grounds that he was undereducated and perhaps also too short. Though he signed up with the Royal Flying Corps and began training in Canada in 1918, the armistice ended his training after only four months. He of course never saw action and probably did not even get to fly. Nevertheless, he came back to Mississippi at the end of 1918 in an RAF uniform, wearing a cap that signified that he'd been overseas, carrying a cane, and walking with a limp—presumably from a war wound.[20] That he created any number of poses and told any number of lies about his war experiences testifies not only to his inventiveness but to his deep need to deny or compensate for what he must have seen as an unspeakable failure. Apparently, Faulkner felt himself a failure as a man, in both love and war.

Faulkner must also have felt his financial dependence a sign of failure. In an earlier presentation during this conference, J. M. Faulkner spoke of living as a child in the house on the campus of the University of Mississippi with his grandparents, his parents, Dean, and William Faulkner. He said that Dean was "legitimately" there because he was still un-

19. See Stonum's *Faulkner's Career* for a detailed treatment of the centrality of the concept of arrested motion in the development of Faulkner's career.
20. *Faulkner: A Biography*, 205–233.

derage.[21] The implication surely is that William and John Faulkner, who were by then grown men, were not legitimate members of their father's household. Surely, William Faulkner was not impervious to that judgment. And to have to remain into his thirties at least a partial dependent of the father who did not understand him and probably did not even like him must have been humiliating for Faulkner. However comic being called "Count No Count" may seem to us now, at the time it meant that the community really thought him worthless. Faulkner responded by arrogant contempt for the community on the one hand or by self-contempt on the other.

His dissatisfactions with his circumstances are to be found in everything he wrote during this period. In 1920, reviewing a volume of poetry by William Alexander Percy, Faulkner wrote that Percy "suffered the misfortune of having been born out of his time"—"like alas! how many of us."[22] Typical of his other reviews are disparaging remarks about modernity and an America which has "no tradition"[23] and is, as he wrote in 1922, "aesthetically impossible."[24] These comments and others like them suggest how the romantic yearning to be elsewhere, a rather adolescent dissatisfaction with the here and now, was a way of thinking for the young Faulkner.

Into his poetry Faulkner poured his distaste for the age and his yearning to be elsewhere. The theme of all of this poetry is longing: for a woman, for a lost golden age, for something of beauty which would be immutable. One of the early but typical poems is "To a Co-ed" published in the 1919–20 issue

21. J. M. Faulkner, "Knowing William Faulkner," (August 4, 1980), University of Mississippi.

22. William Faulkner, Review of *In April Once*, by W. A. Percy, in *William Faulkner: Early Prose and Poetry*, Compilation and Introduction by Carvel Collins (Boston: Little, Brown and Company, 1962), 71.

23. "American Drama: Eugene O'Neill," in *William Faulkner: Early Prose and Poetry*, 87.

24. "American Drama: Inhibitions," in *William Faulkner: Early Prose and Poetry*, 94.

of *Ole Miss*, the college annual. Faulkner compares the co-ed to Venus, Helen, and Beatrice. He ends the poem: "For down Time's arras, faint and fair and far, / Your face still beckons like a lonely star."[25]

That startling disparity between the subject matter—a co-ed—and this inflated treatment is symptomatic of Faulkner's utter unhappiness with the near and the familiar. Longing for release from all that stifles and imprisons one is also the theme of *The Marble Faun*, published in 1924. The search is for a perfect realm beyond time.

There are three problems with this early romantic work. One is that it is terribly derivative. Perhaps if Faulkner had continued writing in that vein, however, he would have become, not another Keats, but at least another Swinburne. But he would have been an anachronism, rather as he said William Alexander Percy was. The second problem with the early work is that it was dated even as it was written. If literary forms evolve, as Scholes and Kellogg insist that they do, the lyric expressing a desire for a more perfect realm was already "dead as a dinosaur." (As Scholes and Kellogg insist, such an evolutionary process does not mean that we do not appreciate the art of another age; it just means that we do not write it anymore.)

The third problem with Faulkner's poetry, perhaps an outgrowth of the first two, is that, embodying a desire for a static condition, the poems remain static. There is no drama; the desired woman or state of being is always impossibly out-of-reach. For purposes of comparison, I find it helpful to imagine diagrams of tensions in literary works. These poems would require only the simplest sort of diagram—a straight line; the line would stretch from subject to object, from desirer to desired. No other marks would be needed on the

25. *Early Prose and Poetry*, 70.

diagram, for these poems do nothing more than express the poet's (or the persona's) impossible yearning for an unattainable object.

Faulkner himself may have realized something of what was wrong with this poetry. But until 1925 he was imprisoned by his psychology and also apparently by his reading. As Cleanth Brooks remarks, the bonds that rendered the young poet (speaking as the Marble Faun) "relatively 'mute and impotent' were not marble but literary."[26] That is, Faulkner's imitation of a rather debased romanticism bound him to outdated conventions and stifled the development of his own art. He later wrote that he had at the time found in Swinburne "nothing but a flexible vessel into which I might put my own vague emotional shapes."[27] In other words, Swinburne provided a sort of ready-made form into which Faulkner poured his dissatisfactions.

Faulkner seems to have sensed what was wrong with this art, but for quite a while he did not know how to break out of this pattern. Consider what he wrote in a 1922 review of Joseph Hergesheimer's novels. He wrote that Hergesheimer's *Linda Condon* "is not a novel. It is more like a lovely Byzantine frieze."[28] Faulkner goes on to say that Hergesheimer's characters "are never actuated from within"; they are "like puppets."[29] He suggests that Hergesheimer "should never try to write about people at all; he should spend his time, if he must write, describing trees or marble fountains, houses or cities."[30]

This passage is peculiar because first of all the very descriptions Faulkner makes of Hergesheimer's work apply more to Faulkner's own work than to Hergesheimer's. Second, it is

26. Brooks, 19.
27. "Verse Old and Nascent: A Pilgrimage," *Early Prose and Poetry*, 114.
28. *Early Prose and Poetry*, 101.
29. *Ibid.*
30. *Ibid.*, 103.

71

precisely because Hergesheimer's figures are so stylized or puppet-like that Faulkner says that he should not try to write novels. And finally Faulkner concludes the review by writing that Hergesheimer is "like an emasculate priest surrounded by the puppets he has carved and clothed and painted—a terrific world without motion or meaning."[31] Note here that Faulkner associates and perhaps equates motion with meaning and masculinity.

But in his own work at the time he expresses a desire for a motionless state, and the work itself was static, like a vase or an urn. Faulkner seems to have set up a dichotomy here between, on the one hand, poetry, effeteness, and stasis and, on the other, fiction, masculinity, and motion. Furthermore, he set up a conundrum for himself in which, because he wrote poetry to compensate for life's failures, the poetry would have to fail. Thus even successful poetry would only prove that art was easier and thus inferior to life. As Cleanth Brooks observes, "in *The Marble Faun* it is the inferiority of art to life that [Faulkner] stressed."[32] In the terms Faulkner was later to give Addie Bundren, his own poems were, in his own mind, just shapes to fill a lack. As he once explained, "Maybe [I wrote] because I wasn't as tall or as strong as I wanted to be."[33] At various times, as Judith Bryant Wittenberg writes, "Faulkner admitted that his compulsion to write developed from an urgent sense of lack." She also suggests that perhaps the best resource for a writer is an unhappy childhood.[34] As we know, Faulkner's childhood, his young manhood, and his adulthood had their share of unhappinesses. But before 1925 Faulkner only desired to escape his circumstances. His poetry expresses that desire.

31. *Ibid.*
32. Brooks, 5.
33. *Faulkner: A Biography*, 1442.
34. *Faulkner: The Transfiguration of Biography* (Lincoln: University of Nebraska Press, 1979), 6.

After 1925, however, he wrote prose which does not express but rather examines desire. This prose is peopled with characters full of romantic longing, but Faulkner distances himself from those characters obsessed with impossible yearnings. Though his characters are romantic, his treatment of them is not; it is realistic and often ironic.

Faulkner's transformation from poetry to prose, romanticism to realism, was sudden and nearly absolute. Before 1925 he had written only four attempts at fiction that we know of—"Moonlight," "Landing in Luck," "The Hill," and "Adolescence." After 1925 he wrote almost no poetry. His second volume of poems, *A Green Bough*, was not published until 1933, but most of the original versions of the poems seem to have been written before 1925, and none later than 1926. Faulkner lived in New Orleans from January through June of 1925. When Faulkner got to New Orleans, in January, he immediately began writing prose sketches for the *Double-Dealer* and the *Times-Picayune*. By the time he left New Orleans, he had completed his first novel. Aboard ship on his way to Europe with his friend Bill Spratling, Faulkner threw overboard an enormous number of manuscript pages; Spratling claims that it was a "mass of MS about four inches thick."[35] We do not know about the contents of those pages, but it seems safe to surmise that they contained the sort of romantic work that Faulkner had put behind him.

What explains the dramatic shift from romanticism to realism, from poetry to prose that Faulkner made in the first six months of 1925? First of all, I believe that the tolerance that Faulkner experienced in New Orleans for the first time had a liberating effect upon him. In his foreword to *Sherwood Anderson and Other Famous Creoles*, Faulkner explained the attraction of New Orleans in these terms: "It has a kind of

35. William Spratling, *File on Spratling: An Autobiography* (Boston: Little, Brown and Company, 1932, reprinted 1967), 31.

73

ease, a kind of awareness of the unimportance of things that outlanders like myself—I am not a native—were taught to believe important."[36] Apparently, the "things" Faulkner referred to were those values of respectability and propriety that his Mississippi background had led him to believe were absolute. In New Orleans Faulkner first found a place where he could at once be at home (as he probably had not been earlier in New Haven and New York) and be accepted (as he was not in Oxford). In New Orleans he was not faulted for not being married, or for not being a veteran, or for not having a respectable job, or certainly not for drinking too much. Accepted as he was, Faulkner had less longing to escape to somewhere else.

New Orleans seems to have not only released Faulkner from a number of psychic bonds, but it also released him from a number of literary bonds, because there he was thoroughly exposed to modernism for the first time. In the 1925 "Mirrors of Chartres Street" series there are a number of allusions of a new sort. Faulkner describes "planes of light and shadow which were despair for the Vorticist schools." He writes that "no one since Cézanne had really dipped his brush in light."[37] Such allusions seem to indicate a new cultural awareness in Faulkner; actually, Faulkner's awareness of modernism was not new, but his acceptance of it was. With Phil Stone in Mississippi and Connecticut, Faulkner had certainly been exposed to modernism. L. D. Brodsky's Faulkner collection, for example, includes a copy of Clive Bell's *Art* dated by Phil Stone 3/18/17 and underlined in pencil throughout.[38] And in

36. Foreword to *Sherwood Anderson and Other Famous Creoles* (New Orleans: Pelican Bookshop, 1926); rpt. (Austin: University of Texas Press, 1966), unnumbered pages.

37. *New Orleans Sketches*, Introduction by Carvel Collins (London: Sidgwick and Jackson Limited, 1959), 54, 101–2.

38. Robert W. Hamblin and Louis Daniel Brodsky, *Selections from the William Faulkner Collection of Louis Daniel Brodsky: A Descriptive Catalog* (Charlottesville: University Press of Virginia, 1979), 20–21.

the early twenties Stone ordered Elie Faure's *History of Art*.[39] Given what we know about Stone's program of initiating the young poet into the current cultural scene and about Faulkner's extensive reading in Stone's library, we can be certain that he knew both these books (and others like them) long before he came to New Orleans.[40] But it seems to have been only in New Orleans that the modern became an exciting and engaging reality for Faulkner. Apparently he imbibed a new understanding of modern art from both Elizabeth Anderson whose brother taught aesthetics at Harvard and from Sherwood Anderson whose apprenticeship to Gertrude Stein was past history in 1925. And of course, Faulkner's months with William Spratling, himself an architect and artist, were a formidable influence. The artist Caroline Durieux who lived in the New Orleans French Quarter during 1925 remembers that Faulkner seemed to consume modernism. Mrs. Durieux recalls that Faulkner mostly just listened to the debates about art that were a regular feature of life in the quarter; he seemed to be, she says, "just soaking it all up."[41] In short, the Faulkner who had in 1920 lamented being born into a modern age which was "aesthetically impossible" was in 1925 beginning to discover the aesthetic possibilities of modernism. He began to sense that being born out of his time was his problem, not the age's.

In Paris between August and October of 1925, Faulkner continued to soak up modernism. On August 18th he wrote to his mother, "I spent yesterday in the Louvre, to see the Winged Victory and the Venus de Milo, the real ones, and the Mona Lisa etc. It was fine, especially the paintings of the

39. Joseph Blotner, comp., *William Faulkner's Library: A Catalogue* (Charlottesville: University of Virginia Press, 1964), 124.

40. In "Elmer" Faulkner has his young artist carry a copy of "Clive Bell" and one of Faure's *Outline of Art*. See Thomas McHaney, "The Elmer Papers: Faulkner's Comic Portraits of the Artist," in *A Faulkner Miscellany*, 48–49.

41. Conversation with Caroline Durieux, April 19, 1980, Baton Rouge, Louisiana.

more-or-less moderns, like Degas and Manet and Chavannes. Also went to a very very modernist exhibition the other day— futurist and vorticist."[42] Perhaps because his friends and acquaintances were mostly artists, Faulkner also got to see private collections of Matisse and Picasso.[43] He wrote a few poems, almost the last he was to do. They showed the influence of Cummings,[44] and one was, as he wrote to his mother in early September, "so modern that I dont know myself what it means."[45] But Faulkner mostly wrote prose. He worked very hard on what was to be a novel about an American artist named Elmer Hodge. The typescript of *Elmer* includes a description of Paris as a "merry childish sophisticated cold-blooded dying city to which Cezanne was dragged by his friends like a reluctant cow, where Degas and Manet fought obscure points of color and line and love, cursing Bourgereau and his curved pink female flesh, where Matisse and Picasso yet painted."[46] Such comments suggest that Faulkner not only knew modern art, he was comfortable with it. His work on *Elmer* shows that he experimented with various modern narrative techniques.[47] Neither *Elmer* nor the modernism experiment was a success, however; when Faulkner returned to the states, he began to work again on prose which developed from the work he had done earlier in 1925 in New Orleans.

We could diagram the poetry simply by a straight line, but we would need diagrams of ever increasing complexity to diagram the prose that Faulkner wrote between 1925 and 1928. A simple triangular diagram would describe the sketches we know as *The New Orleans Sketches*. As with our diagram of

---

42. *Letters*, 13.
43. *Faulkner: A Biography*, 463–65.
44. *Ibid.*, 454, 459.
45. *Letters*, 17.
46. Quoted by McHaney, 51. The passage was revised slightly for "A Portrait of Elmer." See *Uncollected Stories of William Faulkner*, Joseph Blotner, ed. (New York: Random House, 1979), 637.
47. See McHaney, 53.

the poetry, a line would stretch between the subject and the object of his desire, but with these sketches there would also be a third vantage point—shared by the author and the reader—which is at some distance from the subject's. Here, for almost the first time, Faulkner did not use art to express his own dissatisfactions and desires. Instead he wrote of a variety of characters who are clearly not himself; he tried several dialects which had been alien to him before he came to New Orleans, and he treated romantic longing with realism, distance, and some irony. Also there is a new acceptance of this world and of the flesh in these sketches. But they are still desperately static.

In *Soldiers' Pay*, written in New Orleans in 1925, Faulkner apparently tried to multiply the number of characters clustering around the desired object. The situation remains basically static, but apparently Faulkner's strategy was to create movement by moving the reader among the characters, not by moving the characters very much.

In *Mosquitoes* Faulkner tried another way to rescue his work from stasis. He chose a situation—a boating excursion—which in itself provided structure. But the situation remains dreadfully static. Faulkner partially solved the problem with *Flags in the Dust*. Returning to Mississippi both literally and imaginatively, Faulkner tapped the wealth of stories and legends and happenings which were to keep him busy writing for more than thirty more years. In *Flags in the Dust* perhaps too much happens; movement is almost out of control. But the novel remains curiously static.

I think the book is static because both the reader and the writer remain above events. In a diagram, they would be at the apex of a cone while characters would move within a circular pattern below. Such a cone would describe each of these first three novels; though the number of characters increases as does the number of patterns of interaction, in each novel relations between subjects and objects are played out on a circumscribed arena which the reader observes from above.

These books are of this earth and clearly realistic. Cleanth Brooks writes that the major problem with Faulkner's poetry had been its lack of a realistic context. It needed, according to Brooks, "elements of realism sufficient to purge any sense of effete prettiness and faded romanticism."[48] But Faulkner solved that problem not by adding "elements of realism" to romantic poetry, but by rejecting poetry altogether and turning to realistic prose fiction. In his artistic evolution, however, the realistic period was short-lived, not terribly successful, and not purely realistic. His realism was always struggling to be modernism; for he did not structure the novels and stories written before 1928 by the traditional novel's formula of conflict, complication, and resolution. Instead, Faulkner attempted to structure by pattern, as in a modern painting. Except for the abortive *Elmer* experiment, he was not significantly modern enough to try the sorts of structural interruptions which force the reader to participate in assembling the work of art itself. Only with *The Sound and the Fury* did he adapt such cubist techniques; and it seems to me that those techniques, rather than locale or desire, explain the grandeur of that book and of the experiments with the novel form which were to follow.

Faulkner did not reject the devices that he had used in the first three novels, he just further modernized them. The clustering of *Soldiers' Pay* is repeated in *The Sound and the Fury*; the journey device from *Mosquitoes* is repeated in *As I Lay Dying*; and the devices of foiling and juxtaposing from *Sartoris* were used in all the major novels which were to come. The difference between those first three novels, on the one hand, and *The Sound and the Fury*, *As I Lay Dying*, *Sanctu-*

48. Brooks, 20.

ary, Light in August, Absalom, Absalom!, The Wild Palms, The Hamlet, and *Go Down, Moses,* on the other, is partially a matter of control, maturity, and experience. But also in these novels Faulkner adapted the methods that the cubists had first made available to the modern world around 1910, methods which used broken forms to compel the reader to create whatever order the work of art was to achieve. Thus if Faulkner's early poems had expressed desire, and his first prose works had examined desire, his great novels work by creating desire in his readers. They do so first by unsettling our preconceptions.

As the Cézannes and Matisses I described in my first lecture illustrate, flattening startles the eye, unsettling our understandings about both perspective and importance. It also calls attention to the shape of the canvas itself. Faulkner creates something of the same effect in *The Sound and the Fury* with the precise, even laborious detailing of Quentin's preparations for suicide (packing the trunk, mailing one letter to his father, giving the letter for Shreve to Deacon, painting his cut with iodine, and so on). These matters which might be expected to remain in the background become the foreground, while the suicide—the most dramatic event in the book—is omitted altogether. Similarly, in *Sanctuary* Faulkner builds suspense as chapter after chapter delineates Temple's panic, but the rape scene itself is simply omitted.

In the late Cezannes, space became as important as objects. Similarly, the gaps in the narrative of *The Sound and the Fury* and *The Wild Palms* are spaces which resonate because we are forced to fill them in. As Wolfgang Iser explains in *The Implied Reader,* "it is only through inevitable omissions that a story gains its dynamism. Thus whenever the flow is interrupted and we are led off in unexpected directions, the opportunity is given to us to bring into play our own faculty for establishing connections—for filling in the gaps left

79

by the text itself."[49] What is not told, then, becomes as important, or more important, than what is told. Our responses are engaged partly because our preconceptions about importance are overturned.

Our preconceptions are also unsettled by passage of planes. In *As I Lay Dying* the absolute division between space and time blurs as Cash is "sawing the long hot sad yellow days up into planks and nailing them to something."[50] Space, even one's personality, can slip out of itself, "as though the clotting which is you had dissolved into the myriad original motion" (*AILD*, 156). Volume is flattened as Vardaman's face fades "into the dusk like a piece of paper pasted on a failing wall" (*AILD*, 48). A more complicated passage of planes occurs in *Absalom, Absalom!* when Quentin and Shreve become Henry and Charles. Such a flattening of normal distinctions startles readers and provokes us to question the status of those distinctions. Furthermore, it makes us aware of the fictive order of the novel before us.

The sort of peculiar introductions of a visual dimension into narrative that Faulkner makes are collage-like. In *The Sound and the Fury* there is a diagram of an eye: "Keep your on Mottson, the gap filled by a human eye with an electric pupil" (*SF*, 388). *As I Lay Dying* includes a blank space to signify visually the blank Addie experiences when she thinks "The shape of my body where I used to be a virgin is in the shape of a   I couldn't think Anse, couldn't remember Anse" (*AILD*, 165). Also, Tull resorts to a diagram to describe the shape of Addie's coffin: "They had laid her in it reversed. Cash made it clock-shape, like this ⌐‾‾‾⌐ with every joint

49. Wolfgang Iser, *The Implied Reader: Patterns of Communication in Prose Fiction from Bunyan to Beckett* (Baltimore: The Johns Hopkins University Press, 1974), 280.
50. William Faulkner, *As I Lay Dying* (New York: Random House, Vintage Books, 1957), 25. Hereafter references to this edition will be abbreviated *AILD* and included in the text.

and seam bevelled and scrubbed with the plane" (*AILD*, 82). These examples interject the visual into the verbal medium, challenging distinctions between them. In a comparable way, the commissary ledgers in *Go Down, Moses*, which purport to be historical documents, call into question distinctions between non-privileged and privileged writings.

As the cubists stacked different viewpoints together on a flat plane, so Faulkner assembles a number of different perspectives in *As I Lay Dying* and *Absalom, Absalom!* The effect of seeing circumstances from so many different perspectives is to deny any one's claim to absolute truth and to force the reader to search for something which approximates that truth—a fourteenth way of looking at a blackbird.

All of these techniques work by unsettling and then engaging us, but the most complex and brilliant example of such engagement occurs in *Absalom, Absalom!* when we readers are compelled to participate with Quentin and Shreve in creating not just an explanation for why Henry shot Charles, but in creating the novel as we read it. That is, we are engaged in the process of fiction in much the same way that Duchamp wanted to engage the viewer in the painting "Nude Descending the Staircase." To see that painting and to read that novel, we have to participate in the process of creation.

The *petites sensations* of interest in cubist painting tended to create tensions between parts and wholes. Similarly, every Faulkner novel includes episodes which distract us from the central focus of the novel. These episodes are usually integrated into the novel by pattern, motif, or symbol. Examples are Louis Hatcher and his dirty lantern or the boys swimming in *The Sound and the Fury* or Cora Tull and her cakes in *As I Lay Dying*. More elaborate examples are found in the lengthy asides about Joe Christmas's past or Joanna Burden's or Gail Hightower's ancestry. These stories do not advance the plot, though they do present extended exposition, but I

81

think that their real meaning is that in them we see patterns repeating themselves with a difference. Faulkner expanded the method in *The Hamlet* and *Go Down, Moses* so that separate narratives in *The Hamlet* become variations on the themes of love and acquisition: dissimilar sorts of things which finally become similar. And the separate narratives of *Go Down, Moses* are united finally as variations of the theme of confinement and freedom.

Many of Faulkner's novels are structured geometrically. The four sections of *The Sound and the Fury* offer four parallel glimpses of yearning for a lost ideal, only one of which contains the possibility for transcendence. Images of circles and straight lines predominate in *As I Lay Dying*, but they also diagram the patterns the readers are forced to follow in reading the book. In *The Wild Palms* movement also is faceted. That is, in both small and large matters, action repeats a basic pattern of movement. That pattern is first illustrated by the case of the anonymous doctor in chapter one. He has lived *"behind a barricade of perennial innocence."*[51] That barricade is a veil which hides truth and experience from him. Trying to understand his two tenants (Harry and Charlotte), he has a "sense of imminence, of being just beyond a veil from something, of groping just without the veil and even touching but not quite, almost seeing but not quite, the shape of truth . . . " (*WP*, 13). But after the veil parts and he understands something of their relationship, he feels only outrage: "*Why did you have to tell me?* he thought" (*WP*, 19). In that chapter the doctor moves from enclosure, to exposure, to return. That pattern is repeated in a faceted design in the movements of the river, of Harry, and of the tall convict.

51. William Faulkner, *The Wild Palms* (New York: Random House, Vintage Edition, 1966), 16. Hereafter references to this edition will be abbreviated *WP* and included in the text.

When we read the novels which violate sequence, we must keep two orders at once before us: the order in which we read *The Sound and the Fury*, or *Light in August*, or *Absalom, Absalom!*, or *Go Down, Moses* and the original chronological order in which events actually occurred. Working back and forth between those two orders, we conduct perceptual shifts similar to but more complicated than those we make when we look at an arrangement of lines and shapes as they are in a cubist painting and then as they would be as reassembled original shapes.

Obviously, time does not permit major analyses of the structure of all the cubist novels. But I would like at least to suggest something of the way cubist design works in three novels: *The Sound and the Fury*, *The Wild Palms*, and *As I Lay Dying*. As I have explained, the problem with Faulkner's early poetry is that it just expressed his desire. The early realistic fiction observed desire. But with *The Sound and the Fury* Faulkner learned both to project his own desires into the structure of a novel and to create desire on the part of the reader. In *The Wild Palms* he made a similar sort of projection of his own needs, desires, and dilemmas into the structure of the novel. From *As I Lay Dying*, he excluded all desire and created a "pure" aesthetic artifact.

Let me explain.

I have already suggested that Faulkner was never a very happy man and that however unfortunate for his life that fact may have been, it was not entirely unfortunate for his art. It may be that at some level Faulkner knew that and thus cultivated at least some of those miseries. In one of the letters to Helen Baird in the William B. Wisdom Collection at Tulane, for example, he writes: "I hope to come to New Orleans before the winter is over. I dont hate it. I dont come back much because I had more fun there than I ever had and ever will have again anywhere now."[52] The logic of this explanation is that he stays away from New Orleans because he *likes* it so much. In other words, here he overtly acknowledges what Cleanth Brooks, following Denis de Rougemont, has taught us is the romantic's preference for unfulfillment, dissatisfaction, and longing. Faulkner seems to have cultivated some of his frustrations in his early romantic period because he preferred unfulfillment to fulfillment and found that his yearnings intensified his art. In his realistic period, when that letter was written, he seems to have cultivated some frustrations so that he might observe them. He may have continued to do so in his private life, but with *The Sound and the Fury* he began also to cultivate frustration in his readers.

We Faulknerians may be now so far away from our first experience with *The Sound and the Fury* that we have virtually forgotten what an assault upon our sensibilities it first was. Arnold Weinstein calls this an "almost despotic affective technique";[53] that is, Faulkner here is a despot, a tyrant, giving us no order, no coherence, no clues. But I suspect that Weinstein's despotic image is not entirely appropriate for Faulkner. The despot intends to keep his subjects in the dark and enslaved; Faulkner, on the other hand, mystifies his readers so that they will search for enlightenment and thus will liberate themselves.

All the way through the Benjy section we search desperately for some way to order and understand what we read. But instead we find only a reductionist picture of what life would mean without consciousness and feel like without love. Though the section ends with Caddy comforting Benjy, we know that that comfort will be short-lived. Thus we sense that

52. The typed, undated letter seems to have been written in the winter of 1925–26. Permission to quote granted by Jill Faulkner Summers and Ann S. Gwyn, Curator, Special Collections, Howard-Tilton Library, Tulane University.

53. Arnold L. Weinstein, *Vision and Response in Modern Fiction* (Ithaca: Cornell University Press, 1974), 115.

the "*bright, smooth shapes*" (*SF*, 69) of darkness and the smell of death which also end the section more nearly represent this life. Assuming that books must have meaning, we search in this hodge-podge of past and present impressions for some clues to their meaning; in that search we are also asking that life be more than a tale told by an idiot.

In the Quentin section we find consciousness and expect coherence. But here too there is only a scrambling of past and present, desire and disappointment. Looking for meaning in the plot, we find ourselves also looking for meaning in life, but we find little of either. The phrase "reducto absurdum of all human experience" recurs in the Quentin section (*SF*, 93, 105, 111). Tracing with him his deliberate steps towards death we come to realize that Quentin's consciousness is as reductive as Benjy's consciouslessness. Both find meaning only in loss. The Quentin section ends as the last note sounds and Quentin reopens his bag to brush his teeth. The final sentence, after Quentin remembers his hat is: "I had forgotten to brush it too, but Shreve had a brush, so I didnt have to open the bag any more" (*SF*, 222). Here the order Quentin can make is as meaningless as the "bright shapes of darkness" which comforted Benjy at the end of the first section.

We turn to the Jason section with relief: "Once a bitch always a bitch . . . " (*SF*, 223). Here at last, we think, is someone who can think straight and can clarify this muddle. But soon we discover that Jason's sort of rationality is paranoiac and xenophobic. The section ends where it began: "Like I say once a bitch always a bitch. And just let me have twenty-four hours without any damn New York jew to advise me what it's going to do. I dont want to make a killing; save that to suck in the smart gamblers with. I just want an even chance to get my money back. And once I've done that they can bring all Beale Street and all bedlam in here and two of them can sleep in my bed and another one can have my place at the table too" (SF, 329). Again we have order but only meaningless order. We however are still searching for meaning.

In the final section we at last find some of the missing pieces which explain, or begin to explain, what has gone before. But this section ends the book with the restoration of an order which is as meaningless as any which has gone before: "The broken flower drooped over Ben's fist and his eyes were empty and blue and serene again as cornice and facade flowed smoothly once more from left to right; post and tree, window and doorway, and signboard, each in its ordered place" (SF, 401).

That ending offers closure, the resolution of a pattern, but it does not finish a story or answer our questions. In fact, it turns us back into the novel to try to put its parts together. As we do so, we discover how these three ostensibly different brothers—an idiot, an idealist, and a rationalist—are all alike. Each defines his life in terms of loss, each makes Caddy into a symbol, and each is a reductionist. Searching for sequence and coherence among events, we find ourselves also searching for larger meanings, for the hope that life can be more than the meaningless orders each of these brothers achieves. Only once in the novel do we find an indication that life may be more than sound and fury, that downward paths into meaninglessness need not be taken.

That one instance is of course the Reverend Shegog's sermon: "And the congregation seemed to watch with its own eyes while the voice consumed him, until he was nothing and they were nothing and there was not even a voice but instead their hearts were speaking to one another in chanting measures beyond the need for words, so that when he came to rest against the reading desk, his monkey fact lifted and his whole attitude that of a serene, tortured crucifix that transcended its shabbiness and insignificance and made it of no moment, a long moaning expulsion of breath rose from them,

and a woman's single soprano: 'Yes, Jesus!'" (*SF*, 367–68).
Here we have one instance when aloneness, shabbiness, and
insignificance are transcended. They are transcended through
faith and by words. For though they reach a state "beyond
the need for words," words transport them there.

Looking back over the pattern of the four sections of *The
Sound and the Fury* we find a *faceted* design at the end of
each section; for each descends to and closes upon a meaningless order. We realize that the three Compson brothers responded to experience similarly. They also used words as
fixed symbols and those diminished things diminished them.
But the Reverend Shegog and the congregation consider
words containers of and signals toward truth. Because they
look for and expect that truth, they are, for a moment at least,
transformed. I believe that this novel is designed to create a
comparable experience for us.

Faulkner has given us a fragmented novel, splitting even
chronology between four days eighteen years apart, and so
scrambling recollections that we cannot just read this book,
we must reread it. Thus he has taken a device first explored
by the cubists and used it to create meaning in a world otherwise full of sound and fury signifying nothing. Our search
to make sense of this book posits coherence in the book and
thus in the world. Engaged with the pages before us, we
make them move again. This process is evidence that both
words and people may transcend shabbiness and insignificance.

I have already suggested how Faulkner learned in the
1920s to transfer his frustrations into his art. The structure of
The Sound and the Fury is a projection and examination of
the longings he felt. In the late 30s he developed, with at
least one novel, a method of cultivating a more complicated
psychic dilemma and of translating it too into art. That dilemma was one we call putting oneself in a "double bind" or

87

"wanting it both ways at once." Rather than trying to avoid such a destructive psychic habit, Faulkner seems to have nurtured it. A divided man, he cultivated both sides of his personality at once. He could at one and the same time be the romantic and the cynic, the literary man and the dirt farmer, the gentleman and the tramp; or at least, he could try to be both, and never quite succeed. In fact, he seems to have made choices that kept his life torn between irreconcilable and mutually exclusive choices: either Estelle or Meta, either Mississippi or places with no roots at all, either incredibly demanding family responsibilities or none at all. Meta Carpenter Wilde suggests how he set up his life in terms of such irreconcilable alternatives: "When he was in Hollywood, the tug of Oxford kept Bill in a restive state. Now that he had let it draw him back [to Oxford], there was a counterpull to me in Hollywood, a retortion, and again peace of place was denied him."[54] Apparently, it was not just "peace of place" that he denied himself, but peace, because for every pull in his life there seems to have been an equally insistent counterpull. Apparently, at some semi-conscious level, he set up these conundrums in order to transform the impossibility of his situation into art. That is, these conundrums functioned as sexual frustration probably had earlier: to feed his genius.

Faulkner must have felt trapped in the 1930s by both a disintegrating marriage and a lengthening list of personal and fiscal commitments. In such a situation, his fantasies apparently focused upon either a passionate affair with a beautiful woman or an escape from all the familial and social burdens women bring. During several periods in Hollywood he managed to live both of these fantasies at once (as he would later with other young women) through the affair with Meta Car-

54. Meta Carpenter Wilde and Orin Borsten, A Loving Gentleman: The Love Story of William Faulkner and Meta Carpenter (New York: Simon & Schuster, 1976), 101.

penter. Fulfilling both fantasies simultaneously, he probably began to recognize how both the affair with a woman and the desire to escape from women were, paradoxically, expressions of the same urge to be free. But if he felt that urge forcefully, he also felt an equally strong counter-urge to return to Oxford, Mississippi, and accept his responsibilities to Estelle and Jill, Victoria and Malcolm, his mother, his brothers, etc. I believe that he wrote *The Wild Palms* as an expression of that conflict.

As soon as we set aside our conventional expectations about sequence and continuity and read these narratives as they appear, we discover that parallels form the warp and woof of this novel. If we traverse[55] the narratives in the way the book itself teaches us, we discover innumerable ways in which two ostensibly opposite young men are basically alike. Each is carried away from a womb-like existence by a force of nature; each has his life with that force disrupted; each embarks on a journey that repeats his earlier journey in reverse order; and each returns to a womb-like existence similar or identical to that from which he first emerged. Surely, the point of following our final glimpse of Harry, who has willingly chosen to remain in jail, with a picture of the convict, who has willingly returned to jail, is to confirm our sense of how similar the two protagonists really are.

But what then? Normally, when we encounter two alternatives in life or art, we compare them with an eye to choosing. Thus artistic foiling usually works to sharpen outlines, heighten distinctions, and thereby clarify choices. But here the foiling of Harry and the convict finally collapses, so that we discover that Harry's losing the world for love is just as unsatisfactory as the convict's losing it to get away from love; in fact, they amount to the same thing. Traversing the narra-

55. See my article *"The Wild Palms*: Structure, Affect, and Meaning" in *Faulkner Studies II* for a detailed discussion of traversing.

89

tives, we may take aesthetic pleasure in discovering how Faulkner converted opposition to identity; we may admire the novel's formal complexity and be astonished by the neatness with which its design is executed. But our emotions have been too deeply engaged for a purely aesthetic response to satisfy us. I believe that our emotional and intellectual involvement is calculated into the design of this novel just as the viewer's need to reassemble a fragmented still-life is calculated into the design of a cubist painting.

Faulkner designed *The Wild Palms* so that reading it would create an emotional conundrum. That is, we want to escape with the lovers from all the evils that respectability breeds. And we also empathize with the tall convict who wants to unburden himself of all the troubles that women, or domesticity, bring. Through the alternating chapter structure and through the circular design of each narrative, Faulkner brings us to discover how similar and how doomed these escapist dreams really are.

Harry and Charlotte see love and responsibility as mutually exclusive terms. The tall convict sees freedom and responsibility as mutually exclusive terms. Carried by each vision back to death or imprisonment, we readers are forced to discover how absolutist and life-denying is each.

If these visions turn out to be identically deadly, so that we cannot choose between them, our natural tendency to look for an alternative is once again engaged. And, the structural conundrum of this novel should feed our desire to integrate love and freedom with responsibility: to search, then, for a more balanced, less absolutist approach to life than any explicitly depicted in this novel (or ever realized in Faulkner's life).

When Faulkner described *As I Lay Dying* as a "tour de force" he meant something like a clever technical experiment that worked. To Jean Stein he said:

Sometimes technique charges in and takes command of the
dream before the writer himself can get his hands on it. That is
tour de force and the finished work is simply a matter of fitting
bricks neatly together, since the writer knows probably every
single word right to the end before he puts the first one down.
This happened with *As I Lay Dying*. It was not easy. No honest
work is. It was simple in that all the material was already at hand.
It took me just about six weeks in the spare time from a 12 hour
a day job at manual labor. I simply imagined a group of people
and subjected them to the simple universal natural catastrophes
which are flood and fire with a simple natural motive to give
direction to their progress.[56]

Of course the Bundrens' motive for taking Addie Bundren's
putrefying corpse all the way to Jefferson to be buried is neither simple nor natural. In that and other assertions, Faulkner is duping the naive reader. But I think that he was absolutely serious about his insistence that this book was principally
a neat technical or aesthetic experiment. This book is Faulkner's most objective. Not only are authorial comments totally
missing but here none of the characters seem to be surrogate-
figures for the author.

In fact, this novel is something of an aesthetic experiment
in distancing and arranging. As I have already suggested, the
cubists' principal difference from their predecessors was their
determination not to let subject matter engage the reader at
all. Thus they purged from their paintings the easily recognizable and the emotionally affecting. Because there was little
more than form left, the viewer was forced to respond to it.

I think that Faulkner tries a comparable experiment in *As
I Lay Dying*. He gives us not simple natural catastrophes, but
the most bizarre, perverse circumstances imaginable. After
all, here is a story in which a boy bores holes through the face
of his dead mother, in which a broken leg is set in concrete,
and a stinking corpse is carted across the country for nearly a

56. *Lion in the Garden*, 244.

91

week. These are unspeakable horrors. But the book's design so distances us from them that we read it almost without emotional reactions at all.

Instead we are engaged by pattern. The difference between the texture of the book and a statement of what happens is suggested by reading a passage which occurs late in the book and essentially recapitulates the whole plot, such as it is.

> Then he told a long tale about how they had to wait for the wagon to come back and how the bridge was washed away and how they went eight miles to another bridge and it was gone too so they came back and swum the ford and the mules got drowned and how they got another team and found that the road was washed out and they had to come clean around by Mottson, and then the one with the cement came back and told him to shut up. (*AILD*, 194)

Like the chronology at the end of *Absalom, Absalom!* such a summary parodies plot: if we read just to know what happens, these summaries tell us not to bother. But we read forward both teleologically to find out what happens, and also we circle around experientially among the ruminations of various characters. We are forced to circle about because some characters tell us facts before we can understand them, some before they even could know them. Cora tells of Addie's death and the journey's beginning before either happens. Tull, Moseley, and MacGowan recapitulate events before they happen. Cash sees a strange woman and calls her Mrs. Bundren. References to Jewel's illegitimacy early in the book are explained late in it. Vardaman says, "*When I went to find where they stay at night, I saw something Dewey Dell says I mustn't never tell nobody*" (*AILD*, 215), but we have to read on to find that Vardaman saw, and then we circle back to connect our discovery with this reference. And it is only in Darl's last section, as he is riding on the train to Jackson, that we are told that Darl has been "in France at the war" (*AILD*, 244). Belatedly learning that fact, we circle back to determine if it might have affected Darl's disillusionment and disengagement throughout the course of the narrative.[57]

As such examples illustrate, reading forward and forced to circle back, we repeat the basic geometric pattern of the book. That pattern is set up in Darl's first section when Darl follows the path which "circles the cottonhouse" while Jewel follows the path which runs "straight as a plumb-line" right through the cottonhouse (*AILD*, 3). That contrast between circular and linear paths continues throughout the book in the contrast between the rim and the spoke of the wheel and in the journey's linear path with the buzzards circling above. Repeating geometric designs—lines and circles, verticals and horizontals—Faulkner actually facets, like a cubist painting, the design of this book. That is why it is so difficult to speak of theme in *As I Lay Dying*. Here we have a work of fiction that comes remarkably close to being an exercise in pure design, a true tour de force, a cubist novel. Though *As I Lay Dying* is the quintessential cubist novel, it is far from the only one Faulkner wrote. For the modern stage of Faulkner's career, after the romantic poetry and the realistic fiction, began with *The Sound and the Fury* and lasted through *Go Down, Moses*. That is the stage which produced the great novels. Those novels combine an eighteenth-century concern for universals, a romantic intensity of feeling, and a realistic feel for detail with the techniques of cubism. Though cubist techniques are not sufficient conditions for greatness, they do seem to be necessary conditions in Faulkner's works.

Addie Bundren worried, as the young Faulkner had, lest

---

57. The effect of Darl's war experience is a topic explored in detail by Watson G. Branch in "Darl Bundren's 'Cubistic' Vision," *Texas Studies in Literature and Language*, 19, No. 1 (Spring, 1977), 42–59.

words and deeds be so far apart that no one could straddle them. In *As I Lay Dying* Faulkner gives us a book of words which forces readers to read both "longways" and "up-and-down ways" (*AILD*, 35) and both by the line and by the circle. With all Faulkner's cubist novels we similarly join different planes and reassemble narratives. In the process, we disprove Addie as we join words and deeds and make Faulkner's art move again. With the Reverend Shegog's congregation we might say, "'I've knowed de Lawd to use cuiser tools dan dat'" (*SF*, 366).

The Road to *The Reivers*

JAMES B. CAROTHERS

To follow the road to *The Reivers*, to locate Faulkner's last work of fiction through the continuity of his canon, let us first glance briefly at the roads not taken. It is not my intention here to engage in the sort of fictional cartography that aims to identify the "real" Iron Bridge, the "real" Ballenbaugh's, or the "real" mud-farm at Hell Creek Crossing. Anyone who has paused over the photograph of J. W. T. Falkner's Buick mired in the Tallahatchie River bottom, or, for that matter, anyone who has noticed that William Faulkner, like Lucius Priest, had three younger brothers, a father who ran a livery stable, and a family servant called Aunt Callie will have already made a good beginning at discovering how Faulkner, in this particular instance, went about sublimating the actual into the apocryphal.[1] Neither do I care to extend the argument against the highly questionable proposition that *The Reivers* is, in some sense or another, the Golden Book of Yoknapatawpha

---

1. The photograph of Colonel Falkner's car is found in Jack Cofield's *The Cofield Collection* (Oxford, Mississippi: Yoknapatawpha Press, 1978), 25. For attempts to identify sources for geography and characterization in *The Reivers*, see also Edwin Howard, "Anecdote: The Faithful Smith," *Delta Review*, 2 (July-August, 1965), 37, 80; Miriam Weiss, "Hell Creek Bottom Is: A Reminiscence," *Journal of Mississippi History*, 30 (August, 1969), 196–201; Calvin S. Brown, "Faulkner's Three-in-One Bridge in *The Reivers*," *Notes on Contemporary Literature*, 1 (March, 1971), 8–10; Elizabeth M. Kerr, *Yoknapatawpha: Faulkner's "Little Postage Stamp of Native Soil"* (New York: Fordham University Press, 1969), 32, 70, 236; and Joseph Blotner, *Faulkner: A Biography* (New York: Random House, 1974), 1793 ff.

County or Faulkner's version of *The Tempest*, his self-conscious summing up of his fictional world and his valediction to it, his broken pencil to Prospero's broken staff.[2] And although I will discuss some of the connections between *The Reivers* and Faulkner's other fiction, I will assume that many of the parallels and similarities—the way Uncle Bud of *Sanctuary* anticipates Otis, for example—are too obvious to require extended attention. Nor, finally, am I more than incidentally concerned with refuting those reviewers and critics who found *The Reivers*, at best, an engaging entertainment for a juvenile audience, and, at worst, "a surrender to sententious banality."[3]

What I propose to show is that Faulkner had conceived the basic situation, characters, and theme of *The Reivers* at least from the time shortly after he completed *The Hamlet*, that he incorporated elements of that situation, those characters, and that theme into several of his major fictions written after 1940, that when he finally came to write *The Reivers* he drew on imagery, vocabulary, situation, character, and theme from the entire range of his writing, and, therefore, that *The Reivers* is neither a sentimental afterthought, a commercial con-

2. See especially Elizabeth M. Kerr, "*The Reivers*: The Golden Book of Yoknapatawpha County," *Modern Fiction Studies*, 13, No. 1 (Spring, 1967), 95–113; J. M. Mellard, "Faulkner's 'Golden Book': *The Reivers* as Romantic Comedy," *Bucknell Review*, 13 (December, 1965), 19–31; and Ben M. Vorphal, "Moonlight at Ballenbaugh's: Time and Imagination in *The Reivers*," *Southern Literary Journal*, 1 (Spring, 1969), 3–26. James B. Meriwether has challenged the "Golden Book" identification in "The Novel Faulkner Never Wrote: His *Golden Book* or *Doomsday Book*," *American Literature*, 42 (March, 1970), 93–96. See also in this connection Gale Tanner, "Sentimentalism and *The Reivers*: A Reply to Ben Merchant Vorpahl," *Notes on Mississippi Writers*, 9 (1976), 50–58. For a comparison of *The Reivers* and *The Tempest*, see William Rossky, "*The Reivers*: Faulkner's *Tempest*," *Mississippi Quarterly*, 18 (Spring, 1965), 82–93.

3. The last phrase appears in Leslie Fiedler's review in the Manchester *Guardian*, September 28, 1962, 6. Other reviewers who called *The Reivers* "adolescent reading" included Stanley Edgar Hyman, "Taking a Flyer with Faulkner," *New Leader*, July 9, 1962, 18–19; Terry Southern, "Tom Sawyer in the Brothel," *Nation*, June 9, 1962, 519–21; and George Plimpton, "*The Reivers*," *New York Herald-Tribune Books*, May 27, 1962, 3.

JAMES B. CAROTHERS

tradiction, nor a pusillanimous retraction of his great early work, but rather, that *The Reivers* is a fully realized articulation of themes and techniques Faulkner employed throughout his developing career. If *The Reivers* superficially supports the contention that Faulkner repeated himself in his later fiction, it also provides exquisite evidence that he always repeated himself with a difference and to a purpose, and it shows that he retained both his fictional powers and his capacity for risk-taking to the very end. To follow the road to *The Reivers*, then, it is useful to see how far Faulkner's 1940 conception of the novel was consistent with *The Reivers* as finally published in 1962, to see how elements of the 1940 project were employed in his fiction of the intervening years, and to see how, in writing his last novel, he drew on the entirety of his works.

Although it is as difficult to ascertain precisely when Faulkner conceived of *The Reivers* as it is to state with certainty just when and how he first imagined any of his other fictions,[4] we know that he believed he was ready to write a novel very much like *The Reivers* by mid-1940, and we know that, as when he conceived another of his novels that features an excursion to Memphis, his mind was on money as he contemplated the project. In early May of 1940 Faulkner outlined a novel for his Random House editor, Robert K. Haas, as part of a plan by which he might secure a one-thousand-dollar advance from the publisher.

> On the day the plan goes into effect, I will get at a novel. I think I have a good one. It is a sort of Huck Finn—a normal boy of about twelve or thirteen, a big, warmhearted, courageous, honest, utterly unreliable white man with the mentality of a child, an old negro family servant, opinionated, querulous, selfish, fairly unscrupulous, and in his second childhood, and a prostitute not very young anymore and with a great deal of character and

4. Mr. William J. Roane recalls that Faulkner liked to tell a story resembling *The Reivers* "in the early 1930s." Conversation with Mr. Roane, August, 1980.

97

common sense, and a stolen race horse which none of them actually intended to steal. The story is how they travel for a thousand miles from hand to mouth trying to get away from the police long enough to return the horse. All of them save the white man think the police are after the horse. The white man knows the police have been put on his tail by his harridan of a wife whom he has fled from. Actually, the police are trying to return the boy to his parents to get the reward. The story lasts a matter of weeks. During that time the boy grows up, becomes a man, mostly because of the influence of the whore. He goes through in miniature all the experiences of youth which mold the man's character. They happen to be the very experiences which in his middle class parents' eyes stand for debauchery and degeneracy and actual criminality; through them he learned courage and honor and generosity and pride and pity. He has been absent only weeks, but as soon as his mother sees him again, she knows what has happened to him. She weeps, says, "He is not my baby anymore."

May I have the $1,000 at once?[5]

Before we examine the similarities and differences between this outline and *The Reivers*, let us see what detoured the project. Faulkner continued to allude to "the Huck Finn novel" over the next ten months. "If I get at the novel described," he wrote Haas later in May, 1940, "I might need at least a year, during which time I shall have to be underwritten at least $200 a month" (*SLWF*, 124). At the same time he offered Haas an alternative project, "a collection of short stories, most of them from magazines since 33 or 34, perhaps one or two unpublished yet?"[6] Haas preferred the novel to the short story collection, and by the first of June Faulkner was able to summarize their agreement: "I have signed with you a contract for a novel, new, original material, not a collection of short stories" (*SLWF*, 126). But again he proposed the

5. *Selected Letters of William Faulkner*, Joseph Blotner, ed. (New York: Random House, 1978), 123–24. Hereafter cited in the text as *SLWF*.

6. *Ibid*., 124. Faulkner had written Haas in late April, 1940, "I have another in mind similar to THE UNVANQUISHED, but since the chapters which I have written and tried to sell as short stories have not sold, I haven't the time to continue with it" (*SLWF*, 122).

short story book as an alternative. "If I make a connected book-length mss. from material written as short stories, such as Ober now has, you can exercise an option to print this volume in lieu of the one described in the above paragraph, if you wish" (*SLWF*, 126).

When Haas offered as an advance on the new novel only the one thousand dollars Faulkner had first requested, Faulkner began to negotiate with Viking Press. As was his habit in such matters, his behavior with respect to Random House was scrupulous, and he sought to keep Haas and Bennett Cerf informed about the particulars of his negotiations with Harold Guinzburg of Viking. In mid-June he wrote Haas that "in order to get the sum I need, I may have to contract [with Guinzburg] for short story volume to be delivered at once, and a novel to be delivered immediately afterward. Or he may not even want the short story book; it may be I can get this money only by contracting for a novel, to be commenced and completed as soon as possible, in which case I will write the one which I described to you" (*SLWF*, 129–30). About the same time Faulkner wrote Cerf, explaining, "I wrote Guinzburg, told him the sum I wanted, described the short story book and the novel I had to offer against it, explained that I had signed a contract and taken an advance from Random House for a novel" (*SLWF*, 131). These negotiations eventually broke down,[7] and by the end of July Faulkner had turned his attention to the short story book, "a mss. based on short stories, some published, something like the UNVANQUISHED in composition" (*SLWF*, 135). But Faulkner still had some reservations about the short story book, telling Cerf, "Also, it might be best not to publish it, but to wait until I have time to write the Huck Finn novel which I described to Bob. It will be impossible to get at it though before next

7. For further details, see Blotner's discussion, *SLWF*, 130, 132–33.

year at the earliest, unless lightning in some form strikes me a golden blow" (*SLWF*, 135).

Turning once more to writing short stories for quick sales to the national magazines, Faulkner nevertheless alluded twice more to the projected novel. "I am doing no writing save pot-boilers," he wrote Haas in October, 1940. "Ober sells just enough of them to keep my head above water, which is all right. I still have the novel in mind, may get at it when bad weather stops farming and flying and I become better adjusted mentally to the condition of this destruction-bent world" (*SLWF*, 136–77). And in March, 1941, Faulkner spoke of the project in somewhat wistful terms. "I have the book in mind," he wrote Haas. "If I ever get out of hock and settle down to be too old to fight in wars, I will get at it. I will get at it someday anyhow" (*SLWF*, 139).

By the time he got back at it, in 1961, twenty years had elapsed, six other Faulkner novels and three collections of his short stories had been published, and Faulkner was, true to his own prophecy, out of hock, settled down, and too old to fight in wars, or as near to those conditions as he ever managed to be. Yet *The Reivers*, as finally published, was in many essentials the same novel Faulkner had described to Haas in the 1940 outline. From his original summary we can immediately recognize Lucius Priest as the "normal boy" of middle class parents, Boon Hogganbeck as the "utterly unreliable white man," Ned William McCaslin as the "fairly unscrupulous" family servant, Everbe Corinthia as the "prostitute not very young anymore," and Lightning as the stolen race horse "which none of them actually intended to steal." The structure of *The Reivers*, in broad form, parallels the structure of Faulkner's outline; both trios move away from the settled community to a "hand to mouth existence" among scenes of "debauchery and degeneracy and actual criminality," followed by an ultimate return of the boy to his family. The argument

100

of *The Reivers* is anticipated succinctly in the outline, "the boy grows up, becomes a man." The lessons learned by the nameless boy in the outline, "courage and honor and generosity and pride and pity," are voiced, though somewhat differently, by Boss Priest in his famous speech to Lucius at the end of *The Reivers*:

> "I lied," I said.
> "Come here," he said.
> "I cant," I said. "I lied, I tell you."
> "I know it," he said.
> "Then do something about it. Do anything, just so it's something."
> "I cant," he said.
> "There aint anything to do? Not anything?"
> "I didn't say that," Grandfather said. "I said I couldn't. You can."
> "What?" I said. "How can I forget it? Tell me how to."
> "You cant," he said. "Nothing is ever forgotten. Nothing is ever lost. It's too valuable."
> "Then what can I do?"
> "Live with it," Grandfather said.
> "Live with it? You mean forever? For the rest of my life? Not ever to get rid of it? Never? I cant. Dont you see I cant?"
> "Yes you can," he said. "You will. A gentleman always does. A gentleman can live through anything. He faces anything. A gentleman accepts the responsibility of his actions and bears the burden of their consequences, even when he did not himself instigate them but only acquiesced to them, didn't say No though he knew he should."[8]

The Reivers, of course, contains a number of elements altered or omitted from the 1940 outline. Lucius Priest is eleven years old, rather than "twelve or thirteen." Boon Hogganbeck is a somewhat more knowledgable character than his prototype, and Ned McCaslin is far from being "in his second childhood." The sentimental snapper delivered by the boy's mother is omitted from *The Reivers*, though it is vestigially

8. William Faulkner, *The Reivers* (New York: Random House, 1962), 301–2. Hereafter cited in the text as *R*.

present in Boss Priest's injunction, "Persuade Alison to go on back upstairs and stop snivelling" (*R*, 301). Boon Hogganbeck inadvertently acquires a wife rather than attempting to escape from one. The time of the action is reduced from "a matter of weeks" to more nearly a matter of days. The fugitives of the novel are rather more concerned with first escaping from, and finally returning to, their family and community than with eluding the police long enough to return the horse to its rightful owner. The major physical addition to the outline is an automobile, Boss Priest's Winton Flyer, which is as important in the complication and frantic motion of the novel as the race horse itself. New characters who contribute significantly to the novel's texture and development include Reba Rivers, Otis, Butch Lovemaiden, Uncle Parsham Hood, Sam Caldwell, and Boss Priest. Lucius Priest himself must also be considered a new character insofar as he emerges as the mature narrator of the rogues' adventures, himself the grandfather first identified in the shortest frame ever provided for a frame-tale in American literature, "GRANDFATHER SAID" (*R*, 3). Lucius Priest, in his narrative role, makes a sufficient number of comments on the contemporary, i.e., 1961, scene to raise serious doubts about the allegation that *The Reivers* is a product of pure nostalgia.[9] If it is true that *The Reivers* has much in common with the novel Faulkner outlined in

9. Consider, for example, Lucius Priest's description of Mr. Binford in 1905: "(You see? how much ahead of his time Mr Binford was? Already a Republican. I dont mean a 1905 Republican—I dont know what his Tennessee politics were, or if he had any—I mean a 1961 Republican. He was more: he was a Conservative. Like this: a Republican is a man who made his money; a Liberal is a man who inherited his; a Democrat is a barefooted Liberal in a cross-country race; a Conservative is a Republican who has learned to read and write)" (*R*, 109). And his description of Lightning's handling of the bit "as if the bit were a pork rind and he a Mohammedan (or a fish spine and he a Mississippi candidate for constable whose Baptist opposition had accused him of seeking the Catholic vote, or one of Mrs Roosevelt's autographed letters and a secretary of the Citizens Council, or Senator Goldwater's cigar butt and the youngest pledge to the A.D.A.)" (*R*, 169). For an extended analysis of the "nostalgia" question, see Edwin Moses, "Faulkner's *The Reivers*: The Art of Acceptance," *Mississippi Quarterly*, 27 (Summer, 1974), 307–18.

1940, it is also considerably different from that outline in a number of important respects.

To understand some of the differences between Faulkner's original conception and his ultimate execution of the novel, we should consider his use of the projected material in other fiction of the '40s and '50s, chief among them the book he offered Random House and Viking Press, the "mss. based on short stories, some published, something like the UNVAN-QUISHED in composition." The road to *The Reivers* leads first to *Go Down, Moses. Go Down, Moses*, like *The Reivers*, is concerned with the process by which "the boy grows up, becomes a man." Issac McCaslin, like Lucius Priest, undergoes an initiation, through which he learns the lessons of "courage and honor and generosity and pride and pity," by turning away from the comforting certainties of civilization and confronting a different order of reality. Ike and Lucius also have in common a perplexing wealth of mentors, including Boon Hogganbeck, with whom they both take a trip to Memphis. Both protagonists are permanently changed by their experiences.

But the differences between the two protagonists and the two novels are greater than their similarities. Ike McCaslin learns his lessons in the wilderness, whereas Lucius learns his lessons on the road and in the city. What Ike learns is that his heritage is tainted by his grandfather L. Q. C. McCaslin's initial presumption that he could own land and slaves and by his subsequent arrogation of both to satisfy his appetites, with the disastrous compounding of incest upon miscegenation. The consequences of this lesson, for Ike, are guilt and repudiation. What he learns prevents him from making an affirmative return to the settled community, with its sustaining comforts of family and property. Having acquired an anachronistic preference for the wilderness, with its atavistic compact among the hunters, the hunted, and the land, Ike seeks to

103

repudiate the land and his family as well, "himself and his wife juxtaposed in their turn against that same land, that same wrong and shame from whose regret and grief he would at least save and free his son and, saving and freeing his son, lost him."[10] Lucius Priest, by contrast, learns to "live with it." He learns his own capacity for what he persists in calling "non-virtue," and he observes the capacity for "debauchery and degeneracy and actual criminality" that is within others, but he returns, changed and strengthened, to the community in which he assumes a traditional and positive role. Lucius himself becomes a grandfather in time, while Ike remains a childless uncle.

Go Down, Moses, then, is closer in tone and theme to the fiction Faulkner wrote before 1940 than it is to the tone and theme of the 1940 outline or the 1962 novel. The mood of *Go Down, Moses*, like the mood of *The Hamlet*, is often despairing. In spite of his education and initiation, and, paradoxically, because of them, Ike is helpless to prevent the repetition of his grandfather's crimes by his kinsman, Roth Edmonds, and he is helpless to prevent the continued destruction of the land he loves, whether he holds legal title to it or not. Faulkner's outlook about this time was memorably expressed in a 1944 letter to Malcolm Cowley: " . . . life is a phenomenon but not a novelty, the same frantic steeplechase toward nothing everywhere and man stinks the same stink no matter where in time."[11] Though some critics have persisted in seeing Ike's behavior as heroic, Faulkner's position may be inferred from the rebuke delivered in "Delta Autumn" by the woman whose claims on the McCaslin family and on simple humanity Ike has shrilly refused to acknowledge. "'Old man,'

10. William Faulkner, *Go Down, Moses* (New York: Random House, 1942), 351. Hereafter cited in the text as *GDM*.
11. Reprinted in Malcolm Cowley, *The Faulkner–Cowley File Letters and Memories, 1944–1962* (New York: Viking Press, 1966), 15.

she said, 'have you lived so long and forgotten so much that you dont remember anything you ever knew or felt or even heard about love?' "[12] Faulkner's comment on Ike in a University of Virginia interview points up the differences among Ike, Lucius, and Quentin Compson, and goes some way towards describing the change in outlook reflected in the fiction of Faulkner's last phase: "Well, there are some people in any time and age that cannot face and cope with the problems. There seem to be three stages: The first says, This is rotten, I'll have no part of it, I will take death first. The second says, This is rotten, I don't like it, I can't do anything about it, but at least I will not participate in it myself, I will go off into a cave or climb a pillar to sit on. The third says, This stinks and I'm going to do something about it. McCaslin is the second. He says, This is bad, and I will withdraw from it. What we need are people who will say, This is bad and I'm going to do something about it, I'm going to change it."[13]

Faulkner's fiction after 1942 often centers on characters of the third stage, characters who are determined "to do something about it," "to change it." Gavin Stevens, in the title story of *Knight's Gambit*, anticipates a murder and prevents it, whereas his role in the other stories in that volume—all written by 1940—is the more passive one of lawyer-detective. In *Intruder in the Dust*, Chick Mallison, Aleck Sander, and Miss Eunice Habersham confederate to prevent the lynching of

12. *Go Down, Moses*, 363.
13. *Faulkner in the University: Class Conferences at the University of Virginia, 1957–1958*, Frederick L. Gwynn and Joseph L. Blotner, eds. (New York: Vintage Books, n.d.), 245–46. See also Faulkner's comment about Ike to Cynthia Grenier, "I think a man ought to do more than just repudiate. He should have been more affirmative instead of shunning people." *Lion in the Garden: Interviews with William Faulkner 1926–1962*, James B. Meriwether and Michael Millgate, eds. (New York: Random House, 1968), 225. It is, of course, always risky to depend absolutely on any of Faulkner's comments about his own work, and both of the remarks quoted above were made quite some time after he had completed *Go Down, Moses*. They seem to me, however, a fair sample of the way Faulkner evaluated his characters, and man in general, during the last phase of his career.

The Road to *The Reivers*

Lucas Beauchamp and to solve the mystery of the murder of which Lucas has been wrongly accused. In *Requiem for a Nun*, Nancy Mannigoe determines to do something about Temple Drake Stevens's expressed intention to forsake her family, and though Nancy seizes on the terrible expedient of murdering Temple's child, she succeeds in her aim. Nancy, having the courage to die for her choice, assists Gavin Stevens in teaching Temple to "live with it." Numerous characters in *A Fable*, including the rebellious Corporal, the British runner, the Reverend Tobe Sutterfield, and Mister Harry, attempt to stop the war. In *The Town* and *The Mansion*, Gavin Stevens, Chick Mallison, and V. K. Ratliff join forces to oppose Snopesism, with varying degrees of effectiveness. *The Reivers* is, in a sense, the culmination of this developing theme in Faulkner's fiction. To be sure, the extremities of the situation Lucius faces are less pronounced than those confronted by other Faulkner characters, but they are about as much as one could expect a boy of his age and background to have to stand. This is not to deny that *The Reivers* is considerably softer in tone and substance than Faulkner's earlier fiction. It is the first of his novels since *Mosquitoes* in which no death figures centrally in the plot, if we except the death of Grandfather Lessep, and it is the only one of his novels from which the threat of death is essentially absent.[14] But Lucius Priest, more than any of Faulkner's other central characters, not only accepts the responsibility for his own actions,

14. Too, Faulkner avoided in *The Reivers* a complication hinted at in the 1940 outline by establishing Lucius at an age below which he could be presumed to have attained sexual capacity. Lucius Priest himself, as narrator of *The Reivers*, alludes to this point when he describes his reaction to the odor of Miss Reba's hallway: "I had never smelled it before. I didn't dislike it; I was just surprised. I mean, as soon as I smelled it, it was like a smell I had been waiting all my life to smell. I think you should be tumbled pell-mell, without warning, only into experience which you might well have spent the rest of your life not having to meet. But with an inevitable (ay, necessary) one, it's not really decent of Circumstance, fate, not to prepare you first, especially when the preparation is as simple as just being fifteen years old"(*R*, 99).

but also manages to achieve a state of comic affirmation rather than one of alienation.

The tone of conscious didacticism that informs both the 1940 outline and *The Reivers* is typical of Faulkner's later fiction. Although this tone is muted in *Go Down, Moses*, it is readily observable in the version of "The Bear" Faulkner published in *The Saturday Evening Post* in 1942. The final scene of this story, which centers on the encounter between the great bear and the little mongrel dog, bears some striking resemblances to the phrasing of the 1940 outline and to the situation at the end of *The Reivers*. The protagonist of the story, a nameless boy of fourteen, is taught the practical lessons of the wilderness by Sam Fathers, and the abstract meaning of these experiences by his own father, who points the explicit moral. "'Courage and honor and pride,' his father said, 'and pity and love of justice and of liberty. They all touch the heart, and what the heart holds to becomes truth.'"[15] In this passage, as in the 1940 outline, Faulkner uses the rhetoric that would become famous after his address at Stockholm. In *Go Down, Moses*, Ike McCaslin, whose family life is anything but normal, argues and discourses with his cousin, McCaslin Edmonds, rather than learning from his own father, and Ike's interpretation and application of the lessons of the wilderness are radically at variance with the conclusions reached by the boy of "The Bear" and by Lucius Priest.[16]

Examples of such didactic scenes abound in Faulkner's later

15. *Uncollected Stories of William Faulkner*, Joseph Blotner, ed. (New York: Random House, 1979), 295. Hereafter cited in the text as *US*.
16. For a different evaluation of Ike and Lucius, see Haney H. Bell, Jr., "The Relative Maturity of Lucius Priest and Ike McCaslin," *Aegis*, 2 (1973), 15–21. Critics who maintain the position I am supporting here include Cleanth Brooks, *William Faulkner: The Yoknapatawpha Country* (New Haven and London: Yale University Press, 1963), 362; Albert J. Devlin, "*The Reivers*: Readings in Social Psychology," *Mississippi Quarterly*, 25 (Summer, 1972), 327–37; and V. R. N. Prasad, "The Pilgrim and the Picaro: A Study of Faulkner's *The Bear* and *The Reivers*," *Indian Essays in American Literature: Papers in Honour of Robert E. Spiller* (Bombay: Popular Prakashan, 1969), 209–21.

fiction. Gavin Stevens's lengthy disquisitions on the race issue to Chick Mallison in *Intruder in the Dust* come immediately to mind, as do his speeches to Temple in *Requiem for a Nun*, the conversations between the Supreme Commander and the Corporal in *A Fable*, Mister Ernest's encomium on education to the boy who narrates the 1955 short story, "Race at Morning," and Gavin Stevens's attempts to educate Chick Mallison and Linda Snopes in *The Town* and *The Mansion*. Faulkner's earlier fiction also contains didactic speeches from fathers and father-figures, but the earlier instances of this device are more compressed in form and more despairing in substance. Consider Mr. Compson's cynical advice to Quentin in *The Sound and the Fury*, or Ab Shopes's terse injunction to Sarty in "Barn Burning": "You're getting to be a man. You got to learn. You got to learn to stick to your own blood or you ain't going to have any blood to stick to you."[17] Faulkner's fiction after 1940 is characteristically a rhetorical fiction, in which he sought not only to refine and clarify a more affirmative view of the human condition than his earlier work had portended, but also to discover forms and situations in which these affirmations could be rendered credible.[18]

One portion of the 1940 outline that Faulkner developed specifically in subsequent fiction prior to *The Reivers* is the story of the stolen race horse. The story, which was published in three different variants before it appeared for the last time as an embedded narrative in *A Fable*, details the adventures of the three inadvertent thieves who live from hand to mouth

17. William Faulkner, *Collected Stories* (New York: Random House, 1950), 8. Hereafter cited in the text as *CS*.
18. For a general treatment of this development in Faulkner's writing, see Joseph Gold, *William Faulkner: A Study in Humanism From Metaphor to Discourse* (Norman: University of Oklahoma Press, 1966). Edwin Moses discusses this aspect of the narrative structure of *The Reivers* in some detail in "Faulkner's *The Reivers*: The Art of Acceptance" (see above, note 9).

as they endeavor to evade the police.[19] In *Notes on a Horsethief*, an English groom takes advantage of a railroad accident to make away with a valuable race horse. He is joined by an itinerant Negro preacher and his grandson, and the three of them manage to escape capture for over a year, even as they are pursued by five different groups of police, and by numerous amateurs in quest of the reward that has been offered for the race horse. Though the horse, injured in the accident, has only three good legs, the fugitives race it at every opportunity, and are thought to have won a large amount of money in doing so. Faced with capture at last, the groom kills the horse, rather than allowing it to be returned to stud, " . . . where it wouldn't need any legs at all not even a travelling crane geared by machinery to the rhythm of ejaculation because a skillful pander with a syringe and a rubber glove. . . ."[20]

While the *Notes on a Horsethief* story differs from Faulkner's 1940 outline in a number of obvious particulars, it also marks an important point on the road to *The Reivers*. The groom's experience with the horse is the means through which he learns to enter humanity, and in *A Fable* he joins in the futile rebellion against the war. Harry, like Ned McCaslin in *The Reivers*, is a Mason, and both the *Notes on a Horsethief* and *The Reivers* end with evasive answers to queries

19. *Notes an a Horsethief* was published by the Levee Press of Greenville, Mississippi, in a limited edition in 1950. In 1954, two excerpts from William Faulkner, *A Fable* (New York: Random House, 1954) were published in magazines, under the title, "Notes on a Horsethief." The *Vogue* version, 124 (July, 1954), 46–51, 101–7, corresponds to material on pp. 151–204 of *A Fable*. The version published in *Perspectives U. S. A.*, No. 9 (Autumn, 1954), 24–49, corresponds to the material of pp. 151–89 of *A Fable*. See Mary Jane Dickerson, "Faulkner's Golden Steed," *Mississippi Quarterly*, 31 (Summer, 1978), 369–80 for an analysis of the image of the horse in Faulkner's work, and especially pp. 379–80 for *Notes on a Horsethief* and *A Fable*.

20. *Notes on a Horsethief*, 21. The complicated wager between Boss Priest and Colonel Linscomb (*R*, 293–95) also recalls the even more complicated series of wagers between Uncle Buddy McCaslin and Hubert Beauchamp in *Go Down, Moses*.

about the amount of money won by gambling on the horse.[21]
More important than these details, however, is the emphasis
in both narratives on the complicity of the community at large
with the horsethieves. As Lucius Priest voices the discovery,
"All the world loves a lover, quoth (I think) the Swan: who
saw deeper than any into the human heart. What pity he had
no acquaintance with horses, to have added, All the world
apparently loves a stolen race horse also" (R, 135). And
shortly afterward he adds, "And you see what I mean too: all
the world (I mean about a stolen race horse); who serves Virtue works alone, unaided, in a chilly vacuum of reserved
judgment; where, pledge yourself to Non-Virtue and the
whole countryside boils with volunteers to help you" (R, 143).
The same theme is sounded in *The Town*, in which the whole
community of Jefferson seems to be in conspiracy to keep
Flem Snopes from having to discover his wife's affair with
Manfred de Spain.

The Reivers has less substantial affinities and connections
with *Intruder in the Dust*, *The Town* and *The Mansion* than
it does with *Go Down, Moses* and *A Fable*, though there are
numerous characters in common in each of these works.[22]
Each novel, however, is concerned with the ways in which
the individual and the community respond to the discovery
of personal and social evil. Faulkner postponed his Huck
Finn novel to write *Go Down, Moses*, as he later postponed
A Fable to write *Intruder in the Dust*, as he seems to have
discovered *Knight's Gambit* in the process of outlining his
Collected Stories,[23] and as he wrote *The Town* and *The Man-*

21. *Notes on a Horsethief*, 70–71; *Reivers*, 303–4.
22. Many of the parallels between *The Reivers* and Faulkner's other fiction have
been mentioned by Elizabeth M. Kerr in "*The Reivers*: The Golden Book of Yoknapatawpha County" (see above, note 2). Joseph Blotner mentions parallels between Faulkner's 1940 outline and the short story "Uncle Willy" (*Faulkner: A Biography*, 1795), and "Uncle Willy" bears a number of important resemblances to
The Reivers itself.
23. See Faulkner's letter to Haas, *SLWF*, 274–75, 280, 283, 287.

sion to complete the saga he had promised as early as 1934 and outlined—to a conclusion very different from the one he finally reached—in a letter to Haas in 1938.[24] To understand the essential continuity of the Faulkner canon, we may observe that in writing his last novel, Faulkner drew on not only the materials present in his 1940 outline, but also on the work habits and the resulting substance of his entire range of writing.

In selecting a title for *The Reivers*, Faulkner recalled a word that he had employed in some of his earliest poetry and in his first novel. In the poem "The Poet Goes Blind," a typescript of which is dated 29 October, 1924, Faulkner wrote: "What sport is this—the sleeper to awake/Into a day he sought not, then to take/His waking span and rieve its sun and moon?"[25] Rector Mahon, in his first encounter with Januarius Jones in *Soldiers' Pay*, remarks that "Only the ageing need conventions and laws to aggregate to themselves some of the beauty of this world. Without laws the young would rieve us of it as corsairs of old combed the blue seas."[26] Jones himself employs the word in a subsequent scene, in a satiric echo of the rector's phrasing, "Years rieve us of sexual compulsions: why shouldn't they fill the interval with compulsions of food?" (*SP*, 70). In *The Town* Gavin Stevens speculates on Flem Snopes's attitude toward the looting of banks by their owners. Flem, Gavin tells us, would loot his own bank, "decently, with decorum, as they had done and would do: not rieved like a boy snatching a handful of loose peanuts while the vendor's back was turned, as his cousin Byron had

24. Faulkner's 1938 outline of the Snopes trilogy is in *SLWF*, 107–8. Aubrey Starke, "An American Comedy: An Introduction to a Bibliography of William Faulkner," *Colophon*, 5, part 19 (1934), unnumbered pages, forecasts the Snopes saga.

25. William Faulkner, *Mississippi Poems* (Oxford, Mississippi: Yoknapatawpha Press, 1979), 25.

26. William Faulkner, *Soldiers' Pay* (New York: Boni and Liveright, 1926), 58. Hereafter cited in the text as *SP*.

done."[27] Faulkner recalled the word when he came to choose a title for the novel he had called *The Horse Stealers: A Reminiscence* while it was in manuscript. "The title for what they are doing," he wrote Albert Erskine, "would be/ The Stealers. The title I have now is/ The Reavers/ But there is an old Scottish spelling which I like better:/ The Rievers (maybe *Reivers*)/ This sounds more active, swashing, then Reavers, which is the American word meaning the same, but it sounds too peaceful, bucolic: too much like Weavers" (*SLWF*, 456). The *OED* confirms Faulkner's understanding of the spelling variant, and cites uses of several forms of the word by Langland, Chaucer, Spenser, Burns, Scott, and Tennyson, among others. Whatever the specific literary source of Faulkner's title,[28] he was amused by the fact that, for once, he would puzzle his readers with his title, rather than with the story itself.[29]

The narrative strategy of *The Reivers* includes a number of techniques Faulkner had employed previously in his continuing experiment with point of view, and which, taken together, form a combination unique among his novels. The fact that the entire narrative is assigned to a single first-person voice distinguishes *The Reivers* from every other Faulkner novel except *The Unvanquished*. Although *The Sound and the Fury*, *As I Lay Dying*, *The Town*, and *The Mansion* are rendered primarily or exclusively through first-person narrators, each of these novels is structured through alteration among radically opposing points-of-view, and significant portions of both *The Sound and the Fury* and *The Mansion* are assigned to an omniscient third-person narrator. Both Lucius Priest and Bayard Sartoris tell their stories from a mature perspective; both are describing important experiences of their own

27. William Faulkner, *The Town* (New York: Random House, 1957), 265.

28. See Benjamin H. Griffith, "Faulkner's Archaic Titles and the *Second Shepherd's Play*," *Notes on Mississippi Writers*, 4 (Fall, 1971), 62–63, for an argument for one possible source.

29. Reported in *Faulkner: A Biography*, 1801.

youth, telling how "the boy grows up, becomes a man." Bayard Sartoris' narrative in *The Unvanquished*, however, is not given the explicit and precise dramatic frame that Faulkner sets for Lucius Priest. Bayard's maturity can be inferred primarily from the sophistication of his prose, and from the retrospective allusion in "An Odor of Verbena" which recalls the particulars of Ringo's announcement of the death of Bayard's father: "It was not until years later that he told me (someone did; it must have been Judge Wilkins) how Ringo had apparently flung the cook aside and come on into the house and into the library where he and Mrs. Wilkins were sitting and said without preamble and already turning to withdraw: 'They shot Colonel Sartoris this morning. Tell him I be waiting in the kitchen' and was gone before either of them could move."[30] Thus both *The Unvanquished* and *The Reivers* are built on a double perspective, that of the youth who directly apprehends experience, and that of the mature man who recalls, recounts, and explains the meaning of that experience.

Faulkner employed this double perspective in his short stories as well, notably in "That Evening Sun" and "Barn Burning." "That Evening Sun" is told by Quentin Compson, whose sophisticated narrative voice recounts his observation of the crisis in the lives of Nancy and Jesus that had occurred fifteen years previously. Quentin, however, is deliberately ambiguous about the outcome of the confrontation between Nancy and Jesus, and he avoids explicit comment on the meaning of the experience. The boy Quentin's final question, "Who will do our washing now, Father?" (*CS*, 309), indicates that the boy believes that a change is taking place, but the mature narrator declines further comment or explanation. In "Barn Burning" the omniscient narrator distinguishes among several levels of perception and alludes to the passage of years

30. William Faulkner, *The Unvanquished* (New York: Random House, 1938), 244–45.

from the point of the events of the story. "Later, twenty years later, he was to tell himself, 'If I had said they wanted only truth, justice, he would have hit me again.' But now he said nothing" (*CS*, 8). Like *The Unvanquished* and *The Reivers*, "That Evening Sun" and "Barn Burning" are stories of initiation, but only in *The Reivers* does Faulkner establish the narrator as protagonist and endow him with the freedom and capacity to describe fully and to comment upon the substance of both the youthful and the mature perspectives.

A partial explanation of this difference may be found in the fully realized narrative situation of *The Reivers*, a prose equivalent of the Browning dramatic monologue, in which the speaker reveals his character by addressing an identifiable audience for a discoverable purpose. Where Bayard Sartoris of *The Unvanquished* and Quentin Compson of "That Evening Sun" are literary narrators addressing a distant, impersonal audience, and thus reveal very little about their present circumstances, Lucius Priest is presented as a grandfather addressing his grandchildren. Thus he is able not only to recount the past, and to comment on both the past and present, but also to inform his grandchildren about their family and regional heritage. If Lucius is occasionally somewhat sententious, his behavior is at least appropriate to the homiletic character of a grandfather. The dramatic situation of *The Reivers* and the voice of Lucius Priest allow Faulkner to demonstrate the full range of the styles of which he was capable, and even, on occasion, to parody the vagaries of his own prose.[31]

While Faulkner's use of the fluctuating first-person narrative method in *The Sound and the Fury* and *As I Lay Dying* may well constitute his single most important contribution to

31. If the passage, "in the frozen attitude of running or frozen in the attitude of running or in the attitude of frozen running, whichever is right" (*R*, 14), is not Faulkner parodying himself, it is Faulkner parodying academic criticism of his works.

modern narrative prose technique, it raises some nearly un-
answerable questions of judgment for the many readers who
assume that the several narrative voices stand in an identifiable hierarchical relation to one another, for the many readers
who assume that a single narrator must be selected from
among the several as Faulkner's "spokesman," and for the
many readers who assume that a first-person narrator ought
to employ diction and phrasing appropriate to his character
and circumstances. Although there are convincing arguments
against any of these three assumptions, it is nevertheless true
that in *The Reivers* Lucius Priest may be taken as an authorial
figure, where Quentin Compson, Ike McCaslin, and Gavin
Stevens—to name only the three characters most often ana-
lyzed and pilloried as Faulkner spokesmen—are always one
voice among several in the fictions in which they figure. The
great advantage of the technique of *The Reivers* is that it
helps Faulkner to avoid the problems in verisimilitude raised
by his habit of assigning inappropriately sophisticated diction,
syntax, or philosophy to his more primitive characters, and
by his habit of assigning grandiloquent speeches to such characters as Gavin Stevens and by authorial "intrusion" in the
omniscient narrative. Compare, for example, the prose at-
tributed to Darl Bundren in *As I Lay Dying*: "And since sleep
is is-not and rain and wind are *was*, it is not. Yet the wagon
is, because when the wagon is *was*, Addie Bundren will not
be. And Jewel *is*, so Addie Bundren must be. And then I
must be, or I could not empty myself for sleep in a strange
room. And so if I am not emptied yet, I am is."[32] Lucius Priest
voices a similar distinction in *The Reivers*. "Then even the
rage was gone. Nothing remained, nothing. I didn't want to
go anywhere, be anywhere. I mean, I didn't want to be *is*
anywhere. If I had to be something, I wanted it to be *was*"

32. William Faulkner, *As I Lay Dying* (New York: Random House, 1964), 76.

(*R*, 58). Similarly, while Lucius Priest's comments on the mule arise in a densely textured passage eminently appropriate to the method of narration and to the point in the plot in which it occurs (*R*, 121–24), Faulkner's earlier apostrophe to the mule in *Sartoris*, rich though it is in mock-epic rhetoric, remains an obtrusive indulgence for the omniscient narrator.[33]

Lucius Priest also serves, at least incidentally, as the chronicler of Yoknapatawpha County. His narrative manages to encompass—as do the prose interchapters of *Requiem for a Nun* and the fictive essay, "Mississippi"—allusions to a vast range of Yoknapatawpha characters. In fact, each of the other thirteen Yoknapatawpha novels and perhaps two dozen of the short stories are evoked by specific allusions to identifiable characters in *The Reivers*. The novel does not, however, raise the vexing questions of autonomy and interdependence one encounters in dealing with the discrepancies and contradictions among the volumes of the Snopes trilogy, between *The Sound and the Fury* and *Absalom, Absalom!*, or between *Sanctuary* and *Requiem for a Nun*. Many of these allusions are slight, and can be treated as ostentatiously decorative or metafictionally functional, depending on one's point of view, but it cannot be objected that they are either individually or collectively inappropriate to the narrative voice of the novel. Through the voice of Lucius Priest, the grandfather telling his story to his grandchildren, Faulkner, the grandfather who dedicated his last novel to his own grandchildren, discovered the happy combination of teller, tale, and voice which so often eluded him in his other late fiction.

Perhaps the most obvious narrative strategy which connects *The Reivers* to the rest of the Faulkner canon is the device of the perilous journey, and specifically the journey to

33. William Faulkner, *Sartoris* (New York: Harcourt, Brace and Company, 1929), 278–79. For further discussion see William T. Stafford, "'Some Homer of the Cotton Fields': Faulkner's Use of the Mule Early and Late (*Sartoris* and *The Reivers*)," *Papers on Languages and Literature*, 5 (Spring, 1969), 190–96.

Memphis. From the allegorical journey of Sir Galwyn of Arthgyl in *Mayday*, and the chaotic odyssey of the Bundrens to Jefferson in *As I Lay Dying*, through Lena Grove's quest and Joe Christmas's flight in *Light in August*, to Charles Bon and Henry Sutpen's trip to New Orleans in *Absalom, Absalom!*, and the midnight ride of the intrepid trio in *Intruder in the Dust*, Faulkner's novels have depended on the journey for important aspects of structure, episode, and theme. In *The Reivers*, as in dozens of other Faulkner fictions, the destination is Memphis. "(. . . Where else did we have to go? Indeed, where else could anyone in north Mississippi want to go? Some aged and finished creature on his or her deathbed might contemplate or fear a more distant destination, but they were not Boon or me)" (*R*, 57). Memphis represents a variety of goals and discoveries to the dozens of Faulkner characters who venture there. In *Sartoris* Bayard goes to Memphis to acquire an automobile. In *Sanctuary* Temple goes to Memphis under force to be degraded, Horace Benbow goes to Memphis to find her, and Fonzo and Virgil go to Memphis to attend barber college. In *Go Down, Moses* Boon Hogganbeck goes to Memphis to buy whiskey, and Ike McCaslin goes with him to make certain that Boon gets back to the hunting camp with some of it. In the Compson Appendix to *The Sound and the Fury*, Melissa Meek goes to Memphis to find Dilsey, and it is reported that T.P. "wore on Memphis's Beale Street the fine bright cheap intransigent clothes manufactured specifically for him by the owners of Chicago and New York sweatshops."[34] In *The Mansion* Mink Snopes goes to Memphis to buy a gun. The short fiction is equally rich in the matter of Memphis. Dal Martin of "The Big Shot" goes to Memphis to escape poverty. Narcissa Benbow Sartoris in "There Was a Queen" goes to Memphis for an assignation

---

34. William Faulkner, "1699–1945 The Compsons," in *The Portable Faulkner*, Malcolm Cowley, ed. (New York: Viking, 1946), 755.

with the man who is blackmailing her. And in "Two Soldiers" the little Grier boy goes to Memphis hoping to find his older brother and join the army. In each of these stories, and in the majority of the many others which I have not mentioned, the traveler embarks for a specific purpose only to make some unexpected discoveries along the way or within the city itself.

In *The Reivers* this theme is pointed up most prominently by Boon Hogganbeck, who sets out for Memphis for a sabbatical with his whore, only to discover that she has gone and reformed on him. For Lucius we may distinguish between the adventures on the road, such as the crossing of the Iron Bridge, the stop at Ballenbaugh's, and the harrowing of Hell Creek Bottom on the one hand, and, on the other, the discoveries of Memphis itself, including "pugnuckling" and puppy love, from the more abstract discoveries Faulkner had originally contemplated in his 1940 outline. When we recall Faulkner's headnote to *The Mansion*, with its assertion that 'living' is motion, and 'motion' is change and alteration and therefore the only alternative to motion is un-motion, stasis, death,"[35] we may grasp the implications of the journey as metaphor for motion in *The Reivers*, whether the motion is that of an automobile along a road, of mules through mud, or of horses around a racetrack. The characters in Faulkner's fiction who come in for some of the most satiric condemnation, in fact, are those who are reluctant to engage in motion. Jason Compson's futile and desperate pursuit of the girl Quentin in *The Sound and the Fury* is one early important example. The reclusive proclivity of Gail Hightower in *Light in August* is another. In *The Reivers* itself, the theme is manifested in the characterization of Otis, who is afraid to ride Lightning and is terrified by riding a mule. In the short fiction the case is supported by the ironic description of the obese Moketubbe

35. William Faulkner, *The Mansion* (New York: Random House, 1959), unnumbered page.

being carried by his slaves in "Red Leaves," by the withdrawal from society by Miss Emily Grierson and Miss Zilphia Gant, and by the vicious immobility of Old Man Meadowfill in "Hog Pawn." Boss Priest explains the principle to his daughter-in-law. "People will pay any price for motion. They will even work for it. Look at bicycles. Look at Boon. We dont know why" (*R*, 41).

Another sort of repetition in *The Reivers* is the repetition of the situation, common to a number of other Faulkner fictions, in which a woman prostitutes herself in an effort to secure her man's release or escape from the law. In *Sanctuary* Ruby prostitutes herself to pay a lawyer to get Lee Goodwin out of the federal penitentiary in Leavenworth, and she is willing to pay Horace Benbow in like coin for defending Lee in Jefferson.[36] In *The Hamlet* Mink Snopes's wife earns ten dollars to help in Mink's escape by prostituting herself to one of his pursuers. And in *The Town* Gavin Stevens believes that Eula Varner Snopes offers herself to him in an effort to save Flem from prosecution. The characteristic response of the supposed beneficiary of these attempts is shock, outrage, and scorn. Lee Goodwin beats Ruby savagely for getting him out of Leavenworth, and Horace Benbow, in this and other respects anticipating Gavin Stevens, is horrified by Ruby's offer. Mink Snopes flings his wife's offering away, just as Caroline Compson in *The Sound and the Fury* and Dr. Carl Schumann in *Pylon* refuse to accept what they believe to be prostitutes' wages. In *The Reivers* Everbe Corinthia finally yields to the

36. Ruby tells Temple Drake, "When he was a soldier on the Philippines he killed another soldier over one of those nigger women and they sent him to Leavenworth. Then the war came and they let him out to go to it. He got two medals, and when it was over they put him back in Leavenworth until the lawyer got a congressman to get him out. Then I could quit jazzing again. . . ." William Faulkner, *Sanctuary* (New York: Jonathan Cape and Harrison Smith, 1931), 68. And shortly later she explains "I worked night shift as a waitress so I could see him Sundays at the prison. I lived two years in a single room, cooking over a gas-jet, because I promised him. I lied to him and made money to get him out of prison, and when I told him how I made it, he beat me" (*Sanctuary*, 71).

importuning of Butch Lovemaiden, in order to secure the release of the conspirators from the Parsham jail, for which Boon blacks her eye. The scene is a comic repetition of the episode between Ruby and Lee Goodwin, with the difference that by the time he wrote his last novel, Faulkner was delineating more forgiving and understanding characters than in his earlier works.

To illustrate the variety of ways in which Faulkner drew on his early fiction in writing *The Reivers*, let us examine one scene rendered in three distinct fictions to three distinct purposes over a period of 27 years. In "Lion," a short story published in 1935, there occurs this description of Boon Hogganbeck:

> He never could shoot. He never had killed anything bigger than a squirrel that anybody knew of, except that nigger that time. That was several years ago. They said he was a bad nigger, but I don't know. All I know is, there was some trouble and the nigger told Boon he'd better have a pistol next time he came to town and Boon borrowed a pistol from Major de Spain and sure enough that afternoon he met the nigger and the nigger outs with a dollar-and-a-half mail order pistol and he would have burned Boon up with it only it never went off. It just snapped five times and the nigger kept coming, and Boon shot four times and broke a plate-glass window and shot in the leg a nigger woman who happened to be passing before he managed to hit the nigger in the face with the last shot. He never could shoot.[37]

The incident is recounted more succinctly by the omniscient narrator of *Go Down, Moses*. "*Now Boon's going to curse Ash or maybe even hit him*, the boy thought. But Boon never did, never had; the boy knew he never would even though four years ago Boon had shot five times with a borrowed pistol at a negro on the street in Jefferson, with the same result as when he had shot five times at Old Ben last fall" (*GDM*, 230).

<hr/>

37. *Uncollected Stories of William Faulkner*, 189.

And in *The Reivers*, Lucius Priest provides yet another version of the incident:

So Father, Luster and I hurried up the alley toward the Square, me trotting now, and still too late. We hadn't even reached the end of the alley when we heard the shots, all five of them: WHOW WHOW WHOW WHOW WHOW like that, then we were in the Square and (it wasn't far: right at the corner of Cousin Isaac McCaslin's hardware store) we could see it. There were plenty of them; Boon sure picked his day for witnesses; First Saturdays were trade days even then, even in May when you would think people would be too busy getting land planted. But not in Yoknapatawpha County. They were all there, black and white: one crowd where Mr. Hampton (the grandfather of this same Little Hub who is sheriff now, or will be again next year) and two or three bystanders were wrestling with Boon, and another crowd where another deputy was holding Ludus about twenty feet away and still in the frozen attitude of running or frozen in the attitude of running or in the attitude of frozen running, whichever is right, and another crowd around the window of Cousin Ike's store which one of Boon's bullets (they never did find where the other four went) had shattered after creasing the buttock of a Negro girl who was lying on the pavement screaming until Cousin Ike himself came jumping out of the store and drowned her voice with his, roaring with rage at Boon not for ruining his window but (Cousin Ike was young then but already the best woodsman and hunter this county ever had) for being unable to hit with five shots an object only twenty feet away. (*R*, 14–15)

In spite of their superficial similarities, these three passages have relatively little in common. Each concerns Boon Hogganbeck, and each specifies his poor marksmanship through an account of his attempted shooting of a black man with five shots. A few details are shared by two of the three versions. In "Lion" and *The Reivers* one of Boon's shots breaks a plate glass window, and wounds a bystander. In *Go Down, Moses* and *The Reivers* Boon misses his target.

What are the differences? One consideration is that each account emanates from a distinct narrative point of view, in a distinct form. Quentin, the narrator of "Lion," recounts the episode to explain why Boon will not kill Old Ben, and the anecdote contributes to Quentin's portrait of Boon as a man of savage violence. Boon's killing of Old Ben with only a knife, in defense of the courageous dog, whom he loves, is the more remarkable for its contrast with his murder of the black man and his later proprietary attitude toward the gum tree full of squirrels. The omniscient narrator of *Go Down, Moses* also dramatizes Boon's violence and his poor marksmanship, but the summary sentences given to the shooting episode make Quentin's point more economically, and soften the characterization of Boon by having him miss the black man. Lucius Priest's extended narrative serves to introduce one of the novel's principal characters, and to establish the comic tone of the entire work.

The discrepancies among the effects of Boon's shooting are pronounced. If Boon is a murderer in "Lion," and an attempted murderer in *Go Down, Moses*, in *The Reivers* he is merely a buffoon, for there is never any serious question in the novel that Boon will kill Ludus. As John Powell explains, "'Aint nobody studying Ludus. . . . Ludus the safest man there. I seen Boon Hogganbeck . . . shoot before'" (*R*, 10). In this connection we may also note the changes in the descriptions of Boon's target. In "Lion" Quentin repeats over and over that Boon's encounter was with a "nigger," and his numbing repetition of this epithet suggests his own racial attitudes as well as his indifference to the fate of Boon's victim. The narrator of *Go Down, Moses* uses the more neutral term, "Negro," and omits Quentin's ambiguous allusion to the "justice" of the shooting. Lucius Priest's account not only gives Boon's ostensible target a name and a personality, but also provides extensive comic motivation, which establishes Boon as clearly in the wrong.

Another incidental discrepancy we may note is the different setting in time for the three episodes. The time of the action of "Lion" is somewhat vague, but we are told that Quentin is sixteen years old, that Boon is about forty, and that "Boon and the conductor and the brakeman talked about Lion and Old Ben as people talked about Sullivan and Kilrain and Dempsey and Tunney" (*US*, 187). Although the famous Dempsey–Tunney fight took place in 1927, we may legitimately conclude only that Quentin's narration, and not necessarily the action of the story, took place after 1927. The time of the shooting episode in *Go Down, Moses* is 1878 or 1879, and the episode in *The Reivers* takes place in 1905. There are other additions, deletions, and alterations in Lucius Priest's version of the incident—Boon, as Lucius tells it, appropriates a pistol from John Powell, where Quentin has Boon borrowing the pistol from Major de Spain, and the weapon in *Go Down, Moses* is a more neutral "borrowed pistol", and there are significantly altered descriptions of the character and role of Ike McCaslin, and a burlesque embellishment of the description of the wounded girl—but the incident as a whole should serve to illustrate the vast differences between instances of Faulknerian repetition of character, situation, and incident.

There were, of course, risks involved in Faulkner's choice of methods and materials for *The Reivers*, and the mixed critical response to the novel shows that with at least a significant and influential portion of his audience, the risks were unsuccessfully taken. It was no more fashionable among the elite academic audience in 1962, and it is no more fashionable now, for a "serious" writer to endorse affirmative sentiment and nostalgia than it was fashionable to tell the kind of truth Faulkner told in 1931 in *Sanctuary*. By employing so many characters and incidents and situations from his previous writing, and by presenting those materials from an altered perspective, Faulkner made himself vulnerable to the paradoxical charge that he had changed his mind at the same time as he was simply repeating himself. But if we can transcend the spurious mandates of literary ideology, with its distracting accidents of attitudinal fashion, if we can remark the judicious differences as well as the bald similarities between *The Reivers* and the other fictions on which Faulkner drew generally and specifically in writing it, and especially if we can see that *The Reivers* was conceived in financial desperation, delayed twenty years by the sustaining distractions of other fiction and by the debilitating distractions of Hollywood, fame, and domesticity, and completed at last at a time when Faulkner had achieved the perspective from which he could recollect the chaos of his Human Comedy in something like tranquility, then we can see that the road to *The Reivers* was not only a long and circuitous one, but also that it led him, finally, to an honorable place.

The Collector as Sleuthsayer

LOUIS DANIEL BRODSKY

Toward the end of April 1946 a squat little volume, thickly paged, with lavender dust jacket, edited by Malcolm Cowley, was published by The Viking Press of New York. The book, a collection of excerpts gathered with the idea of imposing chronological, thematic, and anthropological order on Faulkner's writing from its beginnings to the present, was called *The Portable Faulkner*. It was intended to be conveniently transported in one's coat pocket, and its editor and publisher had spirited hopes that it might not only sell well, but help redress the imbalance between Faulkner's literary importance and his current neglect.

When Faulkner received his initial pre-publication copy from Viking, his response to Cowley was exuberant. He wrote on April 23, 1946:

> Dear Cowley:
>   The job is splendid, Damn you to hell anyway. But even if I had beat you to the idea, mine wouldn't have been this good. By God, I didn't know myself what I had tried to do, and how much I had succeeded.

The rest of the story is legend. Our presence here tonight is a testimonial to this writer's accomplishment and to his staying power.

When asked to lecture about my Faulkner collection, a sampling of which is currently on display in the John Davis

125

The Collector as Sleuthsayer

Williams Library here, and pondering with outsized pride both the flattering nature of the request and the many paths I've taken to arrive at this pinnacle, a symbol of which is surely this podium, I was immediately reminded of Faulkner's expression to Cowley in the letter previously quoted: "By God, I didn't know myself what I had tried to do, and how much I had succeeded."

Even as I stand here now, I'm renewed with amazement and excitement realizing that my own efforts have been responsible to a modest degree not only for helping to perpetuate Faulkner's reputation, but in expanding others' awareness and appreciation of the legacy he left us. And as if this were not accomplishment enough for one collector to achieve, I am also brought to the realization that what I had set out to do nearly twenty years ago has far outstripped even my most capricious and exaggerated early dreams: I am thus reminded that dreaming has its own special value and reward in that it can sometimes fulfill itself by crossing over into the living, breathing world of action; that it can enhance one's life by becoming pragmatic and beneficial instead of remaining mere stuff the mind gathers to sleep more quietly at night.

What has arisen from the dream, materialized in palpable form, and which until recently I "didn't know I had tried to do" is a broader, more enlightened perspective of William Faulkner, the man and the writer. The current exhibit at the Library, the seemly booklet that accompanies it, the Faulkner and Yoknapatawpha Conference for 1980, and the recent publication by The University Press of Virginia of a book titled *Selections from the William Faulkner Collection of Louis Daniel Brodsky: A Descriptive Catalogue*, all confirm the notion that dreams can become realities.

Curiously, the Virginia Press descriptive catalogue bears some affinity to *The Portable Faulkner* in that it encapsulates the best of my collection, bringing it together for the public, scholarly and otherwise, to assimilate. When Cowley's design for ordering Faulkner's material became clear to him, he wrote Faulkner proposing that they collaborate on the book. Faulkner wrote back on August 16, 1945: "By all means let us make a Golden Book of my apocryphal county. . . ." I believe that my catalogue, made in collaboration with Robert W. Hamblin, who in November of 1977 wrote and made a similar suggestion to me, is somehow my Golden Book.

What began as a youthful gesture to accumulate a few first editions and hopefully a few Faulkner signatures has now become a record, a documentary of one man's literary career. It has resulted from a fanciful amalgam, a salmagundi, if you will, of disparate circumstances and values: partly through prescience, good fortune, sometimes called "luck," perspicacity, accident, "providence"; it is also the child of sheer plodding, endless investigative reading, strategy formulation, letter writing, traveling, loan-taking, stock-taking, and begging. From this quagmire of words, I have extracted the title of my lecture, "The Collector as Sleuthsayer."

Obviously this word belongs to me; it is a portmanteau word that has stuck in my mind for a long time. I intend for the Sleuthsayer to convey a blending of both concepts, "soothsayer," or foreteller of the future, and "sleuth," or detective. Tonight I am going to share with you some insights I've isolated from my experience in collecting Faulkner memorabilia over the past twenty years that substantiate my choice of title.

In *The Evolution Of A Collector: A Pilgrimage*, a piece I wrote to introduce the booklet accompanying a 1979 exhibit at Southeast Missouri State University, I rehearsed the influential motivations and the dynamics responsible for nurturing the obsession which ultimately caused this collection to coalesce. Briefly I would like to refocus on the term "obsession."

It has often been noted that in a crowded auction room it

takes only two bidders to determine the destiny of any object on the block. This applies to items that have little appeal as well as to those which everyone covets. And as we all know, there can be only one winner: the one most obsessed with obtaining the item at hand. He becomes the temporary arbiter of its value. For that one moment the glory is his; the spoils are his reward. A veil of victory surrounds him, no matter how evanescent. That he was shrewd and insightful, that he came away unscathed and with a bargain is a matter to be decided by tomorrow's arbiters. For the present he has conquered his opponents, cast his shadow, raised his heraldic banner above all others; he has corroborated his own existence by a show of total faith in his own understanding of and capacity to control those elements composing his cosmos.

What I am suggesting is that this individual has taken upon himself a special responsibility and obligation to act, imposed from within, from somewhere deeper than the intellect. Let us speculate that this is a soul-motivated response: he acts on his instincts, not without fear, or with complete certitude either, because he realizes that nothing is predictable, or defensible, or invulnerable to change, but with the intuition that what he is doing, the money he is offering in exchange for his obsession, will still be judged worthy of all his enthusiasm and energy when he contemplates his recent act in the silence of his own consciousness.

What brought this person to that emotional precipice on whose edge he was willing to pace back and forth without looking down? What zeal coerced him to seek such heights, let alone convinced him that he would even leap to keep some specific object he valued from slipping forever from his grasp? I would suggest that that awesome compulsive force was nothing short of impassioned faith in self; that what kept his spirit energized was a total sense of commitment to his own decision. And this is the stuff, the obsessional clay that constitutes and informs the make-up of the successful collector.

Rarely does a collector such as myself have the opportunity to retire to his towered library or study long enough to contemplate and analyze the elements which form the basis for his behavior. And I am not altogether sure that it is an endeavor which leads to any important conclusions. Nonetheless, this assignment has meant that I take a searching look backwards and outwards from the compass point that my existence marks at this time.

What I know for certain is only this: the obsession descended on me at age eighteen, illuminating some obscure intuition that William Faulkner was extraordinary among writers and that somehow I was meant to follow that lighted notion to the tunnel's opening. How I could intelligently perceive this is even now difficult for me to fathom, since as a freshman and sophomore at Yale in the late fifties and early sixties I had little skill and even less background in traditional literature by which to judge Faulkner's ultimate merits. Yet, he was the person my psyche and temperament were drawn to: surely my senses recognized in his fictional characters, if not in his own irrepressible omniscience, kindred spirits, conspiratorial voices, a quality of rebellious independence as well as a brooding gloominess bordering at times on madness and brilliance. These must have been the elements that led me from the outset to divine that Faulkner was the writer with whom my spirit identified, the soulmate of my own conscience.

At some point, what I've termed "obsession" metamorphosed magically into inspiration. This transmutation might have been alchemical or oneiric, or it might have been a mere figmental mirage my mind set up to disguise a basic crass materialism threatening to undo the aesthetic nature of my initial urge to collect. On the other hand, it might have been

129

as real as wisdom, as maturity, as the aging process itself. Just as I was growing, so too was the collection.

It seems obvious to me now that there were two decided periods in the development of the collection. The first, or obsession-oriented phase, began with my initiation into the world of literature and higher academic pursuits at Yale and lasted until 1968. A little more than nine years spanned my undergraduate career, my advancement through graduate school, and the culmination of my education with a second Master's degree in creative writing from San Francisco State College. What at Yale began as an unpretentious gathering of miscellaneous Faulkner editions had continued to gain momentum. As long as I was surrounded by academicians and students whose chief concerns were aesthetics and semantics, pedagogics, and literature, and eschatology, and as long as I believed that the be-all and end-all of living revolved around the ever-finely sharpened intellect, it was easy enough for me to perpetuate the collection. Perhaps it had become a kind of status symbol, a waking and sleeping reminder that I, the curator, the maker of the collection, was one of an elite group of intellectuals and that the books were my credentials and my keys to the gates of that exclusive fortress, enlightenment.

Catalogues from book dealers constantly poured in to entice me to purchase every new item that might add bulk if not quality to the group. I made numerous trips to New York where I would wander bemused in a half-light through celebrated bookshops like The House of Books, Ltd, Phillip Duschnes, Gotham Book Mart, The Phoenix Book Shop, Seven Gables. It was a time of haphazard acquisitiveness, and I was reveling in it like Bacchus locked in the wine cellars of the gods.

At this juncture I feel compelled to make a profound confession. My "collection plate" as I now refer to my "income" during those years consisted almost entirely of money that I could siphon from my father and my mother. With my dad, it was always a ticklish matter of dealing in subterfuge, or developing elaborate dissimulations by which to obtain the money. Always it seemed I was the messenger of bad tidings, bringing news of unexpected changes in the winds of fate: either my courses demanded heavier reading than I had anticipated, more texts to be purchased, or my clothing allowance had grown outmoded, or the car required an unexpected replacement of parts . . . always there was some exigency that necessitated his filling the "plate" with additional funds . . . and each time the difficulty was, of course, the same one brought on by the obsession—that of needing money to obtain another prized Faulkner book. With my mother, the situation was never an uneasy one. I could prostitute my pride, sell my soul to her without recrimination because she was always sympathetic to my philanderings; she abetted my "little hobby" whenever she could, and was "on my side," as it were, whenever the truth threatened to demand an unequivocally forthright explanation.

Ultimately, phase one of the collection, which quantitatively overshadows the second level, to be discussed later, was concomitant with my formal education, and like it, was paid for almost entirely, though not always wittingly and certainly not willfully, by my parents. For the record, I must assert this brief plea of innocence: never did I believe that my crime was one against humanity, and always I suspected that my father had more than an inkling of and much more than a little pride in my pursuit. To this day, one of the brochures that accompanied a former exhibition of my Faulkner collection holds a reserved, if cramped, position of honor on his office desk. Like my mother, but in his own way, he recognized that he was abetting something positive, something of intrinsic value, and he allowed my extended prodigality to continue despite the fact that doing so ran counter to all his beliefs in good, sound business ethics and acumen.

In 1968, something cataclysmic occurred: I graduated for a final time from university life. I took my first tentative steps out into the world at large. And what I soon discovered was that there were few people who spoke my language. Turmoil and upheaval began gnawing at my psyche. It was a time of extraordinary change; by degrees my mind was opened to new people, newer concerns, and I found that my obsession in its former guise had come to an abrupt cul-de-sac: that book collecting was no longer compatible with my new surroundings, my new life which placed me in a factory of trouser-making machines. My blue-collar reincarnation required my spirit to don different clothing.

The years between 1968 and 1974 were ones in which I forgot the books and they forgot me. In the crypt-like room at my parents' home which had been my study for more than four years, they remained dormant and unstirring behind sheets draped over them. Meanwhile I was busy giving free run to another obsession; this took the form of antique collecting. Specifically, it was the pursuit of Americana which was at that time in its infancy. When I began to bring home brass cash registers, marble-top furniture, slot machines, outside-horn phonographs, Tiffany-type light fixtures, turn-of-the-century tin wind-up toys, Currier & Ives lithographs, unique typewriters by the dozens, and other "junk," I was immediately labeled prodigal and spendthrift. But I knew better, I had the "call," just as I'd received the call once with the Faulkner books almost ten years before. To my sensibility the items were pleasing and beautiful. The frequent censure that I was wasting my time and money didn't disturb or deter me because I realized that the antiques were filling a vacancy left by the books over which I'd imposed an indefinite moratorium. Americana was the proper yardstick by which I could measure the aesthetic goals of my new life, one salient facet of which was the easily tenable gesture of furnishing my most recent acquisition, a fourteen-room steamboat Gothic house, complete with an equally recent wife. The pleasing accoutrements from past generations provided an endless landscape through which our imaginations could range at will; also, they were the replacement ballast for my stability.

In the Introduction to *Selections from the William Faulkner Collection of Louis Daniel Brodsky: A Descriptive Catalogue,* I refer to this time during which the book collection went fallow as a "hiatus." And it was just that, although for a long time I had no idea that I would ever return to my passion for book collecting. During my antiquing period, I believed that an old love had been freed of all binding ties; that she and I, regardless of our good feelings about each other, had permanently parted. Because I had grown to appreciate the antiques on an aesthetic level, the last thing in the world I would ever have dreamed was that they would someday promote the book collection at their own expense.

Yet something which I could not have foreseen began to interrupt my positive response to the antiques: the public. What I'd undertaken as a labor of love in acquiring Americana was now being spoiled for me, tainted by the money changers outside the temple who had started dicing in droves. By 1974 or 1975, prices were already soaring, auctions were being organized by promoters who would seed their crowds with shills and ringers whose task was inconspicuously to see that the bidding was jumped and double jumped so that unwary enthusiasts would be caught in the middle, forced to claim fraudulent final bids. I don't mean to suggest elitism on my part, and hopefully I won't appear condescending when I say that what had begun as groups of devotees interested in rescuing old things to preserve a heritage seemingly fast-disappearing, persons collecting items for their "beauty" alone, was being subjugated by those interested only in making a fast turnover, a faster buck, or by those who envisioned "great investments." My wife and I discerned these attitudes everywhere; abruptly we ceased going to shops, auctions, reading the journals. The door was closed; we both knew it would never open again for us: it had been a shared hobby we had enjoyed immensely; now it had a sick odor.

This was when, with unexpected zeal, I found myself turning back to the Faulkner collection. My blue-collar clothing had begun to wear a bit thin. I had gained a great education from my work in the factory, and once again changes were in order. Already I'd begun rereading my favorite writers: Faulkner, I discovered, far and away still claimed my highest accolades. In early 1975, my dear friend and proprietress of The House of Books, Ltd, in New York, Mrs. Margie Cohn, informed me that she had a run of exceedingly rare presentation copies which Faulkner had inscribed for his California friend, Hubert Starr, in the early 1930s. Would I be interested in some of them? Any of them? The flame was held in just the right space to reignite my old interest. I traveled to New York with my wife to visit Margie and to see the books.

Despite the clichéd injunction, "You can't go home again," I felt as though I were coming home. Holding the books in my hand, perusing the minute and fastidious printing of their inscriptions, I sensed the old passion returning. And in Margie's shop that day I knew that the faith had come back to me, that I would make a new commitment to the collection, and that I would awaken all my books from their sleepy repose. Thus, the second phase of the collection came about; it was one I knew intuitively would have its foundation set on inspirational bedrock, rather than in obsession's unpredictable sandstone. I realized in an instant that my collecting would be geared toward acquiring only unique, quality items, books and hopefully some manuscripts that would augment and raise the collection to a level of world-class importance.

These inchoate goals were extremely ambitious and somewhat pretentious, since at the outset I suspected the Hubert Starr books were and would remain the soaring pinnacle of my collection. I couldn't imagine that more impressive materials would ever surface since little of significance had passed through dealers' hands or over the auction blocks in all the time during which I had been withdrawn from the market. Regardless, I had just paid a staggering aggregate price for nine Faulkner presentation copies, including a perfectly pristine copy of *The Sound and the Fury*, that magnificent, special book of books. Also, with enormous trepidation I had taken out my first loan knowing that my father would have dourly disapproved of my action.

I had just begun to settle back with an incredible sense of satisfaction and proprietary pride when Margie Cohn called one day a few months later to inform me that the celebrated Mary Killgore collection was being auctioned at Swann Galleries in New York. This would be a test of my self-confidence. For weeks I had the same nervous feeling in my stomach that I always experienced in my Yale days before a Crew regatta. One of the enticements in that auction catalogue was a copy of *The Marble Faun*; another was a signed, limited copy of *Go Down, Moses*, one of only a few of 100 original copies known to exist. The time to make a great decision had arrived. I suspected that to falter here would be to remove myself from the contest, to drop out before being able to test the dream, forever to falter when future moments would arrive. With eyes wide open, I began to pace the edge of the precipice. Once again I prevailed upon my friend at the bank, Rolla Gordon, to show a vote of confidence in me. Then I leaped. To this day I can still recall the ecstasy of that freefalling feeling of having acted on the purest of instincts—guts.

The Collector as Sleuthsayer

In the first phase of the collection all books, magazines, critical pieces, and ephemerae were purchased directly from dealers or out of their catalogues. At the time, these items were inexpensive and not too difficult to locate; this accounts for the wonderful condition of most of the first and signed, limited editions in the group today. I might add that although the early acquisitions required scanty resourcefulness in obtaining, they were responsible for forming the present collection's bedrock. It would be difficult and terribly expensive to attempt to duplicate the thousand or more items that were acquired between 1959 and 1968.

The second phase of the collection, started in 1974, in contradistinction to the first, was marked by an almost systematic turning-away from book dealers. Its development was totally dependent on personal initiative, resourcefulness, and techniques nurtured partly in response to my former dealings in the antique market. It began almost certainly by providence or special design, though not wholly by accident.

One significant event which occurred just about the time my interest in collecting Faulkner was reawakening was the publication of Carl Petersen's book, *Each in Its Ordered Place: A Faulkner Collector's Notebook*. When the book arrived, I was dumbfounded. For weeks I remained in shock, staggered by the massive collection this gentleman had gathered. Not only did it describe copious one-of-a-kind items, but it was rich and expansive in its foreign editions and ephemerae. Each night it became bedside reading. This went on until I believe I'd actually memorized its more than two thousand listings.

I mention this publishing event because it probably had as much to do with motivating me to want to succeed with my collecting as anything before or since. Furthermore, it indirectly gave me the singular insight that I feel to this day was responsible for putting me in touch with fine Faulkner materials. It happened in this way: having been so completely mesmerized by Carl Petersen's holdings, my mind was forced to focus on just a few important items in his book. This phenomenon is similar to that which a spinning skater experiences in avoiding dizziness. I fixated inordinately on a copy of *Soldiers' Pay* which appeared as a graphic plate in the book and was listed as having been inscribed and presented by Faulkner to Sherwood and Elizabeth Anderson almost concurrent with publication of the book in 1926. It is legend to Faulkner scholars and buffs that Sherwood Anderson was responsible for getting Faulkner's first novel, *Soldiers' Pay*, published. It struck me that owning that very book inscribed to the key man himself had to be one of the epiphanies of all book collecting. Also, I was fascinated by a copy of *Sherwood Anderson and Other Famous Creoles*, which William Spratling and Faulkner co-authored: to own the copy on which Spratling and Faulkner collaborated, inscribed by the former to Anderson, was equally epiphanic.

The insight I gained grew very casually out of a phone conversation I had with Margie Cohn. Expressing my amazement over these two particular books, I asked her how Carl could have had the good fortune of obtaining those items. She responded with a characteristic, matter-of-fact phrase: "Oh, he had contacts. I believe he met Mrs. Anderson once— maybe he even visited her. Yes, he got them from Sherwood Anderson's wife." And that was all. On reflecting, I'm sure it didn't take all at once. Rather, that simple insight must have begun rooting downward in my mind. The germ had surely been planted: what I would discover was that for me to succeed it would be necessary to make contacts on my own, to go out in quest of them. I would learn that waiting for unique items to come to the auction block or be offered up in dealers' catalogues, or for me to merely walk into a shop and find some exotic book or manuscript waiting there on the shelf

The Collector as Sleuthsayer

was as unrealistic and improbable as any notion could be.

About a year later, I got involved in my first public exhibition in almost twelve years. Reawakened to the pleasures and the excitement of book collecting by Margie Cohn during 1974 and 1975, and through the example set by the Petersen book, and having regained my old zeal, I realized it was time to take my bearings. Armed with such recent spoils as the beautiful, unjacketed copy of *The Marble Faun*, a signed, limited copy of *Go Down, Moses*, and nine presentation copies inscribed to Hubert Starr, I decided to share my collection with the public.

The exhibit at Washington University in St. Louis, under the direction of Mrs. Holly Hall, lasted from August 23 to October 15, 1976, and it was tastefully presented. I was quite proud to be able to display it and show many of my friends through the various stages of Faulkner's lengthy career; more importantly, it yielded the first of those crucial contacts that I would eventually make.

Just after the exhibit closed, I received a brief note from Tulsa, Oklahoma, from Mr. Vance Carter Broach, who I would soon learn was not only vitally interested in William Faulkner, but was Faulkner's second cousin through a common relationship to Mrs. Walter B. McLean, Aunt 'Bama Falkner McLean, a daughter of the legendary Old Colonel, W. C. Falkner of Ripley, Mississippi. A few tentative letters followed, in one of which I sent Mr. Broach my first modest contribution to Faulkner bibliography, the recent Washington University exhibit brochure. He, in turn, reciprocated with a monograph he had composed on the life of his Aunt 'Bama, entitled *Grande Dame: A Tribute to Bama Falkner McLean*. In a subsequent letter, Mr. Broach also sent me a list of the books in his Faulkner collection, among which was a large group of presentation copies inscribed by William Faulkner to both Aunt 'Bama and to Vance Carter Broach, his kinsman.

That a second run of inscriptions should appear within a year of each other was more than I could imagine. Although I entertained little hope of obtaining any of these items, my imagination was fired. I tried to conceive what offering I might make to break the ice. Against my own better judgment, I wrote back that I had a copy of *The Marble Faun* that I might offer in trade for some of his materials. I knew two things: one, that he would be interested, since a "Faun," being the author's first, privately printed book, is the most desired of all Faulkner books; and two, that I had no wish whatsoever to part with what had only recently become the cornerstone of my collection. I had to be crazy. By the end of April, I was on the road, driving toward Tulsa in response to a very warm invitation by Mr. Broach to spend the evening with him and his wife.

This trip was followed by a number of visits exchanged between my family and the Broachs and by a joyous trading of items. The most unique item that came from Aunt 'Bama through Mr. Broach was the ledger of the Ripley Rail Road which had originally belonged to her father, the Old Colonel, Faulkner's great-grandfather after whom he had fashioned so much of his fiction. Typescripts of early poems were equally significant in that they gave insight into the apprenticeship of the author who would later write *The Sound and the Fury*.

To move ahead, the second important contact, Professor James B. Meriwether, was made just three months later in Oxford, Mississippi, while I was attending the annual Faulkner and Yoknapatawpha Conference held at Ole Miss. We had known of each other for years, but had never met. We quickly found that we had much in common: Jim, as I came to call him, was not only a scholar, but an avid book collector as well. Impressed by the early poems I had recently acquired, he asked me point-blank just how serious I was about furthering my collection. The answer was automatic. Within a week after the conference ended, I was in contact with Mrs. Emily Stone, widow of Phil Stone. Faulkner's early mentor and life-long friend and lawyer, Jim had known Mrs. Stone and her husband for years, and was aware that at one point she had been offering for sale Phil's valuable Faulkner memorabilia. Although Jim had no idea as to their present availability, he would phone Emily at once, and I would write to her. I had no promises, and my expectations, which had risen with the initial thought of possibly acquiring these items, sank in discouragement and remained there until the moment I slit open the letter postmarked Montgomery, Alabama, August 11, 1977, which read:

> Dear Mr. Brodsky,
>   Thank you for your warm and cordial letter, which arrived yesterday, about the Faulkner books and papers. From what Jim Meriwether said to me about you, it would be difficult for me to imagine a person in whose hands I should prefer them to go. . . .

The letter ended:

> I look forward to seeing you.
>   Sincerely yours,
>   Emily W. Stone

To distill the events of the next few weeks, suffice it that there was much chaos and frenzy in trying to make this transaction possible. Unlike the former one, this required fluid cash, a great amount of it to be paid immediately. A week later I made a flight to Montgomery to visit Mrs. Stone and to inspect the collection. It was composed of inordinate richesse. I had never dreamed of seeing Faulkner's early flowery handwriting, that which dated from the late teens and early 20s of this century, much less imagined ever owning a full-blown manuscript. Seated in the company of this wonderfully anecdotic and warm woman who had been the wife of one of Faulkner's most influential friends, I held at various times the six-hundred-page carbon typescript of *The Hamlet*, the forty-four-page bound ribbon typescript of a short story, *The Wishing-Tree*, many inscribed books from Faulkner to Phil Stone including all three books comprising the Snopes trilogy which Faulkner had publicly dedicated to Phil. Also there were Last Wills and Testaments, other legal documents, correspondence from Phil to important scholars of the day regarding Faulkner, and books from the early days when Phil and Bill would go for long walks and read what was current among the novelists and poets and philosophers, books dating 1912 to 1925.

When I returned home, I knew that to pass up this opportunity would be tantamount to self-destructing the collection. These were materials that had belonged to the leading force in Faulkner's early career. This collection was absolutely of the highest significance. With all the self-justification I could muster, assuring myself that I was doing something for the future, not indulging my own greedy instincts for ownership, I handed over to Rolla Gordon a typed schedule of prize antiques to serve as collateral. Ultimately, many of them, including some of the coveted arcade machines, music boxes, and the entire typewriter collection, were sold to provide the necessary funds to float this transfer of materials from the Stone family to my collection.

I was surprised by the lack of pain I experienced in making the sacrifices to acquire the Stone memorabilia. What I had given up had provided enjoyment for my wife and myself. Like the antiques, the new items were also mere objects, material objects with arbitrary value. But, unlike the books and manuscripts and miscellany from Phil and Emily Stone, the antiques were neither particularly unique, nor imbued with personal, intrinsic overtones. Although the antiques had historical relevance and were inherently aesthetic, they did not resonate in the same way the books did. The antiques had

141

served their time well; now they made an honorable sacrifice. Within two years I had embarked on a journey that had taken me to Tulsa, Oklahoma; Oxford, Mississippi; and Montgomery, Alabama. Within another two months, my wife and I would have as our houseguest the gentleman who had so influenced me without knowing it: Carl Petersen. His visit would be a time of incredible reverberations, of fantastic spoken and unspoken sharing; how could it have been otherwise? I brought nearly eighteen years of Faulkner-dreaming and energy and study to the encounter; Carl brought with him almost twenty-eight years of the same enthusiasm and insight. And I would get to thank him in person.

Now it's early August 1980; three years to the month have transpired since the acquisition of the Stone collection. Looking back I see a pattern which takes the form of a jigsaw puzzle, and, although its configuration is incomplete, I discern an overall design: a map of the United States. It seems that for the last six years I've been bringing little pieces of the map back to Farmington, Missouri, and fitting them to other pieces. The result is a metaphorical geography that is beginning to have continuity.

To elaborate, let me explore a concept which I refer to as "Faulkner's Gifts of Friendship." Although not born in Oxford, Mississippi, Faulkner spent his childhood and teens there, and with few exceptions, he preferred to live there where he had family, relatives, friends, and acquaintances; he did most of his "important" writing there as well.

Legend has made us painfully aware that Faulkner was a man who cherished his privacy to a compulsive degree. Nevertheless, he would make frequent trips away from Oxford. Some of these lasted four to six months at a time; these occurred mainly during a ten year period between 1936 and 1946 when he was indentured to the movie industry in California. Although much has been written about how his stays in Hollywood were anathema to him and that he lived a reclusive existence while there, we have evidence to the contrary. There is little doubt that he regarded writing for the movies a cheap and inferior way to make a living, a prostitution of his talents. On the other hand, he made many close friends out West, notably an enamorata, Meta Carpenter. Also, Hubert Starr was there, as well as many people connected with the studio, including Jim Conselman, whose inscribed books form part of the collection of Faulkner materials housed at the University of Virginia.

When Faulkner was most successful at getting away, it would be on short trips to nearby Greenville, where his good friend and later agent, Ben Wasson, and his family resided, and to Pascagoula, Mississippi, or New Orleans during the early years. Later, he would make repeated trips to New York, and always there was Memphis, his stopping-off point, his "watering hole," where his great-aunt 'Bama lived. Of course, the list of places Faulkner chose to visit could be extended to incorporate many many more locations.

I realized that Faulkner's relatives and friends held the key to the development of the collection. Many of them had changed residences at least once, sometimes more often. Some were no longer living, and their descendants were not always easy to locate. Yet, if Vance Broach and Emily Stone still had significant materials in their possession at this late date, I figured it was not implausible that others might also have cherished memorabilia.

Important to my detective work were three sources in particular: *Faulkner: A Biography* by Joseph Blotner, *William Faulkner of Oxford* edited by James W. Webb and A. Wigfall Green, and "A Census of Manuscripts and Typescripts of William Faulkner's Poetry" by Keen Butterworth. From each source I got crucial information about personal friends and "gifts" which once belonged to them. I realized the information I was using was in most cases obsolete in terms of having been gleaned from interviews made a decade or more earlier. Still, I knew that the only way to find out whether these items were available or already disposed of was by first finding out where these people resided, writing them, and following up on my inquiries. In a few instances, the process was straight-forward in that some persons were not only alive, but living in the same location they had occupied when they knew Faulkner. In other cases, it was necessary to write family or friends of friends. There are a few whom I have never yet located.

Ultimately my map began to take shape. I added to those pieces labeled Tulsa and Montgomery and Los Angeles and Oxford, other jigsaw parts with the following names: Green-ville, Mississippi; Athens, Georgia; Columbia and Charles-ton, South Carolina; New York, New York; Reading, Pennsyl-vania; Memphis, Tennessee; White Sulphur Springs, West Virginia; and Sherman, Connecticut. Curiously, many of the persons I contacted had lived originally in Oxford and had subsequently moved elsewhere: this was true of Edith Brown Douds and Calvin Brown, both children of Faulkner's French teacher at Ole Miss in 1920. This was also the case with Myr-tle Ramey, who had moved from Oxford to New Jersey, then to West Virginia where I finally discovered her.

Two facets relevant to my ranging out from Farmington, Missouri, should also be mentioned. First, without having taken this course of action, the materials which form an inte-gral part of this collection undoubtedly would have been scat-tered; some to private collectors through various auctions and dealers, some to public institutions as tax-deductible dona-tions, outright sales or transactions that would have been con-summated by private dealers working on a commission basis for a museum or library or university. Secondly, had I not seized these opportunities by having forced them into the open, I would never have been able to accomplish what I call "dovetailing" which makes this one-author collection unique.

What I'm referring to when I use the word "dovetailing" is this: to take just one salient example, let me mention again the materials from the Stone collection. Most imposing are the poetry fragments, both typescripts and holographs, which Phil had salvaged from a fire at his home in 1942. There is little Faulkner poetry in all the institutions in this country; most of it perished with the fire. What is left tells us much about Faulkner's earliest literary influences because it was the mode he first practiced, the one by which he originally felt he would make his reputation. It is common knowledge that Phil Stone had been Faulkner's early mentor, instructing his reading and writing of poetry from 1914 to 1924. It is also fact that Phil paid the expense of having *The Marble Faun* published; he even linked himself to that project by writing the Preface to that slender volume. Finally, the reason that Phil had all the early manuscripts in his home when the fire occurred was simple: having been teacher and agent for the fledgling writer, he was the obvious custodian for those papers; Phil was settled and ensconced in a law practice. William's future was as unpredictable as his wanderlust.

When I had the opportunity to obtain the holdings of Myrtle Ramey, a gradeschool friend of Faulkner, perhaps a childhood sweetheart as well, as is suggested by the nature of the "gifts" which he periodically bestowed on her, what I discovered was more than just another fine group of inscribed books, or even a uniquely juvenile group of early drawings dating from 1913 and 1916. Among the materials which Myrtle Ramey had clung to for more than fifty years was a sheaf of typed poems with the title "Mississippi Poems" on a separate cover sheet which Faulkner had inscribed to her. More amazing, however, was the fact that all thirteen sheets of poetry comprising twelve poems were signed by William Faulk-

145

ner at the bottom and by Phil Stone across the top in his flowing script. With an air that in retrospect seems appropriately proprietary, suggesting that Faulkner was his protégé, and that he, Phil Stone, was sole agent for this budding genius, Stone wrote similarly on each sheet: "Publication rights reserved. Not to be published without the written consent of the author or that of Phil Stone."

And as if this were not enough, it turned out that three of the twelve poems in this group remained unpublished. To my knowledge, these sheets of typescript poetry, with the exception of a few recorded copies of *The Marble Faun*, represent the only known linkage of the two men's signatures on materials that relate directly to the poetry over which both labored. And to climax this great find, sitting at the bottom of the box in which the books were kept was a copy, with dust jacket, of *The Marble Faun*, inscribed by both Faulkner and Stone to Myrtle Ramey on the same day they had both given her the poetry manuscripts, December 30th, 1924.

What had coalesced and metamorphosed from two disparate contacts I had made was nothing short of a miracle in book collecting. From Montgomery, Alabama, and from White Sulphur Springs, West Virginia, I had brought back to Farmington, Missouri, materials which had originated in Oxford, Mississippi, from the collaborative talents of two young men equally enthusiastic about what each dreamed would bring them fame.

Ultimately, what is miraculous to me is not so much the fact that given an endless amount of items, one can impose order on them, devise elaborate constructs and paradigms by which better to appreciate them and give them integrity from without if not from within; rather, what staggers my own imagination most is that the items which Faulkner had been scattering over a career lasting fifty years keep surfacing; or to relate it back to my previous metaphor, the diffused pieces of the puzzle continue to relinquish their anonymity, begging, as it were, to be fitted contiguously to each other. This, as well as the constant awareness that so many of the rare items still exist, amazes me. Even now, my fingertips have literally shuffled a number of the remaining pieces of the jigsaw over the table on which I've been constructing the map without being able to lift and insert them into the pattern. Perhaps this will yet occur. And, if not, enough of the geography on the map of Faulkner's literary career can be glimpsed by scholars and buffs alike to have made the time spent assembling it spendidly diverting and worthwhile.

At the beginning of this lecture, I referred to Faulkner's comment to Malcolm Cowley in which he distilled a sweeping appraisal of his own work up to that time with the following remark: "By God, I didn't know myself what I had tried to do, and how much I had succeeded." Now, on concluding my thoughts, I am reminded of another characteristic echo from many of Faulkner's public statements. Faulkner was ever wary of self-satisfaction and self-congratulation; always he had the feeling that success meant never never never believing that previous accomplishments were sufficient or self-sustaining, or that one could ever be wholly successful in achieving his high intentions.

In like manner, I confess that what I have done with this collection both amazes me and puts me on my guard. I realize the need to look forward more than to linger on the past, to discover ways of making this collection find its own place exclusive of me, and for me to strive toward my destiny unfettered by it. In truth, it has already outdistanced whatever inchoate goals I might have held personally for its future, and it has surfaced as a grand phenomenon; it deserves to be placed where the reading public will come to pay tribute to it as a legacy and a reminder of the writer whose inspired work they'll undoubtedly still be worshipping generations from

147

now. It deserves to be kept intact. But before its disposition occurs, I would like to think that I will be instrumental in seeing portions of this collection tour various institutions, just as art shows tour the country's leading museums. Also, I would like to contribute a number of scholarly articles for academic journals consisting of insights made possible by some of the as-yet-unknown materials in the group. Finally, I would like to bring to a close those potential acquisitions which I have been nurturing for a long while in the belief that they might lend even greater significance to the already-dovetailed holdings I have brought together.

Lastly, if in pursuing my love of William Faulkner's literature, I, as a poet myself, have been able to achieve a better understanding of what it means to become a successful writer, then I will consider this to have been an extraordinary inspiration and stroke of good luck. Nothing could pleasure me more than to be considered one day the Faulkner of American poets.

If, however, my little celebrity never transcends this moment in history, I will gracefully accept, as God-given, the opportunity that has been mine to indulge my sensibility in collecting artifacts of another artist who before his life was over had been awarded the garland for having run the race well, and won.

Faulkner's Women

ELLEN DOUGLAS

Early this year, in preparation for this conference, I began to reread Faulkner's novels and stories and, indeed, to read some of them for the first time. I glanced at *Soldiers' Pay*, put it aside—as it turned out, permanently—and began instead with *Mosquitoes*. *Mosquitoes*, for all its apprentice quality, its callow pseudo-sophistication, reveals among other things, both Faulkner's early awareness of literary modernism— Joyce and Eliot, for example—and his self-conscious conception of himself as an artist, facts he later tried with considerable success to conceal. It also reveals his early stance toward women and, by its very obviousness, forcibly directed my attention to that stance. I read on—through most of the work of the middle period—the great books—and into the later period; and it came to seem to me that, far from changing, Faulkner maintains his view of women with consistency even when in his middle age he begins to write glosses on himself.

As I explored the novel more closely and began to document this view, I ran into the obvious difficulty that Faulkner often does not speak for himself, but puts his judgments into the mouths of his characters. This is, of course, an almost universally used device of modern fiction—a fiction that declares itself grounded on the principle of "show, don't tell." And it goes without saying that it is a device which can be a boon to critics, who respond by producing endless series of

149

articles and books debating whose side the author is *really* on, what he *really* meant to persuade the reader of. But in the long run, in Faulkner's case, if one reads the body of his work, certain strongly and perhaps irrationally held convictions are evident.

Wayne Booth in his book *The Rhetoric of Fiction* has dealt at length with the problems the critic faces in dealing with our "unreliable" modern writers. The author, he says, "can choose his disguises, but he can never choose to disappear."[1] As he sensibly points out, the "implied author"—that is, the intelligence which the reader senses behind any given work of art—has, must have, a philosophical and moral position with regard to that work. And when the reader has finished reading, attentively, with his whole mind, he should, if the work is successful, grasp the writer's position. This is not to say, of course, that any given character or situation may not be presented as mixed, ambiguously motivated, confused, and so forth. It is to say that every book has the tone and the stance that its author gives it.

It is not true, Booth points out, as Flaubert said of Shakespeare, that we do not know what Shakespeare loved or hated. We know well what our great writers love and hate. Among other things Shakespeare loved courage and hated cruelty. He believed it good to love, wrong to love selfishly. He requires us to believe that it is right to honor our fathers, wrong to kill off old men like Lear. After we have read his plays, we know these and others of his convictions. And we know equally well, for example, that Henry James loved delicacy of sensibility and subtlety of mind and hated vulgarity, that Flaubert hated bourgeois respectability. By the same to-

---

1. Wayne Booth, *The Rhetoric of Fiction* (Chicago: University of Chicago Press, 1961), 20.

ken, we come slowly to know the mind of the implied author behind the Yoknapatawpha chronicles.

Faulkner has said himself that he regards the Yoknapataw-pha books as a single whole, as one book, so to speak, even almost as one long sentence that he produced in his lifetime of trying to understand and put down the human predica-ment. So I think we can safely regard the implied author of the books as one man. Even when, as I wrote above, he be-gins in his middle age to write glosses on himself, one hears, I believe, the same man, scrambling to put things a little less bleakly, and succeeding, instead, only in putting them more sentimentally. Of course, tensions exist in this man, tensions so strong they sometimes tear his works apart. His concerns are various, protean, his view self-contradictory, his *oeuvre* huge. His avowed ambition is to say everything—to fail gi-gantically.

Let's go back and hear what Faulkner says about women, whether it is directly, as commenting author, or through his characters. We can start, as I did, with *Mosquitoes*, a book which presents the reader with a gallery of unrelievedly dis-mal women. First, Mrs. Maurier, a snobbish, silly, brainless poseuse who fancies herself the grande dame of a literary sa-lon in the French style; then her niece, Pat Robyn, equally brainless, shallow, callow, and selfishly cowardly; and on through Miss Jameson with her large teeth, pale gums, and cold eyes, dull, humorless, and sex-starved; and Jenny, plac-idly bovine and also brainless, prefiguring the even more bo-vine and brainless Eula. Only Mrs. Wiseman, of the women, has a grain of sense, and her part in the book is minute. And there is the relentless tone. The book is about men trying to escape women, women trying to trap men, about urbane and superior men, yearning, brainless women. To borrow a line from *The Sound and the Fury*, these people are like "the swine untethered in pairs rushing coupled into the sea."[2] One feels, particularly in the portrait of Mrs. Maurier, an intensity of rage that seems disproportionate to the miserable creature who evokes it.

Let me move on with a series of quotations gleaned from the major works:

Women . . . have an affinity for evil for supplying whatever the evil lacks in itself for drawing it about them instinctively as you do bedclothing.[3]

"They lead beautiful lives—women. Lives not only divorced from, but irrevocably excommunicated from, all reality."[4]

"Didn't the dread and fear of females which you must have drawn in with the primary mammalian milk teach you better [than to believe] you could have bought immunity from her for no other coin but justice———"[5]

" . . . raised and trained to fulfill a woman's sole end and purpose: to love, to be beautiful, to divert . . ."[6]

" . . . that grim Samaritan husbandry of good women. . . ."[7]

"There's not any such thing as a woman born bad, because they are all born bad, born with the badness in them. The thing is, to get them married before the badness comes to a natural head."[8]

In this context badness consists of evidence of sexuality and the implementation of desire, which is by implication O.K. for men, but not for women.

Or, Tull on Cora in *As I Lay Dying*: If Cora had charge of the universe, he says,

2. *The Sound and the Fury* (New York: Modern Library, 1946), 219.
3. *Ibid.*, 119.
4. *Absalom, Absalom!* (New York, Vintage Books, 1972), 191.
5. *Ibid.*, 265.
6. *Ibid.*, 117.
7. *The Wild Palms* (New York: Random House, 1939), 10.
8. "Hair," in *Collected Stories of William Faulkner* (New York: Random House, 1950), 133.

"I reckon she would make a few changes, no matter how [God] was running it. And I reckon they would be for man's good. Leastways we would have to like them. Leastways we might as well go on and make like we did."[9]

Or, on the subject of the female cousin who comes to stay

"penniless and with no prospect of ever being otherwise . . . moving . . . into your home and into the room where your wife uses the hand-embroidered linen, she . . . goes into the kitchen and dispossesses the cook and seasons the very food you're going to eat to suit her own palate . . . it's as though she were living on the actual blood itself, *like a vampire* . . . abrogating to herself, because it fills her veins also, nourishment from the old blood that crossed unchartered seas . . . ."[10]

Or "the fact that women never plead . . . loneliness until . . . circumstance forces them to give up all hope of attaining the particular bauble which at the moment they want."[11]

Or the agreement among all the characters in *Go Down, Moses*, consented to by the writer, that it is better to "receive" one's "blood" from the male rather than from the female ancestor. For it is repeatedly said of McCaslin Edmonds that he is descended "only on the distaff side" or is a McCaslin "only on his mother's side."[12]

And, in one of the later books where Faulkner redeems hatred with sentimentality, let's hear what the genial Mr. Mallison says to his wife: "'You're human even if you are a woman.'"[13] Mallison, let me emphasize, is presented as wise, tolerant, and temperate. This is supposed to be an amusing remark—to amuse his wife as well as the reader. And equally genial Gavin Stevens on women in the same book: "'Yes, they don't need minds at all, except for conversation, social inter-

9. *As I Lay Dying* (New York: Vintage Books, 1964), 70.
10. *Absalom, Absalom!*, 86. (Italics mine.)
11. *Ibid.*, 53.
12. *Go Down, Moses* (New York: Random House, 1942), *passim.*
13. *The Town* (New York: Vintage Books, 1961), 179.

course.'"[14] Finally, Mallison again: You've "'tried always to deny that damned female instinct for uxorious and rigid respectability which is the backbone of any culture not yet decadent.'"[15] It's his wife's poor best and only a little better than the poor best of her respectable sisters. And unpleasant and unattractive as these "sisters" may be, we can all console ourselves that they supply the backbone of all still vigorous cultures.

After a few months of reading, one is ready like Shreve in *Absalom, Absalom!* to say, "Wait! Wait!" To want a hand in rewriting, re-inventing the record. What is all this anyhow? Can we be blamed both for living governed entirely by the mores of the community (respectability) and for having been born evil and sinful? Both for being mindless and stupid and for being capable of taking over the universe from God and running it to suit ourselves? Both for feeding on our relatives like vampires for the practical purpose of surviving and for being "irrevocably excommunicated from all reality"? Both for being very demons of vengeance from whom a man cannot buy immunity and for having as the sole end and purpose of our lives "loving, being beautiful, diverting"? And then can there be thrown in for good measure hypocrisy, vanity, silliness, vindictiveness, and a general capacity to "weaken the blood"? The answer, of course, is *Yes.* By Faulkner's lights we can and must be blamed *as women* for just about everything.

Do you hear my voice becoming slightly querulous? Do you see before you an incarnation of Mammy Yokum, ready to jump up and down with rage and beat Mr. Faulkner over the head with a broomstick? Maybe it's just that I'm in a bad humor from making the immense, staggering effort required of my poor female brain to read all these books. (The writer, he says, is always writing with the ultimate intention "of im-

14. *Ibid.*, 182.
15. *Ibid.*

154

pressing some women that probably don't care anything at all for literature *as is the nature of women.*")[16]

But bear with me. There are other things to be said. Instead of defending myself against the charge of querulousness, let me approach the problem from another direction. Let's glance briefly at the way women function in the novels. Not what anybody—the author or any of his characters—says about them, but what they *do* in comparison to what men do.

In *Absalom, Absalom!* Henry Sutpen kills Bon out of concern, however misguided, for his sister's honor. Bon acts out of his passionate need for recognition from his father. But Judith? Nothing ever contradicts our first view of her avid cold face in the barn loft as she watches a savage fight between her father and a slave. And she destroys Charles Etienne Bon with her "cold, implacable antipathy." Just naturally mean.

Horace Benbow does his best against staggering odds to save Lee Goodwin and to befriend Ruby. Narcissa Benbow, probably the worst of the lot of Faulkner's women, out of her passion for respectability, deliberately makes it possible for the District Attorney to frame Goodwin for a crime she knows he did not commit. As for Temple Drake, she, of course, testifies falsely against Goodwin and sends him to his death. And even the good-hearted whores mimic the hypocritical respectability of their "pure" sisters.

But Ruby Goodwin—*she* is a heroine. Yes, she is courageous and loyal to her man, ready to die for him. But persistently I wonder about her and Faulkner's fondness for her. How grand it is, he says to us, that she is not shaken in her love for Lee even though he beats her and abuses her, allows her to walk a mile for water six times a day, and shows his fondness for her by throwing her across the room. We are made to feel that this curious heroine is proud of her father

16. *Mosquitoes* (New York: Liveright, 1955), 250. (Italics mine.)

for shooting her lover and saying to her, "Get down there and sup your dirt, you whore."[17] This, as she tells Temple, is the true role of a *real* woman.

In *Light in August* Mrs. McEachern is presented as servile, craven, and contemptible for her pitiful efforts to stand between her maniacal husband and the child Joe. Joanna Burden is presented as being evil, precisely in the function of her sexuality. The act itself, the coupling, is evil—on her part, that is, not, so far as we are told, on her partner's part. "It was as though he *had fallen into* a sewer. (Joanna) had an avidity for the forbidden word symbols, an insatiable appetite for the sound of them on his lips and her own" and "the terrible curiosity of a child about forbidden subjects and objects." She wanted to live "not alone in sin, but in filth." She was "in the wild throes of nymphomania." But we get no judgment on Joe Christmas who was the willing partner of this "filth."[18] He does say of himself, when he has taken her brutally and coldly, in rage, "'At least I have made a woman of her. . . . Now she hates me. I have taught her that, at least.'"[19]

And then of course there is Mrs. Compson. I withdraw my statement that Narcissa Benbow is probably the worst of Faulkner's females and award the palm to Mrs. Compson, whose whining self-pity, selfishness, capacity for self-delusion, lovelessness, and obsession with respectability destroy her children's lives. (I might add, however, that if I had a husband who felt the contempt for women that Mr. Compson feels, I might not have retired to my bed—too boring—but it is quite possible I would have killed him.)

As for Lena Grove, although we are repeatedly told that she is quiet, pleasant, friendly, alert, and nobly determined

17. *Sanctuary* (New York: Modern Library, 1932), 67.
18. *Light in August* (New York: Modern Library, 1959), 242 ff. (Italics mine.)
19. *Ibid.*, 223.

to give her child a father, she is presented as perhaps the most mindless of all Faulkner's females. Although the evidence is overwhelming, it never penetrates her thick skull that the father she seeks for her child, even if she found him, would be worse than no father at all. Quaintly and good-naturedly and invincibly stupidly she gains from her travels not the least notion of where she is or how far one place is from another; and at the end of the book she is presented as deliberately making a fool of the shy, kind man who has selflessly befriended her and who loves her with deep devotion.

Addie Bundren in *As I Lay Dying*, by her own account, is unable to make contact with the children she teaches except by switching them until the blood runs down their legs. And, of course, there is Eula. Eula, the cow woman. Eula, the ravishing beauty. Eula the sluggard who is so lazy she literally won't get up off her butt to go any place except to the table. (Until she is rehabilitated in the later books.)

You will have noted that in most of the quotations and situations I have drawn here, the feeling of rage and outrage and fear and hatred is not expressed as directed against one individual woman, but clearly against women as sexual creatures. But Faulkner can write eloquently of sexual love. Listen:

> Then he would hear her, coming down the creekside in the mist. . . . the dawn would be empty, the moment and she would not be, then he would hear her and he would lie drenched in the wet grass, serene and one and indivisible in joy, listening to her approach; . . . the whole mist reeked with her, the same malleate hands of mist which drew along his prone drenched flanks palped her pearled body too and shaped them both somewhere in immediate time, already married. He would not move. He would lie amid the waking instant of earth's teeming minute life, the motionless fronds of water-heavy grasses stooping into the mist before his face in black fixed curves, along each parabola of which the marching drops held in minute magnification the dawn's rosy miniatures . . . .

Then he would see her; the bright thin horns of morning, of sun, would blow the mist away and reveal her, planted, blond, dew-pearled, standing in the parted water of the ford . . . .[20]

I have changed one word in the passage above, and lifted out a couple of clauses. "The same malleate hands of mist palped her pearled body" should read "palped her pearled *barrel*." Because of course this is the account of the idiot Ike Snopes's love affair with Houston's cow. I look in vain in Faulkner's work for passion and gentleness and concern and generosity of spirit and self-sacrifice between men and women commensurate with the passion and gentleness and concern and generosity of spirit and self-sacrifice with which Ike Snopes loves the cow.

Keeping in mind what we have said about Faulkner's view of the nature of women and what we have said about Ike and the cow, let's consider what seems to be a major exception to all that I have suggested above. This exception is to be found in *The Wild Palms*, in the nature of Charlotte Rittenmeyer and in the relation between Charlotte and Harry Wilborne. Briefly, Charlotte and Harry flee from the respectable bourgeois world in the belief that like a modern day Tristan and Isolde they can live for love alone, and in the belief, too, that the everyday world of marriage and respectability is in fact precisely what kills love between men and women. Charlotte and Harry are thoroughly engaging characters. They are intelligent and direct and devoted and unselfish in their concern for each other. They are capable of those abiding nobilities which we see Ike practice in his relationship with the cow. (We should recall here that Ike feeds the cow, milks her when her bag is full, garlands her as well as he can with flowers, lies down and rises up with her night and day in true

20. *The Hamlet* (New York: Vintage Books, 1956), 165.

devotion and even suffers the pain and terror of fire to rescue her.)

One feels with Charlotte the kind of sympathy and identification that one feels with real women grappling with the real world. But Charlotte Rittenmeyer, in the terms that Faulkner presents men, is a man in disguise. Or rather, perhaps more accurately, she is that always androgynous creature, the artist. In the love affair with Harry she is the aggressor, the experienced sexual creature, Harry the hesitant cloistered virgin. She takes the lead in deciding under what circumstances the affair will be consummated. She makes the decision to leave the bourgeois world. Harry is assigned the questionable (again in Faulkner's own terms) part of stealing the money that will finance their venture. She is the bread winner. He is the one who loses his job because of his "immoral" sexual situation. He worries about Charlotte's children, she never gives them a thought. He, like a pregnant woman, has moral reservations about abortion, when she is ready to go ahead with it, first for her friend, then for herself. Her life is filled with work toward which she feels passionate commitment, his with make-work that fills the time until they are together again. And the work that he finally does is woman's work, writing true confession stories in which he, as narrator, transforms himself into a woman, and as writer even uses a female penname.

But if Charlotte is a hero, not a heroine, it is also true in *The Wild Palms* that Faulkner was able to assign to Harry as heroine the kind of true heroism that he always begrudged his women. In the long run Charlotte dies, but Harry accepts responsibility for his acts and himself and becomes a whole human being. There is something else that strikes me strongly about Harry and Charlotte. Even though Charlotte tells us repeatedly how much she likes "bitching," I never felt that their love was presented as primarily sexual. I felt instead a rough comradeship, a bluntness and honesty, a taking-for-granted that was more like the love between brothers or sisters, or perhaps between brother and sister. And in Faulkner's world brothers and sisters can and do love each other, and women in their roles as sisters are loving. Caddy and Quentin love each other. Horace Benbow and Narcissa love each other—in her early incarnation in *Sartoris*, not in the later one in *Sanctuary*. Margaret Mallison and her twin brother are so close that they read each other's minds and anticipate each other needs.

Much has been made of the incest motives in Faulkner's work, but I would submit that incest in these instances never comes even close to being consummated. Quentin's anguish in *The Sound and the Fury* comes from his failure to protect his sister's honor and his humiliation as a man, and his suggestion to his father that he and Caddy have committed incest is meant, of course, as a last ruse to preserve the intimate—not sexual—relationship that her impending marriage will break. Margaret Mallison has a "happy" marriage. Benbow's sexual attention is directed toward Belle. In fact, it is *only* as brother and sister that men and women can feel affection for one another. With the exception of Harry and Charlotte, as soon as there is the least possibility of sexual connection, love is out of the question. A man can love his sister, can even desire her, and continue to feel affection for her precisely because he must not possess her, or to put it another way, perhaps because he will not be required to demonstrate his potency with her.

But men and women as sexual partners? Over and over he gives us the inevitability of misunderstanding, the cold silence, the eager masochism, the awful sadism, the furious hatred between lover and lover, between man and wife: Benbow and Belle, Sartoris and Narcissa, Mrs. and Mrs. Compson, the Houstons, the Armstids, the Hightowers, Eula and Flem, Sutpen and Ellen, Sutpen and Rosa, Sutpen and Milly, Addie and Anse, Lucas and Mollie, Uncle Buck and Miss Sophonsiba, Ab Snopes and his wife, Joe Christmas and Joanna Burden.

"Because you cant beat them," Faulkner writes in *Absalom, Absalom!*, "you just flee (and thank God you can flee, can escape from that massy five-foot thick maggot-cheesy solidarity which overlaps the earth, in which men and women in couples are ranked and racked like ninepins; thanks to whatever Gods for that masculine hipless tapering peg which fit light and glib to move where the cartridge-chambered hips of women hold them fast)."[21]

Now, to be fair, we need to go back and look for instances of Faulkner's stance toward men in comparison with what we have indicated he felt toward women. And there is more than enough evidence, of course, that the men in Faulkner's world are less than perfect. One has only to consider the weakness and ineffectuality of Mr. Compson, the overweening pride and self-absorption of Thomas Sutpen, the gross cruelty of Henry Armstid, the rapacity of Flem Snopes, the obsessiveness of Gail Hightower, the craven whining self-promotion of Anse Bundren, the wholly evil natures in entirely different ways of Popeye and Jason Compson. And one could go on and draw further instances, for one of Faulkner's great strengths is his boundless inventiveness.

As I have looked through the books, though, there seems to me to be a radical difference between the author's attitude toward evil in men and evil in women. It is very seldom, indeed, that the evil in men is presented as a function of their maleness. It is presented, rather, as the evil of the particular character. We almost never find male characters (much less

21. *Absalom, Absalom!*, 312.

161

female ones) comfortably agreeing together, "Yes, that's the way men are." (Cruel, rapacious, self-deluding, obsessive, whatever.) The only repeated generalization I find about "men" is the one laid down in opposition to the statement in *The Town* that "women dont care whether they are facts or not just so they fit" and "men dont care whether they fit or not just so they are facts."[22]

From my reading of Faulkner, in short, I find that the evil nature of men is presented as individual, that of woman as general to all white women of child-bearing age. For, as has been pointed out before, old women and black women—Miss Rosa Millard and Dilsey, for example—are usually O.K. (I could say parenthetically here that you don't run across many good preachers in Faulkner and that therefore he probably makes a sweeping generalization about the nature of preachers, but it would be a bit outside the subject we are exploring, except that he sometimes presents preachers and women as perpetrating their evil schemes in cooperation with one another.)

Briefly, not to belabor a point that has been made over and over in other contexts, it was true in the world in which Faulkner grew up as well as in his work that the role of women was defined as almost exclusively sexual. A woman was an innocent virgin, a mistress, a wife, a mother, an old maid, a widow, a prostitute. Men on the other hand in that same world were farmers, soldiers, pilots, bankers, lawyers, merchants, bootleggers. Here, I believe, lies the reason for the individuality of male villainy. Male villainy (or goodness) is radically altered on the basis of the circumstances of the man. Men use the law, they use the bank, the land, their airplanes, their horses, their stores, to work out their greed,

22. *The Town*, 330–31.

to get revenge, to hold onto power, to destroy their rivals. But for women circumstances are always the same, always sexual. Women can impinge on the world and on men only through their sexuality. They have no weapon with which to control their destiny, to fight for themselves or their children except sex.

It was (in objective reality) a world in which women used sexuality to reward and punish men and to control the behavior of men. What other tools did they have? Political power? No. Not even, to begin with, the vote. Economic power? No, not even, usually, over their own money. Professional power? No. They were barred from all professions except teaching. They had not even the final power over their own children or their own bodies, so long as men were physically stronger than they. In this world women were unable to express their sexuality except in the framework of marriage, and frustrated old maids were known to make hysterical accusations of rape against innocent men, as in "Dry September." In this same world female cousins did indeed come to stay and feed like vampires on their families. What else could they do? If they were poor and unmarried or widowed, they lived on their families or starved.

It was indeed true that women were meant to "lead beautiful lives, lives excommunicated from all reality." Excommunicated by males. That they were "raised and trained to fulfill a woman's sole end and purpose: to love, to be beautiful, to divert." A purpose defined by males. That there was a "grim Samaritan husbandry of good women." A goodness defined by the male-controlled society as chastity, fidelity, respectability. It is interesting to note here that the women in Faulkner's books who escape being sexual villains are precisely those who define their lives not only sexually, but in some other terms—Miss Rosa Millard, for example, who steals horses; Mrs. Littlejohn, who runs a boarding house; Drusilla, who fights in the Confederate Army; and particularly Charlotte Rittenmeyer, who is an artist.

It seems to me, then, that Faulkner has accepted without examination or question his own society's evaluation of women, that it never once crossed his mind that women *must* define their lives in sexual terms in order to survive at all in a world which is wholly controlled by men. He believed that what is sometimes a societal problem is always an unalterable genetic predicament. Please note here that I say *sometimes*. I am not making a case that the passage of the ERA will magically resolve all problems between men and women or that getting to be chairman of the board of General Motors will make some bright aggressive woman better in bed or kinder to her husband. I am saying that Faulkner did not often make the connection in his work that *I* (and my mother in her own and Faulkner's generation) made, and that, I feel sure, most other women of our generations made, early in adolescence, between the facts of our society and our own behavior. The world was such that women often had to manipulate men in order to effect their wills. It was such that they often had no say-so in the spending of money they helped to earn. It was such that, like blacks, they were sometimes forced to be duplicitous, treacherous, and servile to survive. It was a world in which their destinies *had* to be worked out largely in terms of their sexuality. And in consequence they vented their rage in myriad ways on the men with whom they lived.

But instinct tells me that something else is also true about Faulkner's view of women—that he has loaded us with an even heavier burden than our sexuality—a burden that, to be traced out, would require another paper. Let me, in concluding, only suggest what I mean. I think, for example, of the role of the wilderness as female. In *Go Down, Moses* Faulkner suggests that to Ike the wilderness is wife, mistress, and mother. But, if this is the case, she betrays him in the end. She succumbs to rape, vanishes, dies. If she is a symbol of virginity, innocence, that virginity and innocence are lost, just as already in the beginning of *The Sound and the Fury* Caddy's drawers are muddy. And it seems to me that here is a further, a triple connection which Faulkner makes. Both the wilderness *and* the South are female. Both the wilderness and the South are symbols of lost innocence.

All this spring and summer, as I read, I kept thinking over and over again of a scene I saw on television during Barry Goldwater's campaign for the presidency. It was in Montgomery, Alabama, I believe, the capital of the Confederacy, at a football stadium, and Goldwater was greeted there by what seems in my memory to have been a veritable sea of Southern ladies—a field entirely filled up with Southern ladies in hoop skirts, each carrying a single magnolia blossom. (Thinking back, I say to myself, Could it have been? It doesn't seem possible. Maybe I made it up. But I do remember them.) The crowd in the stadium, looking down at the ladies on the field, went wild. The roar was like the roar in the football stadium in Jackson, Mississippi, when Governor Barnett walked in that memorable day during the Meredith crisis at Ole Miss. Why? Because those ladies in hoop skirts carrying magnolia blossoms, like Governor Barnett, stood for the Old South: in his case, for its ferocious racism; in theirs, for its purity, nobility, simplicity, endurance. For that never, never land of swashbuckling courage and noblesse oblige and innocence that we, every one of us, sometimes long to inhabit.

Faulkner, as artist, must and does contain in himself and embody in his books both these emotions—the Southerner's ferocious hatred and his yearning for purity—just as we all contain within ourselves the capacity for all noble and ignoble

165

emotions and acts. For this is not, of course, a Southern predicament. It is the human predicament. Faulkner, in practice, just as he makes the wilderness female, makes the South
female. She is human innocence sullied, the lost virgin per-
sonified. She is the lady with the flower, but she's been raped
with a corncob. This is the burden Faulkner's female characters must bear, a burden too heavy sometimes for their individual shoulders. For in the characterization of individual
women and in the presentation of relations between men and
women in Faulkner's books, the projection of human purity
onto women is doomed always to failure, doomed to produce,
inevitably, disappointment and hatred.

This particular projection has, of course, been a fact of hu-
man society at least since Adam said, "She gave it to me."
"She gave it to me," Faulkner says. She—the woman, the
South, the beloved region, the earth-mother-wilderness. *She
failed me.*" I think in this connection of the end of *Absalom,
Absalom!* where Quentin says, "I dont hate the South. I dont.
I dont." Quentin, of course, does hate the South that he loves,
just as Faulkner hates the South that he loves and hates, *as
symbol*, the women who universally symbolize the South.
Faulkner says to us that man is filled with fear and outrage
and bafflement by women, that he blames them for his predicament, that he yearns for a world in which they are sinless
and he is noble, that his heart is filled both with the need for
love and the aspiration toward perfection, with guilt and
hatred for his own failures and the need to blame somebody
else for his predicament. In this sense, woman is wilderness,
is South, is lost innocence, is failed and sinful humanity. Of
course, Faulkner hates women. Of course, Quentin hates the
South.

Here, if ever, Faulkner speaks not only with his own voice,
but with the voice of his region, the voice of America, the
voice of the human world. Quentin/Faulkner is saying, "From

166

this story that we have spun together I see that human beings are evil by nature and by act, that the human world is filled with sin and suffering and violence and despair. But the human world, *the South*, is what we have and I am of it. I have complicity in it. I do not, *will* not hate it."

Cooper, Faulkner,
and the American Venture

CHARLES H. NILON

When the Leatherstocking Tales are ended with the trapper's
death in *The Prairie*, it appears that Cooper accepts the passing of the wilderness as inevitable and that he has confidence
that the American civilization will continue to be a strong and
good one. He was in Europe when he finished that novel,
and it appeared to him then that the responsibility for direction of the American venture could be safely entrusted to the
landed gentry, the class to which he belonged and the class
that he believed had the knowledge and power to direct it.

When he returned to America after being away for almost
eight years, he was disturbed by what he found, and he
feared that the landed gentry could not do what he had assumed it could in *The Prairie*. His fear for the success of the
American venture is the subject of *Home as Found*, *The
Chainbearer*, and *The Crater* and several other novels that
were written after his return to America. *Home as Found* and
The Chainbearer emphasize the danger to the American venture that may come because men are vicious and materialistic. In these novels he continues to trust the values of the
gentry, but he fears that in a free society where the public
will is strong this class cannot have the power to enforce its
values. He fears that the changes that disturbed him when he
returned to America, the products of Jacksonian democracy
and the settling of the West, are too powerful to be stopped

168

by ordinary means. The Effinghams and Littlepages of the country, he thought, were powerless against them.

Faulkner in another time and place is concerned in his fiction about many of the things that Cooper is concerned about, and he is more optimistic than Cooper. Cooper's characters try to escape civilization or to arrest it, but Faulkner's characters know this is impossible. They regard nature positively, much as some of Cooper's characters do, and gain a knowledge from it that permits them to deal with the stress of civilization. Because Cooper placed so much confidence in a class society and the leadership of a landed gentry (his aristocracy) to secure the promise of the American venture, a considerable understanding of both authors may be gained by comparing their treatment of aristocrats.

Cooper appears to believe as his friend the meliorist Henry C. Carey did that "man's misery stems from his innate capacity for viciousness rather than from the form of his social organization."[1] He also appears to have believed that the product of viciousness that affected communities could be controlled by attention to the form of the social organization. Faulkner believes that men are vicious—rapacious is the word that he uses to describe them in *A Fable*. Both authors believe that man's being greedy and grasping is responsible for materialism, and they agree that materialism is a danger to the American venture.

Cooper accepted the notion that man was vicious, but he believed also that viciousness could be controlled by those who were best suited to govern—the landed gentry who had wealth and education and manners and were guided by a proper religious ethic.

Cooper and Faulkner each have in their fiction two kinds of aristocrats—the natural aristocrat and the aristocrat who has

1. Thomas Philbrick (ed.), James Fenimore Cooper's *The Crater; or, Vulcan's Peak* (Cambridge: The Belknap Press of Harvard University Press, 1962), xvii.

169

his place in society because of his family, his wealth, his education, good breeding, and the general respect of his community. In Faulkner's fiction, at least in Isaac McCaslin's case, the natural aristocrat and the other kind are found in the same family and in the same person. The McCaslins would not be considered aristocrats by Cooper's Effinghams, although in Faulkner's world they are. Cooper's Natty Bumppo, like Isaac McCaslin, is a natural aristocrat—a man who lives in harmony with nature.

Cooper's gentry, such as the Effinghams, are not neatly matched among Faulkner's families. They resemble the English landed gentry in style and in their assumptions about themselves and their role in society. Manners, propriety, and social form are of considerable importance to their status as are power and respect. Cooper does not show much of the origins or the beginnings of such families, but the Littlepages, it appears, were always people of importance, responsible and courageous, who may have had wealth and family connections when they came to America. One of Cornelius Littlepage's ancestors had received a charter grant to thousands of acres of land in Connecticut which a Littlepage is engaged in protecting from squatters in *The Chainbearer*. Frequently Cooper's aristocrats are people who have created their estates as the Littlepages have, and towns have grown around or near them. Actually Cooper's family and his family estate appear to be models for the gentry in his fiction, and he felt that people of this kind, his kind, were the mainstay of the American venture.

Faulkner's aristocrats become aristocrats as a result of the roles that they play in communities. The way in which this process of making aristocrats is different from being an aristocrat in a Cooper community is made clear in the first paragraph of act one of *Requiem for a Nun* that is called, "The Courthouse (A Name for the City)." In this chapter Faulkner tells not only how Jefferson got its name but who its early settlers were, where they came from, what their relationships were, and what they did in the town. From the discussion of this pioneer group of settlers it can be seen who the town's aristocrats are and why they are aristocrats. In many ways what makes aristocrats in this chapter has to do with how individuals bear the burden of their humanity.

The first paragraph of the novel provides a starting point for an examination of Faulkner's views of aristocracy because it provides a situation in which Faulkner's aristocrats, or men who are or whose descendants are to be aristocrats, can be seen working. Faulkner believed as Cooper did that men were vicious, or rapacious, and materialistic. Cooper felt that a social organization governed by the gentry could reduce the effects of these tendencies in men and serve to protect the American venture against the harm their expression might cause. Faulkner felt that aristocrats were equally subject to these human weaknesses and sources of evil as other men were. His aristocrats are different from Cooper's aristocrats because they work with other members of the community to control the rapacious and materialistic tendencies in the community and in themselves. They attempt to find ethical means to face the problems that result from change. Faulkner's aristocrats are, in a sense, those persons in his communities who bear the infirmities of their humanity best, who control them through moral and ethical means, and sometimes, for periods at least, escape them. The first paragraph of the courthouse chapter implies that attitude and activity: "The courthouse is less old than the town, which began somewhere under the turn of the century as a Chickasaw Agency trading-post and so continued for almost thirty years before it discovered, not that it lacked a depository for its records and certainly not that it needed one, but that only by creating or anyway decreeing one, could it cope with a situation which

171

otherwise was going to cost somebody money."[2] A good deal is said in this paragraph about the nature of man and, by implication, about materialism.

What is implied in the paragraph is demonstrated in the remainder of the chapter. The Chickasaw Agency trading post was a commercial venture and, if it prospered, profits could be made. Ratliff, who kept the accounts of Indian purchases from his store that were paid for by the federal government, could have changed the names of the items or the prices in such a way when he sent his bills to the federal government as to have brought himself a profit. He had thought about it, but he had never changed them. As an agency the trading post provided a connection between the Chickasaw Indian tribe, the federal government, and the community that was to become Jefferson. The time had come in the community when there was a need to keep records in such a way that there was public access to them—records of land transaction, or loans, of sales of animals, of taxes, and fines and sentences (the town had a jail before it had a courthouse). Actually its having a jail led to its becoming a town.

A lock worth fifteen dollars was borrowed from the U.S. Circuit Mail Rider's bag to lock securely in the jail three members of a dangerous gang from the Trace for whose arrest a reward had been offered. Two groups claimed the reward and drank and argued together noisily while they watched the locked jail until they went to sleep. The next morning they discovered that the prisoners had escaped and that they had taken with them the lock that belonged, in a sense, to the United States. It was suggested to Ratliff that the lock be called axle grease and listed in the account book of the Chickasaw Indians, as an item to be paid for by the government as other items purchased by the Indians were. The suggestion

2. William Faulkner, *Requiem for a Nun* (New York: Random House, 1951), 3.

was not followed because Thomas Jefferson Pettigrew, the mail rider, rejected it as a matter against ethics and morals.

He was, in fact, called a damned moralist by Compson, another one of the community's early settlers. His rejection of the town's rapacious idea on moral grounds causes the men of the community who decide to have a town to name it Jefferson (because Pettigrew's morality has stopped their rapacious urge) and to build a courthouse. Pettigrew had the influence on his community in this affair of the lock that Faulkner felt aristocrats should. He helped to encourage respect for the norms of the American venture by setting in motion an action that would prevent similar emergencies in the future. This rather inadequate summary of the tale of Jefferson's naming and of the building of its courthouse is sufficient to show what is implicit in the first paragraph of the chapter. The men who settled Jefferson were by nature rapacious and materialistic, and building the courthouse was their way of imposing controls that would, to some extent, protect them against themselves. They recognized change, and they prepared as a community to meet it. Although Pettigrew is not an aristocrat in Faulkner's world, Compson, who is to be one, recognizes the rightness of his judgment, and he and the others of the community act on his suggestion.

Faulkner's aristocrats who lived in Jefferson were, with the exception of Grenier, Sartoris, and Sutpen, not wealthy when they came here. The three men who were the first settlers—Dr. Habersham, his son, and the man who served them—possessed education and some refinement. Grenier, the French Huguenot who was granted a big land patent by the government, brought the first slaves into the country and became the first cotton planter. Although he lived apart from the community in a grand style, he shared in the community's emergencies or sent his slaves to share. But he was never to have the influence, the moral and social impact upon the community, that Pettigrew did. His aristocracy in its externals resembles Cooper's, but it lacks social and political force. In Faulkner's world Grenier is an aristocrat only in a social sense. He had no lasting impact on the county, except he left his name for the land that he had owned.

Sartoris was in the conventional sense a member of the aristocracy who had refinement, education, and money and who became ethically responsible in the county and was to offer it leadership and moral support at various times. Sutpen was by origin a poor penniless boy from the mountains who deliberately chose to make himself a copy of what he supposed a plantation aristocrat was and who, except for the outward forms (the land, the money, the slaves, the mansion), never discovered what it was to be human or to recognize the humanity of others. Compson, who came after these three, gained a material stake in the county by swapping Ikkemotubbe a race horse for a square mile of land.

None of these families is free of viciousness and greed. The McCaslins wished to be. Uncle Buck and Buddy worked hard to free themselves of what was vicious and material. Uncle Buck's son Isaac was the most successful at guarding against the influence of materialism.

Cooper writes in *Home as Found* about the beginning of settlements and the relationship of the gentry to other settlers that is established in the early years of a community's existence. "At the commencement of a settlement," Cooper says, "there is much of that sort of kind feeling and mutual interest which men are apt to manifest towards each other when they are embarked in an enterprise of common hazards. The distance that is unavoidably inseparable from education, habits, and manners is lessened by mutual wants and mutual efforts; and the gentleman, even while he may maintain his character and station, maintains them with that species of good-fellowship and familiarity, that marks the intercourse between the officer and the soldier in an arduous campaign."[3] He suggests that this is the kind of relationship that existed in Templeton when the Effinghams and members of the lower classes settled there. Examples of interaction similar to this are shown when Cornelius Littlepage goes to survey his land or to visit his tenants. Evidence of kind feeling and mutual interest is shown in the relationship between Littlepage and his tenants, but he does in all his contacts with them maintain his character and station. This barrier the Effinghams feel must always be maintained.

Faulkner's description of the settlement of Jefferson is far more informal. The new settlers help each other, but they are socially unequal in education, money, and talent. There is no requirement, however, that aristocrats maintain a posture in order to assert their station. The settlement at Jefferson has existed for some time before the jail is repaired (after it is broken open and the lock is stolen and the decision is made to add a room to serve as a repository for records), but all of the men of the community work as equals to repair it. Grenier's slaves work beside the white men. If distinctions are kept in this group, they are kept between those who are white and those who are black. (And this is not entirely the case. Legal barriers are kept between black and white people. Human barriers often are not; for this reason the McCaslins recognize their black relatives. Dr. Habersham's son marries an Indian woman.) Leadership and direction, when the jail was repaired, came from those, without regard to their status, who had the necessary knowledge and skill. Faulkner's aristocrats receive, generally, the respect that they merit.

Aristocrats in the community that becomes Jefferson face change, easily anticipating the new. In the instance of the courthouse they prepare for change before the need arises.

3. James Fenimore Cooper, *Home as Found* (New York: Hurd and Houghton, 1872), 162.

Building a room onto the jail is a gesture to stabilize and regularize, but it is also a gesture to accommodate change. Building the new courthouse gives a permanent character to the town, both to its geography and its legal procedures. The French architect, who is captive to Sutpen, draws the plans for the building and for the courthouse square and points out that a geography and forms of intercourse are being set by his design. This does not mean that a function of aristocracy will be to maintain what is in the design against change at some time in the future.

Because he feared change, Cooper's aristocrats function to keep things as they are or were. This is what the Effinghams assume their role to be. When they return to Templeton they find it changed from what it had been when they left, and assume that it is worse because it is different and that they must try to restore what is changed to its earlier form. They have no flexibility. Their inflexibility is intended to protect men against their natural tendencies to viciousness and greed and in that way to protect the American venture. They not only wish to protect Templeton: they are concerned to have it appear flourishing and prosperous in European terms. The pull of Europe influenced strongly Cooper's sense of what was appropriate in a class society.

Faulkner's settlers, aristocrats and others, do not feel the pull of Europe as Cooper's do. They know that they have European origins—their names remind them and those around them of this, although they have often forgotten how to spell and pronounce them correctly. They are freer in their choices. They have kept the names and some of the European customs, but they have not been reluctant to take what they want from the region where they are. Freedom from the European pull permits them a greater openness to their own time and place. The influence of wilderness, for example, is recognized by Cooper and shown in the making of his natural

aristocrat Natty Bumppo, but Middleton and Inez pass
through the wilderness without being much affected by it. It
is a background against which their European profiles are
seen. It does not appear to make a difference to them. Most
of Faulkner's aristocrats are not influenced by the wilderness
as much as Isaac is, but some of them are influenced by it
significantly, and most of them, particularly those who hunt,
can live in it on its terms, though not to the extent that Isaac
can. Like him, however, it appears that their values and standards have been affected by the wilderness.

A crucial difference between Cooper's aristocrats and
Faulkner's is in this area of values and standards. Faulkner's
aristocrats appear to derive many of their standards of behavior from the practicalities of everyday living and from nature.
Isaac as the son of a McCaslin and Sophonsiba Beauchamp is
descended from persons who are in a social sense aristocrats,
but the Beauchamp manners and pretensions make them
comic and ineffectual human beings—and dishonest. Isaac's
real aristocracy, which is described in "Was," "The Old
People," and "The Bear," comes from the McCaslin side of the
family, from people who bear the burden of their humanity
and have the courage to be honest and different.

Isaac McCaslin's grandfather, a wealthy land and slave
owner, does not violate the conventions of his region by publicly announcing his relationship to his black offspring; but he
does leave money to them in his will, and his sons Buck and
Buddy accept them as relatives. Buck and Buddy are different enough to reject slavery. They move out of their father's
house and build a cabin and care for themselves, cook, sew,
and support themselves by running a country store. They try
to free their father's slaves by permitting them to work and
buy their freedom. They also, as is described in *The Unvanquished*, establish a constructive, socially equal relationship
with the poor white people of their region and work with

them to improve their skills as farmers and aid them in marketing their crops. They work with free black people in the same way. Faulkner's aristocrats have the freedom to be different from their class, the freedom to be eccentric. This does not mean that they are free from criticism by their fellows. As humans they may not like criticism, but they must, as aristocrats, accept it.

The norms of Isaac's status are from his family, and they are modified by his special relationship to Sam Fathers who guides his learning about himself and from nature to a point where through his wilderness experiences he knows the old verities. His uncle identifies the knowledge that Sam Fathers guides him in acquiring with the truth and beauty that are the subject of a Keats poem. He knows the Book (the Bible). These provide him a code, give ethical and moral perspective to his aristocracy. The result of this is a kind of humility and a certain denial and sacrifice of the self in his behavior. Isaac assumes that he has learned to function in a way that is consistent with fostering the well-being of the American venture, avoiding materialism (to an extent), discharging his family's responsibilities to his black relatives, and leading an essentially aristocratic life. Although his life is not free from error, he becomes for the community a kind of philosopher-guide; he comments on community action and sometimes gives warnings.

In "Delta Autumn" when Uncle Ike—the name used for Isaac when he is old—and the men with whom he is going hunting talk about man's predatory nature, which may not be precisely the same as viciousness, he argues that it is natural for men to hunt. He says God knew they were going to hunt when He created them. The hunting is not bad, Isaac says, unless the hunter behaves improperly to the thing he hunts and kills. The conversation about men who are less good than they might be continues until Isaac says that, given their circumstances, men behave rather well. Ike would probably not agree that education, refinement, money—the products of good society and being associated with the aristocracy—make men good.

His role as philosopher-guide, as one who is concerned about the outcome of the American venture, is an important function that is performed by Faulkner's natural aristocrat. This role, however, has no real force to implement what is desirable nor does it indicate that Isaac is free of viciousness or other evil. One of the men in the car questions him about the adequacy of American leadership in that period when Hitler's power was in ascendency. Will Legate answers, before Isaac can, "We will stop him in this country. Even if he calls himself George Washington." Isaac adds, "I ain't noticed this country being short of defenders yet, when it needed them . . . I reckon, when the time comes and some of you have done got tired hollering we are whipped if we don't go to war and some more are hollering we are whipped if we do, it will cope with one Austrian paper hanger, no matter what he will be calling himself. My pappy and some other better men than any of them you named tried once to tear it in two with a war, and they failed."[4] His reference to the disagreement among Americans over what should be done about Hitler is followed by a list of weaknesses that affects the country. Edmonds, Isaac's cousin, says that there are people without jobs, strikes, and closed factories, and people on welfare who will not or cannot work. Against Isaac's optimism he points out that the country raises too much cotton and corn and too many hogs, and that there is not enough food for the hungry. Isaac's confidence remains secure in face of this argument. He is not disturbed by it, although much of it emphasizes the rapacity and materialism that were rampant in the 1940s, be-

4. William Faulkner, "Delta Autumn," in *Go Down, Moses* (New York: Random House, 1942), 338–39.

cause he was reassured by the performance of Americans in emergencies in the past.

As Isaac does in "Delta Autumn," Faulkner's characters usually have history to reassure them when they become nervous and fear that the American venture is failing or threatened. Cooper did not have as much history in the younger America as Faulkner had to learn from, and he does not appear to have regarded history as Faulkner does. His gentry are given the task of restoring the norm of the past, of stopping change, and, in that way, determining the nature of the American venture and its preservation. Faulkner's attitude is different from Cooper's. He regards time as a continuum and his aristocrats who want to stop time (the Compsons in *The Sound and The Fury*, for example) are destroyed. Isaac's sense of the present and the future grows from his knowledge of the past, and he can gain confidence from the past. He cannot return to it; he cannot stop time's movement. These things he knows, and they add to his difference from Cooper's aristocrats.

Although Isaac has confidence that the American venture will survive the threat from Hitler, and his confidence is supported by America's past history, he feels that there are costs that America must pay for rapacity and materialism. These costs, man's punishment for his violation of nature, become clear to him as he becomes aware of his moral failure and as he thinks, following that awareness, in "Delta Autumn," about how man has abused the land to make money:

> This land which man has deswamped and denuded and derivered in two generations so that white men can own plantations and commute every night to Memphis and black men own plantations and ride in jim crow cars to Chicago to live in millionaires' mansions on Lakeshore Drive, where white men rent farms and live like niggers and niggers crop on shares and live like animals, where cotton is planted and grows man-tall in the very cracks of the sidewalks, and usury and mortgage and bankruptcy and mea-

180

sureless wealth, Chinese and African and Aryan and Jew, all breed and spawn together until no man has time to say which one is which nor cares.[5]

Cooper's trapper was also certain that there was a price to pay for waste and destruction of the environment. On this point Faulkner and Cooper are in agreement.

Cooper appears to believe that his gentry can govern in a way that will protect society from the effects of rapacity. Although Isaac is confident that the American venture will survive, experience has taught him that Americans will make costly mistakes and that no class, gentry or other, can prevent this. These mistakes, however, as he sees them, will not destroy the venture. Faulkner appears to feel that history, observed retrospectively, shows that man's rapacity, paradoxically, contributes to the progress that societies and governments make. He says in *A Fable*:

Rapacity does not fail, else man must deny he breathes. Not rapacity: its whole vast glorious history repudiates that. It does not, cannot, must not fail. Not just one family in one nation privileged to soar comet-like into splendid zenith through and because of it, not just one nation among all the nations selected as heir to that vast splendid heritage; not just France, but all governments and nations which ever rose and endured long enough to leave their mark as such, had sprung from it and in and upon and by means of it became forever fixed in the amazement of man's present and the glory of his past; civilization itself is its password and Christianity its masterpiece; Chartres and the Sistine Chapel, the pyramids and the rock-wombed powder-magazines under the Gates of Hercules its altars and monuments, Michelangelo and Phidias and Newton and Ericsson and Archimedes and Krupp its priests and popes and bishops; the long deathless roster of its glory—Caesar and the Barcas and the two Macedonians, our own Bonaparte and the great Russian and the giants who strode nimbused in red hair like fire across the Aurora Borealis, and all the lesser nameless who were not heroes but, glorious in anonymity, at least served the destiny of heroes—the generals and admirals,

5. *Ibid.*, 364.

the corporals and ratings of glory, the batmen and orderlies of renown, and the chairmen of boards and the presidents of federations, the doctors and lawyers and educators and churchmen who after nineteen centuries have rescued the son of heaven from oblivion and translated him from mere meek heir to earth to chairman of its board of trade . . . it is in and from rapacity that he [man] gets, holds, his immortality. . . .[6]

Similar ideas are expressed by Natty Bumppo in *The Pioneers* when he says that man's greed for gold is no less rapacious than the wolf's desire for his prey.

Cooper's aristocrats, with the exception of the trapper in *The Prairie*, never become Uncle as Isaac does (leader, friend, teacher, protector) to their communities. The trapper is uncle, or philosopher-guide, to those persons who have come on the prairie—to Ishmael Bush and his family, to Helen and Paul, and to Inez and Middleton (perhaps to Dr. Battius), and he becomes father to a young Indian brave. To be uncle or father to a person or a group of persons implies a relationship in which there may be respect, and in which the role is related to function. The role suggests, on the one hand, a lack of equality in knowledge, experience, and power, but not a lack of equality in humanity. This is not the relationship of Cooper's gentry in *Home as Found* to the lower classes.

Nathaniel Bumppo was becoming the philosopher-guide for some time. His progress toward the wisdom and goodness that are his in *The Prairie* is implied from book to book in the sequence of the Leatherstocking Tales. As the names that the Indians give to him which measure his growth change, he becomes straight-tongue, deerslayer, and pathfinder, and his growth continues to be marked until he becomes what he is in *The Prairie*. In *The Pathfinder* Cooper says he was "a fair example of what a just-minded and pure man might be, while

6. William Faulkner, *A Fable* (New York: Random House, 1954), 259–60.

untempted by unruly or ambitious desires, and left to follow
the bias of his feelings, amid the solitary grandeur and enno-
bling influences of a sublime nature; neither led aside by in-
ducements which influence all to do evil amid the incentives
of civilization, nor forgetful of the Almighty Being whose
spirit pervades the wilderness as well as the towns."[7]

In *The Prairie* where he is to die, when he is close to Isaac's
age and status in "Delta Autumn," he is called the trapper,
and Cooper says he is "of great simplicity of mind, but of ster-
ling worth. . . . He was a man endowed with the choicest and
perhaps rarest gift of nature; that of distinguishing good from
evil. His virtues were those of simplicity, because such were
the fruits of his habits, as were indeed his very prejudices. . . .
'In short, he was a noble shoot from the strong stock of human
nature, which never could attain its proper elevation and importance, for no other reason, than because it grew in the
forest.'"[8] The trapper has lived in the forest for many years,
and he knows how to find food and to provide shelter; he
knows how to cut down trees, how animals respond to men,
and how to deal with stampeding buffalo. In another time and
place, he killed a man and responded ritually to that death as
Isaac did to the killing of his first deer. He has placed his life
in danger to save other lives. He respects the Indians, and
they respect him. He confesses his weaknesses, has humility,
and is ethically responsible. His role in *The Prairie* is similar
to Isaac's role in "Delta Autumn"—a natural aristocrat's role
that Cooper's gentry are unable or unwilling to play.

Cooper introduces him to the reader and to the Bush family
in a way that symbolizes his aristocracy. The Bush family sees
him first framed by the brilliant color of the setting sun where

7. James Fenimore Cooper, *The Pathfinder* (New York: W. A. Townsend and
Company, 1860), 144.
8. James Fenimore Cooper, *The Prairie* (New York: Rinehart & Co., Inc.,
1950), 128.

he looms larger than life, and they are held in awe when they see "in the center of this flood of fiery light a human form . . . as palpable, as though it would come within the grasp of any extended hand."[9] Seen, as he was by the Bush family, in the "red glow of the setting sun" the figure was larger than life and its attitude was musing and melancholy. Throughout the novel this large presence is not diminished as the trapper is seen in action from day to day. His intelligence judges and guides the other white persons who are on the prairie, and it understands the Indians and can explain their behavior. His attitude toward himself and his role is expressed when Ishmael Bush asks him for advice and he answers that "advice is not a gift but a debt that the old owe to the young." As an aristocrat, he assumes that he has debts to others and he pays those debts throughout the novel. As he pays them, he demonstrates the characteristics of the natural aristocrat. The debt he refers to in his response to Ishmael Bush suggests his awareness of his responsibility for the American venture and reminds the reader that he has, when there was danger and need, left the forest to fight in America's wars. But he has given more than that to the venture. He understands it and says that its object is the protection of the ties that bind one "'to his fellow-creatures best,'" and he recognizes that this national objective is more difficult and to be mourned because "'color, and property, and tongue, and l'arning . . . make so wide a difference in those who, after all, are but the children of one father!'"[10]

The trapper listens to Ishmael Bush's statement about land ownership and is in general agreement with him when he says "'I am as rightful an owner of the land I stand on, as any governor of the States! Can you tell me, stranger, where the law or the reason is to be found, which says that one man

9. *Ibid.*, 8.
10. *Ibid.*, 60.

184

CHARLES H. NILON

shall have a section, or a town, or perhaps a county to his use, and another have to beg for earth to make his grave in? This is not nature, and I deny that it is law.'"[11] Isaac McCaslin makes the same argument to his cousin McCaslin Edmonds in "The Bear" when he is trying to explain to him what is said in "The Book" and to persuade him of the evil consequences of materialism. Isaac says, "I can't repudiate it [the land]. It was never mine to repudiate. It was never father's and Uncle Buddy's to bequeath me to repudiate because it was never grandfathers."[12] The trapper's response to Ishmael is "I cannot say that you are wrong . . . and I have often thought and said as much, when and where I have believed my voice could be heard.'"[13] This argument between the points of view of the trapper and Isaac about land ownership is not meant to suggest that Faulkner is not (as Cooper is) concerned about the protection of property. His concern to make the protection of property adequate, just, and certain of attention is suggested in the sequence of events in Jefferson's early history that lead to the building of the jail and the courthouse—necessary institutions whose function is to assure that voices can be heard, an assurance the trapper did not have.

Although they are philosopher-guides, essentially good men, Isaac and the trapper are not without imperfections, and the scope of their influence is limited. Isaac fails morally, paradoxically (and remains innocently unaware of his lapse for many years) in his attempt to live according to the law of "The Book." Through his earnest effort to free himself from the evil threat of his family's property which he inherits, he persuades his cousin McCaslin Edmonds to accept the money and the land, apparently without concern for the harm that its possession might do to Edmonds and his descendants or for the fact

11. *Ibid.*, 63.
12. William Faulkner, "The Bear," in *Go Down, Moses*, 256.
13. James Fenimore Cooper, *The Prairie*, 64.

that their moral stamina might be less than his. He discovers in "Delta Autumn" that money has affected the morality of Edmond's grandson and, during the same episode in which he is engaged in conversation with one of his black relatives, a woman who has borne a child for Edmonds' grandson, that he is not free of prejudice against black people. When he responds to her race rather than to her humanity, she marks his failure and asks him, "old man, . . . have you lived so long and forgotten so much that you don't remember anything you ever knew or felt or even heard about love?"[14]

The trapper is limited because he cannot live outside the wilderness, and, when he knows that it will be destroyed, he goes willingly to his death before it is gone. Cooper's aristocrats are generally idealized as the trapper is, but in different ways. Faulkner's are not; Isaac is rather typical of them. They are not free of flaws, although they frequently rise above them and perform well in spite of them. Except that he cannot live in civilization, the trapper is a more idealized person than Isaac.

In *Home as Found*, Cooper presents his gentry, aristocrats who are engaged in the task that he feels is their particular responsibility and for which they are particularly suited. Mr. Effingham is a gentleman which means that, as Cooper defines gentleman in *The Chainbearer*, he has the best qualities of man unaided by God, and he is distinguished from the Christian whose graces come directly from God's mercy.[15] Mr. Effingham, the members of his family, and those like them express opinions that are based on intelligence and cultivation and they have taste and manners. Cooper chooses him and those like him as the natural leaders of society. The proper gentry are the landed gentry whose money is not from

14. William Faulkner, "Delta Autumn," 363.
15. James Fenimore Cooper, *The Chainbearer* (New York: W. A. Townsend and Company, 1860), 161–62.

commercial sources and is not used for commercial purposes. Money alliances may bring the aristocrat into compromising relationships with political factions or lead him to accept the current errors of the general populace. John Effingham, a commercial person and a cousin of Edward Effingham, is, because of his commercial alliances and because he has no land, not a proper member of the gentry. Edward Effingham is disengaged and free, and he is not selfish. The task that is provided for the Effingham's when they are again, after travelling in Europe and visiting in New York, at home in the Wigwam is defined in the preface to *Home as Found*. There Cooper says "that the American nation is a great nation, in some particulars the greatest the world ever saw, we hold to be true . . . but we are also equally ready to concede, that it is very far behind most polished nations in various essentials, and chiefly that it is lamentably in arrears to its own avowed principles."[16] It is Edward Effingham's and his family's responsibility to work to see that America does not continue behind the most polished nations.

The Effinghams are an aristocratic family in every sense that Europeans are. They keep the forms of gentility. They have lived in Europe and stood the tests of European inspection. They are sensitive to and able to describe the social changes in America that they find on their return and which they fear. They want to establish again the social and political norms that existed before they went to Europe, to stop change, and to establish their class in the role of leadership. Through them the situations that are described in *Home as Found*, and the talk about them, Cooper makes clear the threat that he felt to his class and the way he felt the American venture was endangered by that threat.

The Effinghams are greatly disturbed when they return to

16. James Fenimore Cooper, *Home as Found*, vii.

Templeton, because of the new persons who have come to live in the town and their new ways. These new persons, whom they call migrants, threaten the established value and social system, and this threat is exemplified in their claim (or the town's claim) of the Point, property that Mr. Effingham believes to be his. Cooper's argument in this novel is made to protect the property rights of the landed gentry as well as a complaint against the greed and egalitarianism of the new people. When speaking of the threat they posed, Mr. Effingham says "that unequalled pecuniary prosperity should sensibly impair the manners of what is termed the world, by introducing suddenly large bodies of uninstructed and untrained men and women into society, is a natural consequence of obvious causes; that it should corrupt morals even, we have a right to expect, for we are taught to believe it the most corrupting influence under which men can live."[17] Because economic success is not dependent upon those refinements that make a gentleman, Templeton has come under this "most corrupting influence" and the Effinghams call attention to it in a variety of ways. Also because economic success is not dependent upon those refinements that make a gentleman, Mr. Effingham is powerless to do more than complain that manners are impaired and people do not know how to behave when they have more money than members of the class to which they belong usually have. He also feels that the morals of newly prosperous persons may be corrupted. These unavoidable consequences of changing or changed economic status in the society he appears willing to accept. As he continues his discussion of the faults of the new people who have come to Templeton, he points out his most serious objection to them: "'I confess,'" Edward Effingham says, "'I did not expect to see . . . the day when a body of strangers, birds of

17. *Ibid.*, 224.

passage, creatures of an hour, should assume a right to call on the old and long-established inhabitants of a country to prove their claims to their possessions, and this, too, in an unusual and unheard-of manner, under the penalty of being violently deprived of them!'"[18] The new people who have come to Templeton claim the Point as the property of the city. Mr. Effingham regards the property as his although he has permitted the town to use it as his father from whom he inherited his claim to it had. The threat of the loss of his property causes Mr. Effingham to engage in conversations with a representative group of the migrants (new people) and to express opinions about them that show Cooper's fears and the role he hoped the landed gentry could play in the protection of the American venture. In so far as the episodes of this novel treat the ownership of property, it is clear that Mr. Effingham's attitudes toward land ownership are quite different from the trapper's. They are also different from Faulkner's.

Although this novel defines the role of the landed gentry, it is not necessarily a document that convinces the reader that people like Mr. Effingham could do what Cooper wanted them to. The new people who migrated to Templeton during the Effinghams' absence do not value the gentry as they do themselves. The novel shows convincingly the difference between the old people and the new people, but it does not show in an equally convincing way that the Effinghams have the power to stop change and to give direction to the social and political choices of the new people in the way that the trapper leads others in the wilderness. The Effinghams may be a threatened class, but their behavior, as they face the threat, does not provide sympathy for them from the contemporary reader, because they do not make, against the background of history, a convincing case.

18. *Ibid.*

The vigor and energy of the new people who disturb the Effinghams most are exemplified in Steadfast Dodge and Aristabulus Bragg who, in spite of the criticism that Cooper makes of them and others in Templeton who support their effort and viewpoint and in many ways are like them, are shown to possess many of the qualities that are prized in a democracy and qualities that contributed to the making of Faulkner's aristocrats who are their historical contemporaries.

Dodge, the editor of the newspaper, and Bragg, who is a lawyer, represent the new forces that threaten the Effinghams. They argue against their claim to land which they feel is public property. They defend the public's right to know several points of view on issues and encourage public discussion of all issues of the moment, although Mr. Effingham objects to young inexperienced men engaging in such discussions. "'Look,'" Mr. Effingham says, "'into the first paper that offers, and you will see the young men of the country hardily invited to meet by themselves, to consult concerning public affairs, as if they were impatient of the counsels and experiences of their fathers. No country can prosper where the ordinary mode of transacting the business connected with the root of the government commences with this impiety.'"[19] Bragg and Dodge in their different ways encourage public discussion of this kind—discussion that Cooper regarded as gossip. They welcome social change and are aware that they are likely to become the new aristocrats; or, perhaps more meaningfully, they are likely to take the new positions of leadership in American society. From their portrayal, it is clear that they are going to make money and that they know how to gain political power. They advocate freedom and change and call attention to the Effingham's fear of a leveling process in society.

19. *Ibid.*, 225.

CHARLES H. NILON

In addition to his general disapproval of Dodge and Bragg, Mr. Effingham calls attention to Dodge's natural endowment of energy and enterprise which he considers indications of his capacity for rapacity. He finds Bragg, however, "bold, morally and physically, aspiring, self-possessed, shrewd, singularly . . . intelligent after his tastes, and apt." He argues that if it had been Bragg's luck to have been thrown earlier into "a better sphere," those same natural qualities that make him so competent "would have conduced to his improvement" and made a gentleman of him. On the other hand, Mr. Effingham argues that Steadfast Dodge is "a hypocrite by nature, cowardly, envious, and malignant," and he says that his circumstances added to his natural tendencies. Both of these men exhibited what Cooper called animal force and a tendency to viciousness.[20]

Although he admired Bragg with reservations, Mr. Effingham fears what he represents. Bragg has proposed to his daughter, Eve Effingham, and to another young lady of her class and has been rejected by both of them without injury to his ego and without learning through their rejection. Refusal did not teach him a lesson. After these two ladies rejected him, he proposes to Annette, Eve Effingham's French maid, and the maid tells her mistress that she intends to marry him, "Je vais me marier avec un avocat."

Cooper explains Bragg's behavior in choosing a wife by saying

Mr. Bragg had no notion of any distinction in the world, beyond those which came from money and political success. For the first he had a practical deference that was as profound as his wishes for its enjoyments; and for the last he felt precisely the sort of reverence that one educated under a feudal system would feel for a feudal lord. The first, after several unsuccessful efforts, he had found unattainable by means of matrimony, and he turned

20. *Ibid.*, 222–23.

191

his thoughts towards Annette, whom he had for some months held in reserve, in the event of his failing with Eve and Grace, for on both these heiresses had he entertained designs.[21]

Annette afforded the practical Mr. Bragg certain advantages. She was attractive and she was a dressmaker. He was acceptable to her because being "un avocat" he offered her a chance to better her condition. After their marriage they were going to emigrate to the far West, where "Mr. Bragg proposed to practice law, or keep school, or go to Congress, or to turn trader, or to saw lumber, or, in short, to turn his hand to anything that offered," as many who have contributed to the American venture have done.[22] Bragg was an opportunist who would do what he must to achieve his ends.

Among Cooper's aristocrats, Mark Wollston in *The Crater* is much closer in his competence as a leader to the trapper than he is to the Effinghams. Like the trapper he is for a time a successful leader and builds in the crater a community, a sort of utopia, that the Effinghams would have liked, a community that is free of all of the social and political evils that disturbed them when they returned to live in Templeton. Mark is like the trapper in his ability to plan for people and to protect them from dangers. His leadership appears to be as much the product of his energy and enterprise as it appears to be the product of the special advantages of his class. Mark's role in the creation of the utopia does support the theory that the gentry can provide leadership, but he is a qualified embodiment of that theory. Mark builds and governs successfully, for a time, the kind of community that Cooper felt was desirable to combat the evils of the Westward movement, of Jacksonian democracy, and of Fourierism as it was defined by Horace Greeley in the 1840s.

After he and Bob Betts, a common sailor who is his friend,

21. *Ibid.*, 431.
22. *Ibid.*, 432.

are shipwrecked in the South Seas, he finds and acquires a reef on a volcanic crater and with Bob's help they make it safe and suitable for a community to live on. After the carefully selected settlers come to live on the crater, Mark governs and leads them effectively in all of the affairs of the community until its agriculture, industry, and commerce are securely established, the barbaric tribes of the area are controlled, and they have attained power and ease. During the early years of the colony's existence, Mark, who owned the land, provided a constitution under whose law he became governor and administered the government of the community with the aid of an elected council that had tenure for life. Other political officers were appointed by the governor and council as there was need for them in the community, and served at their pleasure.

For a time the people of the community have a good life, but this does not last. Mark ceases to be a good leader or an effective aristocrat. He becomes increasingly concerned about his role in society, ceases to be fully human, and becomes the self-conscious gentleman. As he becomes something of a prig, he becomes ineffectual as a leader. His obsession with the forms of gentility makes the necessary openings for those forces of diversity and confusion that destroy his social experiment. Because the people want it, representatives of several religious groups are permitted to join the community, a lawyer comes, and the *Crater Truth-Teller*, a newspaper, is published. Generally, care is relaxed in choosing the settlers.

The result is that what was a successful utopia, according to Cooper's definition, becomes a dystopia. Human greed and rapacity are free to express themselves, as they were in Templeton, and the counterparts of Bragg and Dodge are active. The newspaper argues successfully for a new constitution which like the New York Constitution of 1846 made all of the communities' political offices elective, and Mark is made ineligible for office. The crater which he owns is leased to the public, and later his ownership of the land is challenged as Mr. Effingham's was in Templeton. A lawsuit is brought against him to take away his title to the crater, and it is won. After this loss in the court, Mark and his family leave the community.

Shortly after his departure an earthquake destroys the crater and the entire colony. This event may suggest symbolically that nature takes its own revenge, as Isaac McCaslin suggests near the end of "Delta Autumn," when man uses it unwisely. The suggested parallel is not a good one, but Mark's failure as a leader and the consequences of that failure do show that Cooper believed man's viciousness and his rapacity, when they were not controlled, produced destructive consequences.

Whether Cooper intends it or not, it appears that Mark's success in the establishment of his community in its utopian period is dependent upon human qualities effectively used and upon qualities not too different from those of the trapper or of a Faulkner aristocrat. Actually his enterprise and energy are close to those of Bragg and Dodge, whom Cooper rejects as rapacious, materialist, and animal in *Home as Found*. It is his energy, his leadership, his concern for the welfare of the people who come to the crater to live—his action and his participation, his quality as a human being—that make that venture successful. His social status, education, and culture are not enough alone to make the venture's success, and it fails when his human qualities are no longer dominant and active in him, and he becomes essentially a social form.

To an extent Mark's change of character indicates something of the two opposite pulls that appear not to have been resolved in Cooper. His social theory required him, Henry

Nash Smith says, "to believe that civilization is better than nature" and that "the violation of nature by civilization is necessary and its ultimate consequences are good."[23] When Mark is shipwrecked and lives with his Quaker friend through the use of their physical skills, they find the crater and live and work in the natural world, although not precisely in a wilderness. During this period and the period of the settlement when the natural or wilderness character of the crater is being transformed, Mark continues to be a strong human figure. When the crater has become a civilized rather than a wilderness or natural world, Mark becomes a civilized form and ceases to be an effective person.

When Faulkner's aristocrats are looked at as a group (Grenier, Compson, Sartoris, McCaslin, Sutpen, and Habersham), it is easily seen that they have many of the characteristics of Cooper's trapper, of Steadfast Dodge, and of Aristabulus Bragg. In the pioneer world of Jefferson, as they made their places there, these characteristics proved useful to them and to the town. They are never like the Effinghams, but some of them do resemble Mark Woolston. They have energy and enterprise, and they are sometimes vicious and materialistic. In various ways they and the community recognize the harmful and evil tendencies that are in them and suffer from them. The jail and the courthouse were built because of the recognition of the need for control and punishment and because of the need to support the ethical and the moral.

Faulkner's aristocrats earn their status, at least initially, by their quality as human beings and not by approximating and maintaining the norms of a particular mode of social behavior. Individuals among them often accept roles of leadership or act to persuade the community to take a desirable action, but Faulkner's aristocrats are not unified by a common set of char-

23. Henry Nash Smith, Introduction to James Fenimore Cooper's *The Prairie* (New York: Rinehart and Company, 1950), xvi-xvii.

195

acteristics and in his world the responsibility for the American venture is shared among all of the people. Grenier has the outward attributes of the class that Cooper has confidence in, but he lives by disposition and choice a life apart from the community and makes no clear mark on it. He may be compared to the Littlepages in *Satanstoe* and *The Chainbearer* in that like them he has a grant to a large tract of land, but there the comparison ends.

In *Absalom, Absalom!* Sutpen probably comes closest to illustrating the dangers that Cooper finds in the possible success of men like Bragg and Dodge; and Mr. Compson's father argued that his failures, not so much as an aristocrat but as a human being, were the product of his innocence. He is accused by Miss Coldfield in that novel of "abrupting" his way into the community. As Bragg and Dodge are supposed to have, he has plans that are sufficiently formed when he arrives in Jefferson to be called a design. He acquires the externals of aristocracy through force and energy or viciousness and materialism as Cooper fears Bragg and Dodge will. His failure, however, comes not because he does not discharge the responsibilities of his class, but because he fails to know how to treat human beings. He is not what Isaac McCaslin or Cooper's trapper would call a good hunter. His failure affects primarily his own family, but it also destroys Jones's family and the decency and life of his father-in-law. It can also be judged (insofar as it can be related to the causes for the South's defeat in the Civil War) as being dangerous to the American venture. Faulkner shows through Wash Jones's judgment of Sutpen and some of the men of his class—those who come to punish Wash, after he has killed Sutpen—that aristocracy as a form in the South had divided men, class against class; had supported slavery; and had divided families so that brother fought brother. Sutpen's legend shows these things, and, in that short period before his death, Wash Jones

CHARLES H. NILON

becomes aware of them and makes a judgment against Sutpen's class because he believes it was responsible for the loss of the war.

Faulkner's aristocrats are not always protectors of the American venture. Their goals are sometimes selfish, and their acts are sometimes harmful to others. Isaac's moral failure (and he is a good man) illustrates this. They rise and they fall, and, as families, they are never uniform in type as the Effinghams are. The Compsons and the Sartorises illustrate this. In *The Unvanquished* the men who join John Sartoris's regiment testify to his quality as a person, as does his respect for the values of Uncle Buck and Uncle Buddy. After the Civil War, in which he is brave and full of courage, his effort to maintain white control causes him to become a murderer, a sin for which he pays with his life. Some of the things that he does during this period are probably stupid and cruel. The edict that no black woman should appear on the streets of Jefferson unless she wore an apron was stupid and cruel and a contrast to the understanding and kindness he shows when he persuades the city of Jefferson not to tax Emily Grierson's property. John Sartoris's failure comes when he tries to stop change—to maintain the South as it had been before the Civil War. It comes when he has selected for himself the role that Cooper's Effinghams try to play.

Cooper thought the past could die. Faulkner knew that it was never dead and that change was inevitable. In *The Sound and The Fury* the Compson family is destroyed because it is unable to accept change and wants to stop time. In this novel it is the servant Dilsey who understands that time is a continuum and who, because of this knowledge, is able to understand and serve the Compsons. Cooper's aristocrats are a product of his own fears of the evil in man and of the social and political change that affected him personally. They are also a product of his unresolved attitude toward the advan-

197

tages of nature and of civilization. Because of his place in time, Faulkner began writing knowing the results of some of the things that troubled Cooper. He knew that it was not possible to stop the march of civilization and he knew, as Cooper did, that man is rapacious. Like Cooper he is sometimes not content with the state of the American venture, but he knows that aristocrats as a class cannot keep it safe. He shows in his fiction that aristocrats have only human powers and that their status does not indicate how they will behave nor how people who are not aristocrats will respond to them. Cooper's restraints, those that he wished to impose through the authority and power of his aristocracy, were essentially denials of freedom. Faulkner assumes and suggests through his aristocrats that denials of freedom are harmful to the American venture. Although he believes, or at least has Gavin Stevens say on one occasion that "apparently no man can stand freedom," he appears also to believe that all men should be free to confront it. Faulkner's aristocrats show that a landed gentry of the sort that Cooper wished to establish could not fix in time the civilization that Cooper admired.

The Gothicism
of *Absalom, Absalom!*:
Rosa Coldfield Revisited

FRANÇOIS L. PITAVY

—Croyez-vous aux fantômes?
—Non, mais j'en ai peur.

MME DU DEFFAND

La cave est de la folie enterrée.

GASTON BACHELARD

Of the nineteen novels of William Faulkner, *Absalom, Absalom!* appears as the one which in every sense resorts to and appeals the most to the imagination. An enquiry into the Sutpen mystery fused with a quest for meaning by the narrators, the novel sets up a circular movement in which the consciousness endlessly reverts to the same questionings, like Rosa Coldfield's outraged "Why? Why? and why?"[1] Thus the design of the novel can best be represented by a spiral, which figures the imprisoning of the consciousness laboring under the burden of the past, social and individual, and sinking into its own phantasms, as it tries to unravel the story of the fall of the house of Sutpen.

Phantasms/phantoms: the reverse and obverse expressions of the same inner reality.[2] *Absalom, Absalom!*, the Faulkner

1. William Faulkner, *Absalom, Absalom!* (New York: Random House, 1936), 167. The Modern Library College Edition has the same pagination. All subsequent page references will be given within parentheses after the quotations.
2. The German *Phantasie*, like the English phantasy, means not so much the faculty itself as the imaginary world, its contents, and its creative activity.

199

novel which so remarkably manifests a phantasmatic activity, is also the one which borders the most on the fantastic, or rather the world of phantoms, shades, shadows, demons, fiends, ghosts, and djinns—words which seem to recur more frequently in this novel than in any other by Faulkner. This conjunction phantasm/phantom is already an indication as to the nature and function of the Gothicism of *Absalom, Absalom!*—imaginative rather than imagined, that is, not so much a spectacle (however spectacular the novel can be) eliciting the reader's sense of wonder, or terror, as a means of bringing him into active participation with the narrators' quest: instead of a more interested spectator, he is made into an inhabitant of the house of fiction.

Before coming to a specific study of the Gothicism of the novel and more precisely of Rosa Coldfield's narrative, it is appropriate to define further the structural design of *Absalom, Absalom!* and the critical method which the structure of the novel makes almost inevitable.[3]

A DREAM NOVEL

Absalom, Absalom! could be called a dream novel, both in and outside of the text—for the narrators, for the reader, for

3. On the Gothic novel, see Maurice Lévy, *Le Roman "gothique" anglais, 1764–1824* (Association des Publications de la Faculté des Lettres et Sciences Humaines de Toulouse, 1968); Leslie A. Fiedler, *Love and Death in the American Novel* (New York: Criterion Books, 1960); Peter Brooks, *The Melodramatic Imagination: Balzac, Henry James, Melodrama and the Mode of Excess* (New Haven: Yale University Press, 1976). On the Gothicism of *Absalom, Absalom!*, Fiedler's excellent remarks are still valid (op. cit., passim). Max Putzel, in "What Is Gothic about *Absalom, Absalom!*" (*Southern Literary Journal*, 4 [Fall, 1971], 3–14), has little to say on the subject. By trying systematically to recognize in Faulkner's novels Gothic themes, settings, and character types, Elizabeth M. Kerr, in her recent *William Faulkner's Gothic Domain* (New York: Kennikat Press, 1979), brings in a little indiscriminately all she can muster on the subject and ends up looking at Faulkner's work only through Gothic glasses darkly. Her inadequately coordinated listings do not add up to a new and comprehensive understanding of Faulkner's aims in fiction.

the critic. The novel is indeed made up of successive and seemingly interlocking narratives, each one of which generates images of the Sutpen mystery more dreamed than real, as none of the narrators' visions rest on objective ground. Objectivity, of course, does not refer to an incontrovertible truth outside fiction—say historical truth. Keeping to the space of fiction, the only legitimate field of the literary critic, there hardly exists any foundation for each narrator's imaginary construction, except that construction itself; what is known of the Sutpen family really amounts to shaky certainties or inadmissible evidence: rumors, accounts biased or misunderstood by the narrators relaying them, a forlorn plantation and the gutted shell of a mansion, a letter "without date or salutation or signature" (129), rodent-scavengered tombstones with their faded and inaccurate lettering—vanishing traces all, bearing the marks of destruction, dust, and death: "It's just incredible. It just does not explain. Or perhaps that's it: they dont explain and we are not supposed to know. We have a few old mouth-to-mouth tales; we exhume from old trunks and boxes and drawers letters without salutation or signature, in which men and women who once lived and breathed are now merely initials or nicknames out of some now incomprehensible affection which sound to us like Sanskrit or Chocktaw" (100–1).

Not only must each narrator invent, or dream, the object of his narrative—so that the truth of the narrative finally rests in the fact that it is told, and that the creative act alone legitimates the truth of the creation—but, precisely because they are expressions of different sorts of consciousness, these narratives do not complement one another neatly, nor do they coincide; the result is neither a completed puzzle, nor an exact superimposition of images. Hence the tensions and ruptures, the breaks and blanks between the several narratives, which allow—or rather render necessary to the functioning of

The Gothicism of *Absalom, Absalom!*

fiction—the work of the reader's imagination. The reader has indeed his own version, or vision, of the Sutpen story; he partakes in the creative process. This is what Faulkner meant at the University of Virginia, answering a student who paraphrased Wallace Stevens in a question about the four narrators:

> Q. . . . does any one of the people who talks about Sutpen have the right view, or is it more or less a case of thirteen ways of looking at a blackbird with none of them right?
> A. That's it exactly. I think that no one individual can look at truth. It blinds you. You look at it and you see one phase of it. Someone else looks at it and sees a slightly awry phase of it. But taken all together, the truth is in what they saw though nobody saw the truth intact. . . . It was, as you say, thirteen ways of looking at a blackbird. But the truth, I would like to think, comes out, that when the reader has read all these thirteen different ways of looking at the blackbird, the reader has his own fourteenth image of that blackbird which I would like to think is the truth.[4]

Even though Quentin Compson comes closer to the truth (he is indeed the only one to *see* it, in the joint vision he has, together with Shreve, of the confrontation between Sutpen and his son Henry on the battlefield in Carolina), his view does not invalidate those of Rosa Coldfield or Mr. Compson, who respectively propose a Gothic and what could be called a Greco-romantic view of the Sutpen story.[5] All of these visions are valid, and necessary to an overall view of the truth about Sutpen—not a fourteenth, autonomous vision, but one comprehending and evaluating those of the narrators. So *Ab-*

4. *Faulkner in the University: Class Conferences at the University of Virginia, 1957–1958*, ed. Frederick L. Gwynn and Joseph L. Blotner (Charlottesville: University of Virginia Press, 1959), 273–274. Further references will be given after the quotations, with the abbreviation *FU*.

5. See the clear, but somewhat simplistic article of Lynn Gartrell Levins, "The Four Narrative Perspectives in *Absalom, Absalom!*," *PMLA*, 85 (January, 1970), 35–47. In *Faulkner's Heroic Design: The Yoknapatawpha Novels* (Athens: University of Georgia Press, 1976), Levins develops, but does not substantially alter, her view of this novel.

salom, Absalom! is not a perfected text, self-sufficient in its completion, but a magnificently *imperfect* novel.

A dream novel then it is, for the reader, for the readers-in-the-fiction (the narrators), and for the critic, too, who could indeed dream of few, if any, other novels in which the distinction between the three aspects of fiction, story, narration, and narrative, would be more clearly written into the text itself, since the act producing the narrative is itself fictionalized.[6] These concepts can prove remarkably operative in helping define, at the three different levels, the nature and specificity of the Gothic in *Absalom, Absalom!*, and finally the sense of the Gothic vision of Rosa Coldfield.

The word *story* refers to the content of the novel, its signifier, what is also called the diegesis—the diachronic view of the events that together make up the fall of the house of Sutpen. The story covers roughly one century of history, from the birth of the founder of the dynasty in 1808[7] to the fire which makes the house a gutted shell, around Christmas 1909—a fire in which Henry and Clytie disappear, leaving only the idiot Jim Bond as the living proof of that history—which disappearance in turn brings about the death of the last eye-witness, Rosa Coldfield.

The *narration* means the narrative act, the act producing the narrative which is itself the product, or, more broadly speaking, the narrative situation, remarkable for its being fictionalized, and set at a second remove, as the four narrators

6. I am indebted here to the remarkable and now standard study of Proust by Gérard Genette in *Figures III* (Paris: Editions du Seuil, 1972). This study has been translated recently: *Narrative Discourse: An Essay in Method* (Ithaca: Cornell University Press, 1979).

7. According to Shreve's surmise (220). It seems, however, that Sutpen "became confused about his age": "he told Grandfather that he did not know within a year on either side just how old he was" (227). The "Chronology" at the end of the book sets the date as 1807. In case of discrepancies, one should accept the authority of the fiction rather than the author's afterthoughts or working sheets. See Cleanth Brooks, *William Faulkner: The Yoknapatawpha Country* (New Haven: Yale University Press, 1963), 424–26.

are a secondary agency, in relation to a primary agency, the anonymous narrator—"Faulkner"—who initiates the narrative, before the narration-in-the-novel begins, or takes it up when there is a change of narrator, or a break in the storytelling.

The *narrative* is the signified, the narrative text, made up for the most part of the discourse of the narrators, whether actually spoken, or remembered, or heard as in a trance ("without listening")—a discourse at times taken up by the anonymous narrator himself, who then puts the secondary narrators in perspective: thus "Faulkner" is at the junction of the narration and the narrative.

That the Gothicism of *Absalom, Absalom!* is no mere decorative element, but a clue to the design and significance of the novel, appears in the fact that it can be seen working at each one of the three levels just defined, that is, not only at the surface level of the story, but more profoundly in the narration and in the narrative. Thus it touches on these three aspects of the novel, or faces of fiction.

THE STORY

The Gothic character of the story proper is not so evident as one might think at first, as the Gothicism of *Absalom, Absalom!* pertains most significantly to the telling of the story and to the viewpoint of the first narrator. The story of *The Sound and the Fury* is also one of destruction and death—the fall of the house of Compson; yet, for all the insistence on incest and death, it cannot be called Gothic. Moreover, in *Absalom, Absalom!*, the story has very little of the usual paraphernalia of the Gothic novel, almost an obbligato accompaniment of the genre. Here is, for instance, the description of the castle of Lindenberg in *The Monk*: "The castle, which stood full in my sight, formed an object equally awful and picturesque. Its ponderous walls, tinged by the moon with solemn brightness; its old and partly ruined towers, lifting themselves into the clouds, and seeming to frown on the plains around them; its lofty battlements, overgrown with ivy; and folding gates, expanding in honour of the visionary inhabitant [the Bleeding Nun], made me sensible of a sad and reverential horror."[8] No description of this sort makes its way into *Absalom, Absalom!*, as Faulkner does not resort to the trappings of Gothicism, but to its spirit: the house is hardly ever described because it is above all an active force, a sign, or rather an expression of evil. Admittedly, this can also be said of the somber castles or the walled-in, prison-like monasteries of Horace Walpole, Ann Radcliffe, or Matthew Lewis. But in *Absalom, Absalom!*, the darkness and the evil and the sense of doom are interiorized and so do not have to rest on physical evidence: they become an index to the rationalizations and phantasms of one of the narrators, Rosa Coldfield.

So what may best define the Gothicism of the story is the darkness—in the last analysis the essence of the genre.[9] The phenomenal success of the Gothic novel during the half century following the appearance of *The Castle of Otranto* in 1784 can be explained partly by its answering a need which classical or sentimental literature could not answer, the exploration of the dark side of consciousness and the power of the unconscious and sex, at a time when these were not quite legitimate or acceptable objects of fiction. (It is true that *The Memoirs of Fanny Hill* created a shock the same year *Clarissa* began conquering Europe; but the acknowledgement of underground emotions, the awareness of man's duality, even the fascination for obscenity, which can also be seen in Diderot's

8. Matthew G. Lewis, *The Monk* (New York: Grove Press, 1952), 165–66.
9. "The sentimental fable" reveals "the power of light and redemption," insists "that virtue . . . is triumphant," whereas "the gothic fable . . . is committed to portraying the power of darkness" (Fiedler, 108–9).

The Gothicism of *Absalom, Absalom!*

Bijoux indiscrets—also published the same year—and which would soon culminate in Sade, had not yet created a dominant mode in fiction: that would be the role of the Gothic novel.) However, even though Faulkner perfectly understood the significance and potentialities of the Gothic, he boldly transcended with *Absalom, Absalom!* what the genre had already achieved and which he had superbly put to use in *Sanctuary* and *Light in August*: he did not make it a means of exploring the consciousness in fiction (the reading of Conrad and Joyce had opened up new avenues) so much as a tool to question fiction itself.

In Faulkner's mind, the central metaphor of the novel may have been that of a "dark house," the original title when he started working on a new novel in February 1934: "I believe," he wrote to his publisher Harrison Smith, "that I have a head start on the novel. . . . [It] will be called DARK HOUSE or something of that nature. It is the more or less violent breakup of a household or family from 1860 to about 1910."[10] Such was also the former title of *Light in August*: the new title demonstrates the shift in emphasis from the Joe Christmas and Joanna Burden story of darkness and violence— which does smack of the Gothic—to the slightly comic character of Lena Grove walking in the tremulous August light, unconcerned by the power of darkness: she is indeed the alpha and the omega of the novel's structure.[11] Such a title could also apply to *Sanctuary*, another novel in which Faulkner chooses the Gothic mode: here again, the description of the "gutted ruin rising gaunt and stark out of a grove of unpruned cedar trees"[12] tells something of that Gothic strain of

10. *Selected Letters of William Faulkner*, ed. Joseph Blotner (New York: Random House, 1977), 78. On the several beginnings of the novel, see Joseph Blotner, *Faulkner: A Biography* (New York: Random House, 1974), 828–30.
11. See my study of the structure of the novel in *Faulkner's Light in August* (Bloomington: Indiana University Press, 1973).
12. *Sanctuary* (New York: Jonathan Cape & Harrison Smith, 1931), 6.

Faulkner's imagination. The irony of the title, however, is better suited to the doings and undoings of characters seeking spurious temples and illusory sanctuaries. But *A Dark House* would have been appropriate to *Absalom, Absalom!*: indeed, there is even a ghost in the place, "something living in it" (172).

It comes almost as a matter of course that in keeping with this focal image, most of the major scenes in the novel should be nocturnes, scenes occurring at night, or in the darkness of a shuttered house. The novel opens in Miss Coldfield's office, "a dim hot airless room with the blinds all closed and fastened for forty-three summers" (7), and of the three scenes narrated by her in Chapter I—the races to the church on Sunday mornings, Judith's fit when she realizes the racing has come to an end, and Sutpen's fight with his Negroes—the last two take place in the dark, the one in the "quiet darkened room with the blinds closed" (26), the other at night in the stable, in the center of "a hollow square of faces in the lantern light" (28).

Mr. Compson, too, seems to display a liking for dark scenes. In Chapter II, Sutpen's wedding—that is, the rehearsal and the ceremony itself—is a superb double nocturne, showing the confrontation between the town and Sutpen in "a sort of arena lighted by the smoking torches which the negroes held above their heads" (56). The same dark setting prevails in most of the striking scenes told by Mr. Compson: the library scene on Christmas Eve, the last waltzes at night before the Confederate company departs from Jefferson, later the visit of the octoroon to Bon's grave. The initiation of Henry by Bon into the mysteries of New Orleans is an initiation to the darkness of sex with dark women, the conclusion of this initiatory ritual being the introduction to the octoroon, "a woman created of by and for darkness" (193). The Harvardian part of the novel is framed by the midnight visit to Sutpen's Hundred: the ride in the darkness is told at the beginning of Chapter VI, but the remembering of the visit itself, the entering through the last door into the room of the "ghost"—a confrontation with death, or with nothingness—is delayed until the end of the novel, as the conversation with Henry does not establish or warrant the truth of Quentin's surmises, but confirms *a posteriori* what he has painfully discovered and came to acknowledge in his long journey into the night.

In that second part of the novel, one scene is of particular interest: the telling by Sutpen himself of the history of his design. It is told to Grandfather Compson, at night, by campfire and with lighted pine knots for torches, during a break in the hunting of the architect. The climax, retold by Quentin to Shreve, at a fourth remove from the original narrator, is the episode of the burning of the plantation in the Haitian night: "This anecdote was no deliberate continuation of the other one but was merely called to his mind by the picture of the niggers and torches in front of them" (246). This is a remarkable statement, at the meeting point of story and narration, a commentary on the functioning of fiction, showing how the selection of scenes in the story and the ordering of the narrative can be determined by the narration, or rather the narration-in-the-narration. So one is led to reconsider the nocturnality of the novel: it characterizes the story *because* it originates in the narration. The Gothicism of *Absalom, Absalom!* would then seem to belong to the production rather than to the product. By no means an accessory, one of the trappings of the traditional Gothic fiction, it is one of the "tools" (to use one of his favorite words) Faulkner has at his disposal to carry on his questioning on the production of fiction and the legitimacy of his undertaking—a reflection which is one of the forces at work in the novel. Thus the Gothicism of *Absalom, Absalom!* characterizes the fiction proper, but even more significantly, it also characterizes the metafiction.

THE NARRATION

The study of the Gothicism of the narration calls for a preliminary remark about the continuity in the time of the narration. Rosa Coldfield tells her part of the story to Quentin "from a little after two o'clock until almost sundown" (7). Then Mr. Compson takes up the narration at dusk, after supper, while the fireflies blow and drift "in soft random" over the lawn, "until it would be time for Quentin to start" for Sutpen's Hundred with the old lady (31)—when it is "dark enough to suit Miss Coldfield" (88). That "day of listening" ends with the trip to Sutpen's dark house in the heart of night, undoubtedly on both sides of midnight, because of the slow twelve-mile ride in the heat-laden September dust, which Quentin remembers so vividly (175–76).[13] As the joint narrative of Quentin and Shreve in the cold Harvard room also takes place in the heart of night, from before eleven o'clock to after one,[14] there is an obvious continuity in the narration, in spite of the four months' break, and even more importantly, a superimposition of the narration at Harvard in January and the story of the visit in September: such concomitance is rendered necessary by the final convergence narration/story, when Quentin identifies with Henry and thus becomes at last capable of (re)creating the truth. Yet, to be conscious and accepted, the identification requires distance—both in time

---

13. Out at Sutpen's Hundred, Miss Coldfield remarks to Quentin: "Maybe this far from town, out here alone at midnight . . . " (364).

14. See the numerous references to the ringing of the chimes: pp. 275, 293, 303, 325, 373, 374.

The Gothicism of *Absalom, Absalom!*

and space: hence the *sundered coincidence* of the narration and the story.

The time continuity stresses the similarity of the three places of narration, all dark, darkened, or darkening. Miss Coldfield's office is above all a dark place, like Mr. Compson's gallery in the twilight; like the two students' room at Harvard, it even seems "tomblike."[15] It is important here that daylight—any light from the outside—should be shuttered off. Thus "the dim coffin-smelling gloom" of Miss Coldfield's house becomes the appropriate locus for the apparition of the ghost ("man-horse-demon") conjured up by the old lady "out of quiet thunderclap" (8); it becomes the realm of imagination, creation, *poiesis*, just as the Harvard room at night turns into a "monastic coign," dedicated to "the best of thought" (258), where there is no need for any light, no reference to any "objective" reality: here, as in Miss Coldfield's office or on Mr. Compson's gallery, the only truth is the one told by the narrator. That is why the narrators must know next to nothing about the Sutpen family: as has already been remarked, all the "objective" facts on which their constructions rest are unreliable, evanescent, or obliterated. And is not the keystone of the whole narrative edifice a nocturnal confrontation with a *ghost*, climaxed by a circular, hollow conversation, telling nothing but its own void, revolving around the verb "to die" (373)? Truth here is founded on itself, originating as it does in the narration: in *Absalom, Absalom!*, rather than the story, *the narration is the event.*

In such dark or sepulchral places, the narrator—at least two of them—appears dead or ghost-like. Rosa Coldfield, outraged by Sutpen forty-three years before, tetanized in her rage and hatred, has been stopped in her growth, immobilized in a death-like trance, "sitting so bolt upright in the

15. See pp. 10, 299, 325, 336, 345, 346.

straight hard chair that was so tall for her that her legs hung straight and rigid as if she had iron shinbones and ankles, clear of the floor with that air of impotent and static rage like children's feet" (7). The qualifying adjectives all tell of her rigidity, motionlessness (for Faulkner, a synonym for death): "grim," "straight," "static," "impotent," "implacable," "rigid," "lifeless," "hard," "dead." Similarly, in his Harvard room, Quentin appears brooding, sullen, his face lowered, speaking in a "flat, curiously dead voice" (258).

This is why the narration brings forth only shadows, shades, ghosts, phantoms, or demons; it creates a narrative freed from any diurnal logic, unanchored in objective, countable reality—a nocturnal narrative which has the logic, or illogic, of a dream: "It (the talking, the telling) seemed (to him, to Quentin) to partake of that logic- and reason-flouting quality of a dream which the sleeper knows must have occurred, stillborn and complete, in a second, yet the very quality upon which it must depend to move the dreamer (verisimilitude) to credulity—horror or pleasure or amazement—depends as completely upon a formal recognition of and acceptance of elapsed and yet-elapsing time as music or a printed tale" (22). The paradox time/timelessness is just apparent: only in the awareness of the irreversibility of time and in the recognition that the creatures of the past are shades or ghosts can the narrative obtain its coherence and the imagination assert the autonomy of its creation which, occurring complete in one second, gives the illusion of transcending time into timelessness—every artist's yearning for the absolute, what Faulkner called his dream of perfection, to him exemplified by Keats's "Ode on a Grecian Urn." The characters in the story must be ghosts, so that the narrative may assert the triumph of the word, the transcendance of the imagined over the actual, or, to speak in Faulkner's words, of truth over reality—the pre-eminence of what Rosa Coldfield

211

calls the "might-have-been" (143). In this sense, every creator of fiction is, or should be, a Gothic writer.

Such pre-eminence of the word—of literature—is evinced in the structure of the second part of *Absalom, Absalom!*, in which the truth about the Sutpen mystery is perceived at last. The visit to Sutpen's Hundred is only a deceptive frame, no guarantee as to the truth of Quentin's vision. The real, and only appropriate, frame is Mr. Compson's letter: the whole narrative of Quentin and Shreve is wedged in the hiatus of the interrupted letter. The presence of the letter on the student's table is recalled several times, and all through the night Quentin stares at it, as in a trance: his brooding—his imaginative (re)creation—seems to originate in the letter, the medium of the narration:

> He sat quite still, facing the table, his hands lying on either side of the open text book on which the letter rested: the rectangle of paper folded across the middle and now open, three quarters open, whose bulk had raised half itself by the leverage of the old crease in weightless and paradoxical levitation, lying at such an angle that he could not possibly have read it, deciphered it, even without this added distortion. Yet he seemed to be looking at it, or as near as Shreve could tell, he was, his face lowered a little, brooding, almost sullen. (217–18)

That weightless and paradoxical levitation is the paradox of fiction, creating, in Faulkner's own words, "flesh-and-blood people that will stand up and cast a shadow" (*FU*, 47). The position of the letter framing the Shreve and Quentin narrative signifies that for the artist, say the fiction writer, the word is its own ultimate reference, that literature finds and founds in itself its own legitimacy. The enveloping presence of the letter is homage paid in the fiction to literature.

Thus, even more than it does the exploration of consciousness and of the significance of Southern history, the creation of shades and shadows in *Absalom, Absalom!* serves the artist's questionings on fiction—his epistemological quest.

Indeed, from the outset of the novel, the Gothic vision is a vision of the creative power. The demon Sutpen, in the last analysis, is a demiurge—a figure of the *poet*, a persona of the novelist. Admittedly, this is only one of several ways of looking at the blackbird, Rosa Coldfield's way, but it is also the first, thus creating a lasting impression, the foundation for the other ways, just as, in *The Sound and the Fury*, Benjy's narrative of the degradation and destruction of the Compson family offers a flattened panorama, outwardly devoid of any sense, to which the other narratives bring perspective and meaning. Yet, unwittingly, Benjy tells everything there is to tell about the lack of love in the family. Similarly, although Rosa Coldfield is often mistaken and does not understand the Sutpen mystery, her vision goes beyond the appearances to the essential truth about Sutpen.[16] True enough, she does take up some of the conventions of the genre, but to transform them, giving a new dimension to the Gothic vision, as can be seen in the use of the setting and the conception of the protagonist in her narrative.

A. The house

The privileged locus of the Gothic novel has always been the haunted, doomed castle, or some variant of it.[17] In Rosa Coldfield's narrative, Sutpen's house is not the baronial, castle-like mansion later described by Mr. Compson, but "the strong-

16. One of my aims here is clearly to rehabilitate what has often been dismissed or deprecated as a Gothic vision. Cleanth Brooks, however, has long since recognized that Rosa Coldfield is a true poet, not just "the county's poetess laureate" (11): Faulkner must have written her part—her score in that superb opera of voices—"con amore," Brooks says ("The Poetry of Miss Rosa Coldfield," *Shenandoah*, 21 [Spring, 1970], 199–206).

17. "Le château est au centre du roman comme l'araignée dans sa toile," as Jean Roudant writes aptly in a fine article on "Les demeures dans le roman noir," in *Critique*, 147–48 (August-September, 1959), 713–36, 717.

hold of an ogre or a djinn" (23). To be true, one can hardly visualize it through her words, because she refrains from any description of it. The particular quality of her evocation lies precisely in its absence of realism. With her, no space neatly circumscribed, no setting observed at close range contains an imagination thus set free to create, and be coextensive with, its own realm.

Her first memory of the house, at the age of four, goes back to her visit to Sutpen's Hundred on the day of Judith's fit. A remarkable text, not a Gothic description, but the description of a Gothic mind at work, it deserves to be quoted at length:

As soon as papa and I entered those gates that afternoon and began to go up the drive toward the house, I could feel it. It was as though somewhere in that Sunday afternoon's quiet and peace the screams of that child still existed, lingered, not as sound now but as something for the skin to hear, the hair on the head to hear. But I did not ask at once. I was just four then; I sat in the buggy beside papa . . . looking at the house. I had been inside it before too, of course, but even when I saw it for the first time that I could remember I seemed already to know how it was going to look just as I seemed to know how Ellen and Judith and Henry would look before I saw them for the time which I always remember as being the first. No, not asking even then, but just looking at that huge quiet house, saying, "What room is Judith sick in, papa?" with that quiet aptitude of a child for accepting the inexplicable. . . . Yes, a still hot quiet Sunday afternoon like this afternoon; I remember yet the utter quiet of that house when we went in and from which I knew at once that he was absent without knowing that he would now be in the scupper-nong arbor drinking with Wash Jones. I only knew, as soon as papa and I crossed the threshold, that he was not there: as though with some almost omniscient conviction, knowing that he did not need to stay and observe his triumph—and that, in comparison with what was to be, this one was a mere trivial business even beneath our notice too. Yes, that quiet darkened room with the blinds closed and a Negro woman sitting beside the bed with a fan and Judith's white face on the pillow beneath a camphor cloth, asleep as I supposed then; . . . and so I stood just outside the quiet door in the quiet upper hall because I was afraid to go away even from it, because I could hear the sabbath afternoon quiet of that house louder than thunder, louder than laughing even with triumph. (25–27)

Crossing the threshold, Rosa enters no physical space, but the true domain of her imagination. Oblivious to what is inessential, she immediately perceives "the living spirit, presence of that house" (27), what she will later call the voice of the house.[18] Using organic metaphors, she will even envision the house as the "suppuration" of Sutpen (138)—alive, exuding his evil presence, making it manifest. Thus, that there should be a ghost, "something living in it" (172), is in the logic of her vision and needs no explanation, no proof. Indeed, she *knows* what is inside even before crossing the threshold, and her certainty has no other foundation than itself: hence, the almost obsessive recurrence of the verb "to know," and the assertion of her "omniscient conviction."

So the house is doomed. When she enters it in 1865, it has not been ruined by the war, but marked by "*some desolation more profound than ruin*" (136). She sees it as a rotting shell because, like the house of Usher, it is the *expression* of evil: only fire is appropriate for the final, cleansing destruction. It is remarkable that Quentin should also see it as a "monstrous tinder-dry rotting shell" (375): when it burns down, it is made of wood, "melting clapboards" (376), not bricks. Like Rosa, Quentin does not care for reality (Antonin Artaud calls it "an excrement of the mind"), or verisimilitude, which has nothing to do with truth. His vision has its own logic, that of the imagination: like her, he is a *poet* of truth. No wonder the old lady chooses the young man for her confidant, summoning him "out of another world almost" (10): "Maybe you will enter the literary profession as so many Southern gentlemen and gentlewomen too are doing now and maybe some day you

18. "*the house itself speaking, though it was Judith's voice*" (142).

215

will remember this and write about it. You will be married then I expect and perhaps your wife will want a new gown or a new chair for the house and you can write this and submit it to the magazines" (9–10).

As in horror stories, or films, she neutralizes reason, acting directly on the senses: her apprehension of the house is sensory ("I could feel it"), and appeals to the synesthetic conjunction of two senses, hearing and touch, at once imprecise and impressionable: "something for the skin to hear, the hair on the head to hear." She suppresses every proof or justification; to her listener, as the mystery grows in inverse ratio to knowledge, *not to know* is frightening: so the house is quiet, too quiet (the word recurs nine times), and the little he knows is nothing in comparison with what *she* knows.

Such technique of suspending the information is no doubt one of the tricks of the trade. However, what makes it so revealing of the work of a Gothic mind is that it permeates even the style of the narrative, making it a superb instance of what could be called a Gothic rhetoric, as can be seen in the more frequent use of oxymorons in her speech than in any other narrator's (a way of letting in the irrational), and above all in her rhetoric of negation and accretion—her constant use of "even," her incremental repetitions, and the succession of negations heightening the expectancy and making the long-awaited affirmation almost a physical relief, even though temporary. Her rendering of Ellen running into the stable at night is a fine instance of that Gothic rhetoric:

> Ellen running down the hill from the house, bareheaded, in time to hear the sound, the screaming, hearing it while she still ran in the darkness and before the spectators knew that she was there, hearing it even before it occurred to one spectator to say "it's a horse" then "It's a woman" then "My God, It's a child"—ran in, and the spectators falling back to permit her to see Henry plunge out from among the negroes who had been holding him, screaming and vomiting—not pausing, not even looking at the faces

which shrank back away from her as she knelt in the stable filth
to raise Henry and not looking at Henry either but up at *him* as
he stood there with even his teeth showing beneath his beard
now and another negro wiping the blood from his body with a
towsack. (29–30)

The true dimension of the Gothic structure is not horizon-
tal, but vertical. Whereas the classical edifice is reasonable—
square, or round, with recognized limits: the work of clear
consciousness—the Gothic castle or cathedral lets in the irrational, plunges deep underground and surges up into the
sky, partakes of the earth and the air, of the dark powers of
the unconscious and sex, and creative imagination, of the id
and the superego. Admittedly, the American house does not
have—or has suppressed—those steps leading down to darkness, to the subterranean or the irrational part of the consciousness; yet the stable, where the "scum and riffraff" (28)
of Jefferson sneak in nightly, unseen from the house higher
up on the hill, where Ellen runs *down* at night, where mys-
terious horrors and unnameable rites are enacted, figures as
the profound part of the Sutpen house. The coherence of
Rosa Coldfield's narrative in Chapter I then becomes evident:
the surface life of the Sutpen house appears as the attenuated
expression of its profound life; the race to the church and Judith's fit find their significance in that last scene.

There is, however, a staircase in the house, as Rosa and
Quentin know too well. Instead of going down, Rosa goes *up*
into her consciousness, *"up a nightmare flight of steps"* (149),
to what she calls *"the full instant of comprehended terror"*
(137), as she knows that beyond the door at the end of the
upper hall lies the corpse of Charles Bon: opening it would
mean the death of dream and the overcoming of truth by reality. So the door must remain closed to fact—thus opened
onto the possibility of imagining truth: *"there is a might-have-
been which is more true than truth, from which the dreamer,*

217

The Gothicism of *Absalom, Absalom!*

waking, says not 'Did I but dream?' but rather says, indicts high heaven's very self with: 'Why did I wake since waking I shall never sleep again?'" (143). The structure of her narrative at this point expresses her poetics: it is precisely because she is stopped by Judith in front of the closed door that she can dream and (re)create the scene of her vicarious love for Charles Bon (143–49)—not so much a flashback as the projection of frustrated desires, creating the only true world that renders possible her surviving the outrage. She must not see, so she can dream. When at last she opens that door and sees the corpse-like Henry, she becomes comatose and dies.[19]

Whether dramatically or symbolically, the closed door has always been a favorite resort of the writers of Gothic fiction. But here again, Faulkner's use of the motif points at once to the Gothic tradition and to his reflection on fiction.[20] As has just been seen, the closed door determines the *narrative* of Rosa Coldfield, who has indeed spent her life beyond closed doors and thus been forced into a life of vicarious dreaming, "that aged and ancient and timeless absence of youth which consisted of a Cassandralike listening beyond closed doors" (60).

The motif also works at the level of the *narration*. At the end of Chapter V, Rosa is no longer heard because Quentin no longer listens to her: he is already committed to his own quest (hence the change from italic to roman). It is remark-

---

19. So Shreve is right in thinking that the perpetuation of the sense of outrage in Rosa precludes the death of the object of her rage: "hating is like drink or drugs and she had used it so long that she did not dare risk cutting off the supply, destroying the source, the very poppy's root and seed" (373–74). This explains why she refused to accept Sutpen's death: "'*Dead? You? You lie; you're not dead; heaven cannot, and hell dare not, have you!*'" (172). It is significant that this outcry ends her narrative in Chapter V, and is followed immediately by her revelation of the existence of the "ghost": indeed, she dares not cut off the supply.

20. John B. Rosenman's article, "A Matter of Choice: The Locked Door Theme in Faulkner," *South Atlantic Bulletin*, 41 (May, 1976), 8–12, is little more than a catalogue of instances culled from some of Faulkner's works, to show the treatment of poor whites in Southern society.

218

able that he should at this point find himself stopped by a closed door:

> Quentin was not listening, because there was also something which he too could not pass—that door . . . : the two of them, brother and sister, . . . speaking to one another in short brief staccato sentences like slaps. . . .
>> *Now you cant marry him.*
>> *Why cant I marry him?*
>> *Because he's dead.*
>> *Dead?*
>> *Yes, I killed him.* (172)

What Quentin cannot yet understand in the Sutpen mystery boils down precisely to the reason for this confrontation between the brother and the sister separated by the unfinished wedding dress—a scene purely "fictitious" (as Quentin himself should know after having heard Miss Coldfield), a scene at once true and screening the truth. That closed door becomes the metaphorical threshold of his narration, just before the Harvardian section of the novel, in which Quentin and Shreve will try to understand the Sutpen mystery and finally visualize the truth in another confrontation scene, between the father and the son, at the end of Chapter VIII.[21] But at this point in the narration, the door is closed to proof, verification (indeed there can and must be none), so as to be opened to the possibility of comprehending the truth—to the *intelligence* of the Sutpen story.

Faulkner's perfect control of his metaphors is evinced in that he also uses the closed door motif in the *story* itself. Sutpen's design originates in that axial scene of the novel, where a Negro slave prevents the young Sutpen from entering the front door of the planter's mansion. (In the sequence of the

21. The closed door image is aptly recalled just at the beginning of Chapter VI: "he had not been listening, since he had something which he still was unable to pass: that door, that gaunt tragic dramatic self-hypnotized youthful face like the tragedian in a college play, . . . the sister facing him across the wedding dress which she was not to use . . ." (174).

219

novel, this scene comes *after* the closed door motif has been used in the narrative and the narration: possibly an index as to their preeminence in *Absalom, Absalom!*) Then, in the closed door and the "balloon face" of the "nigger," the boy suddenly sees himself as in a mirror, and conceives of such a design as will never put him again in a position where a door can be closed to his face (234–38). But instead of dreaming the "might-have-been," like Rosa, he tries to *realize* in his design what he cannot see beyond the closed door. The actual and the ideal are not on a par: it is precisely Sutpen's "innocence" to believe in the interchangeability of the two realms. Such "innocence" is emphasized throughout the novel by the ironical reenactment in Sutpen's life of what he had precisely tried to render the repetition impossible: he lets his son Henry shut the library door forever, symbolically shuts his door on his other son by refusing to acknowledge him, and repeats with Wash Jones the exact scene which started his design: Clytie bars him even from the kitchen door. Far from subverting the established order, Sutpen's design is indeed radically conservative.

B. Sutpen, the Gothic protagonist

Devil, demon, or fiend, Sutpen is, in Rosa's eyes, doomed from the beginning, not only selected by Satan, like the monk Ambrosio, but the Prince of Darkness himself, "the evil's source and head" (18). Intruding upon Jefferson on a Sunday morning, he seems to Rosa's listener enclosed by an "effluvium of hell" (13), with "sulphur-reek still in hair clothes and beard" (8). Using the "mythical method" which T. S. Eliot recognized in *Ulysses* as a sign of modernity in fiction, she views Sutpen as Hades taking Ellen-Persephone into his private hell, allowing her to return occasionally, "through a dispensation of one day only, to the world which she had quitted" (23), or as an incubus, begetting his demon children on Ellen-Niobe "in a kind of nightmare" (13). A demon, he is ubiquitous, present in the form of his two children, who have to be protected from themselves, or in his wild, tiger-like slaves. That is why he does not even have to be present at the Sunday morning races: he triumphs *in absentia*: "his face had been in that carriage all the time" (25).

The realm created by Rosa can thus appropriately be called a magic or a fantastic domain, one in which the spatial distinction interior/exterior no longer obtains, where the whole is completely present in any of its minutest parts. Different from the geometrical world of actualities, the fantastic world is ridden with causality, working any and every way: the very definition of fatality. In Rosa's view, Sutpen is indeed an outrage to reason, the irruption of the irrational into the rational: that is why she cannot resist his power.[22]

In Chapter V, however, it appears that Rosa Coldfield experiences a reversal of viewpoint: Sutpen the ogre belongs to her childhood, "*no ogre, because it was dead, vanished, consumed somewhere in flame and sulphur-reek perhaps among the lonely craggy peaks of my childhood's solitary remembering*" (167). The Beast (with hair, teeth, fur, attended by tiger niggers) has become the charming Prince—no longer an object of terror, but of desire: "*the incorrigible flesh*" then betrays her into a "*sewer-gush of dreaming*" (163), as is expressed in the numerous sexual images which crop up in her narrative, particularly in her evocation of Charles Bon, to the point that her imagination becomes completely (bi)sexualized:

---

22. Hence the obsessive recurrence in her narrative of such words as: "destined," "doomed," "curse," "fatality," "helpless," and the structure of the plea by which she initiates her narrative proper, beginning negatively: "I hold no brief for myself," "I don't plead," because the fatal conclusion is foreordained: "Yet I agreed to marry him."

The Gothicism of *Absalom, Absalom!*

"*I became all polymath love's androgynous advocate*" (146).[23] At the time of the awakening of her senses and of her sexual frustrations, "*the miscast summer of* [her] *barren youth*" (144), her desire reveals itself as the obverse side of the terrors of her childhood in which she seems to have repressed her fascination for Sutpen (indeed, her narrative in Chapter I is an *a posteriori* rationalization of the outrage forty-three years before). This relationship terror/desire thus appears not unlike the one Freud saw between the uncanny and the familiar: "the unheimlich is what was once heimish, home-like, familiar; the prefix 'un' is the token of repression."[24]

Acknowledging that her creation—Sutpen—can be the projection not only of terror but also of desire, Rosa becomes aware of the creative power of the imagination.[25] She then becomes capable of recognizing that quality in Sutpen: he, too, is a creator, a demiurge, "creating the Sutpen's Hundred, the *Be Sutpen's Hundred* like the oldentime *Be Light*" (9); then, after the war, setting to himself "the Herculean task" (157) of restoring his plantation to its original, immutable condition; by stopping or freezing time, his aim is no less than to make himself into a God. Dramatically, such *hubris* must be punished and Sutpen is cut down by a too symbolical scythe. But poetically, it is recognized as a desire for eternity—the aim of the creator, i.e., the poet—a design which Faulkner

23. She conceives of sex as an indefinite and indefinitely delayed "polymath" orgasm, "*one anonymous climaxless epicene and unravished nuptial*" (145).
24. Sigmund Freud, "The Uncanny," in *On Creativity and the Unconscious: Papers on the Psychology of Art, Literature, Love, Religion*, ed. Benjamin Nelson (New York: Harper & Row, 1958), 122–61, 153. Cf. "The uncanny proceeds from something familiar which has been repressed" (155).
25. As appears in this striking remark: "*I know this: if I were God I would invent . . . something . . . which would adorn the barren mirror altars of every plain girl who breathes with such as this . . . pictured face. It would not even need a skull behind it; almost anonymous, it would only need vague inference of some walking flesh and blood desired by someone else even if only in some shadow-realm of make-believe*" (147).

saw forever represented in Keats's urn,[26] and which, as Rosa knows, partakes at once of madness and divinity: "*I . . . did believe there was that spark, that crumb in madness which is divine*" (167). That she speaks of "*the white glare of* [Sutpen's] *madness*" (166) may be on Faulkner's part a wink to Melville, who, together with Keats, has always remained one of his acknowledged masters.[27]

Rosa Coldfield's view of Sutpen as a poet is confirmed by one of her strangest—but most appropriate—images: "*a madman who creates within his very coffin walls his fabulous immeasurable Camelots and Carcassonnes*" (160). Those fabulous cities are Faulkner's private metaphors for the realm of the imagination, the domain which the poet has elected to inhabit and of which he asserts himself as the "sole owner and proprietor." More than twenty years later, in Virginia, Faulkner would resort to the same metaphor when trying to account for the Southern renaissance: "I myself am inclined to think it was because of the bareness of the Southerner's life, that he had to resort to his own imagination, to create his own Carcassonne" (*FU*, 136), which of course sends the Faulknerian back to "Carcassonne," a strange short story, rather a prose poem, dating back to 1926, or even 1925,[28] in which the poet protagonist transcends his mortal being, "his very coffin walls," into the immortal realm of the imagination: "*me on a buckskin pony with eyes like blue electricity and a mane like tangled fire, galloping up the hill and right off into the high*

26. On the image of the poet in Faulkner's work and on "Carcassonne," discussed below, see my article, "Faulkner poète," in *Etudes Anglaises*, 39 (July-Sept., 1976), 456–67. Cf. Faulkner's statement in Virginia: "It's one single urn or shape that you want to do" (*FU*, 65).

27. See Michael Millgate's brief but excellent article, "Faulkner's Masters," *Tulane Studies in English*, 23 (1978), 142–55.

28. Blotner suggests 1926, but is not too sure about the date (*Biography*, 502). I would prefer 1925, as the time when Faulkner probably came to acknowledge that he was "a failed poet" and set himself to writing fiction for good (though he went on writing poetry for years).

heaven of the world."[29] Significantly placed at the end of *These Thirteen*, then again at the end of *Collected Stories*, this text represents in Faulkner's fiction the signature of the poet.[30] The reference to Carcassonne by Rosa Coldfield signifies that, a bad poet herself, the local rhymester, she can however recognize in Sutpen the true poet.

Rosa Coldfield, it is true, is mistaken; she does not know who Bon is, why the marriage was forbidden "without rhyme or reason or shadow of excuse" (18), why Henry killed Bon. But beyond the outward appearance, she sees into the profounder significance of Sutpen, which is confirmed at the outset of the novel, by the first tableau of the Sutpen family which Quentin envisions as he listens to Miss Rosa. The scene, "peaceful and decorous as a schoolprize water color" (8), with Sutpen in the center of a formal group, before the "band of wild niggers like beasts half tamed to walk upright" and the manacled French architect, is "historically" inaccurate, as appears from Mr. Compson's narrative. Yet, beyond surface inaccuracies, it is true, aptly expressing the interplay of forces in Sutpen's story. In spite, or rather *because*, of its Gothicism, Rosa Coldfield's vision is profoundly true: avoiding ponderous pronouncements on madness and creation, her narrative asks fundamental questions fictionally, by subverting and transforming one important mode of American fiction, the Gothic. Hence its position in the novel: it initiates the inquiry into Sutpen's story, frames the narrative of Mr. Compson, and leads Quentin to an intelligence of the mystery which, too close a witness, petrified by her impotent rage, lacking in sympathy and love, she must remain unable to achieve.

29. *Collected Stories* (New York: Random House, 1950), 895.
30. Faulkner said of the story in Virginia: "that's a piece that I've always liked because there was the poet again" (*FU*, 22).

It may be that Rosa Coldfield does not *really* think that
Sutpen is a demon, but she must believe it, and tell it, if she
is to survive what would otherwise be the collapse of her
whole tetanized life. As Shreve knows, she dares not take
such a risk. To justify her outrage and terror, she has to con-
jure up irrational creatures which uphold her own rationality
(to the irrational mind, nothing can be fantastic): the irrational
characters in her narrative are not the expressions of reason
disproved, but of reason outraged. By making herself adhere
to her Gothic view and by recounting it, she makes into autonomous beings what might have been only figures of
speech. She substitutes the proper sense for the figurative,
which may well be the very definition of the fantastic.[31] Admittedly, the reader never forgets that she is one of the narrators in the narration and that her vision is at a second remove (unlike *The Turn of the Screw*, where the narrative
frame dissolves away and allows for that hesitation between
the rational and the fantastic). But as her language, distinctly
that of the Gothic fiction, places her within a recognizable
literary tradition, her narrative carries the reader's aesthetic
adhesion—which frees the Gothic vision to become an instru-
ment to question fiction itself.

So the Gothicism of Faulkner in *Absalom, Absalom!* is not
the object of his writing, but the means of questioning the
legitimacy of his undertaking, the creation of fiction: at once
a tool to explore all the aspects of fiction, and the tightly controlled central metaphor of his first narrator's vision, which
probes into the significance of the creative act—an act giving
expression to the irrational in the writer's consciousness, and

31. See the excellent article on the art of terror by Louis Vax, "L'art de faire
peur," *Critique*, 110–11 (Nov. & Dec., 1959), 915–42 and 1226–48. See also his
book, *La Séduction de l'étrange. Etude sur la littérature fantastique* (Paris: Presses
Universitaires de France, 1965).

implying a recognition of the relation of the creative imagination to madness and divinity. That is why the ghosts here
are not a reality in the space of fiction (as they can be in
Lewis), but a metaphor—which does not mean that they do
not exist and that the writer should not acknowledge their
presence in himself.

Blacks in Motion

CHARLES H. NILON

There are two kinds of black movement in Faulkner's fiction. There is the movement of individual characters who live their lives from moment to moment or day to day, and there is the overall movement which is the product of the general meaning of the movement of those individual lives—the product which permits Faulkner to say, when speaking of them, they survived. The second kind of movement provides an image of the black man; he is a pilgrim going to cross Jordan. "Going to cross Jordan" is a phrase that is said repeatedly by the newly freed black persons in *The Unvanquished* which expresses their longing for freedom, their purpose, and the meaning and central effort of their lives. This phrase includes not only an overall impression of the sum of the quality and effort of Faulkner's black characters, but is equally descriptive of individual characters or of the first kind of movement.

The two kinds of movement are effectively controlled by narrators, or the omniscient author, whose presentation of black movement forms pictures that define the black journey as "going to cross Jordan," and they are illustrated below in the discussion of "Centaur in Brass" and "Pantaloon in Black" and in the discussion of episodes from other Faulkner stories and novels. Before these are discussed something must be said about the black journey, the narrators' relationships to the narratives and how their presentation of black movement results in pictures that illuminate the crossing Jordan figure.

Symbolically going to cross Jordan means becoming persons and being free to confront freedom—whether it can be endured or not. Faulkner may have taken the phrase from the spiritual that contains the lines: "River of Jordan is chilly and wide, Going to cross over to the other side." Going to cross Jordan is a journey, a metaphor for the journey of black life—a kind of pilgrim's progress—whose daily trials and whose rigor are only suggested in the confused and violent movement of the scene at the river where the black people in *The Unvanquished* see the bridge destroyed that they would have used to cross to the other side and break the link with their past. The phrase is also a metaphor for the intention or the purpose of the movement of individual characters in Faulkner's fiction.

The journeys that his black characters make are sometimes quests and pilgrimages that they have initiated. Frequently the pattern of quest or pilgrimage is changed to a pattern of escape and pursuit. Rider in "Pantaloon in Black" wants a good life and has begun to move in the pattern of that life, but the pattern changes; his movements change, and he is pursued and killed. Tom-Tom and Turl, characters in "Centaur in Brass," find themselves caught in a movement that is designed by Flem Snopes, diverted from the patterns of their choice, and forced for a time to move in opposition to each other until they are able to join forces and move against Flem Snopes. Sometimes the journey is quiet and the movement of a character is less dramatic and violent than that of Rider and Tom-Tom and Turl, but in the quieter life a character's values and his need to control his life by living it on his own terms are still revealed in his movement as he does ordinary things. This quiet life and movement are illustrated in the life of Emily Grierson's old black servant who is seen going in and out of her house with a market basket. After Miss Emily's death, he "met the first of the ladies at the front door and let them in." Then, "he walked right through the house and out the back and was not seen again."[1] Whether a character remains relatively in control of his movement and free to make his own quest or whether he is pursued and killed as Will Mayes is in "Dry September" is perhaps not significant. It is the movement during the journey, completed or interrupted, that is.

Through his movement the black character discovers the power to give his life meaning, frequently to give doomed lives meaning as Rider and Joe Christmas do. Richard Chase says that Joe Christmas gains the power to do this by "insisting as long as he can on his right to be human." This movement, he says, "outbalances his [Joe Christmas's] being a murderer."[2] Movement demonstrates the insistence of Faulkner's black characters on their right to be human even when their movement, as is true in the encounter between Caspey and Old Bayard Sartoris, does not meet the approval of the narrator or of the white participants in the scene. Crossing Jordan is a quest for identity and what Robert Penn Warren calls "a demonstration of the human will to affirm itself."[3] Loosh more than hints at this when he announces that he is leaving John Sartoris's service. He says, "'I going. I done been freed; God's own angel proclamated me free and gonter general me to Jordan. I don't belong to John Sartoris now; I belongs to me and God.'"[4]

Each of the individual characters seen in motion makes clearer the content of the metaphor that Loosh alludes to

1. William Faulkner, "A Rose for Emily," in *Collected Stories of William Faulkner* (New York: Random House, 1950), 129.
2. Richard Chase, *The American Novel and Its Tradition* (Garden City, N.Y.: Doubleday Anchor Books, 1957), 213.
3. Robert Penn Warren, "Faulkner: The South, the Negro, and Time," in *Faulkner: A Collection of Critical Essays* (New York: Prentice-Hall, 1966), 263.
4. William Faulkner, *The Unvanquished* (New York: Vintage Books, 1966), 85.

through the picture-making, or breaking, that results from movement. Frequently the pictures that are made contradict pictures of black people that exist in the popular mind. This is picture breaking. In a section of Thomas Jefferson's *Notes on Virginia*, after careful observation of his slaves and perhaps of other black people, Jefferson concludes that they are amorous, but he doubts that they are capable of love.[5] The image of the amorous black person was probably already a popular image before Jefferson mentioned it and is still alive. Some of the pictures produced through black movement in Faulkner's fiction contradict the opinion that blacks are incapable of love. Lucas Beauchamp's movement produces pictures that convince the reader that he loved Molly. Rider loved Mannie, and his love for her is proved through his movement. Offering evidence that stereotypes are not true is picture-breaking. Picture-breaking, changing images, also occurs when the cause for the stereotype is revealed. Turl's behavior in "Centaur in Brass" is amorous, and he fits the stereotype elegantly. Through the movement in "Centaur in Brass," through the pictures produced by the movement, Turl and the reader understand why he behaves as he does.

The showing and interpreting of black movement in Faulkner's fiction are the responsibility of his narrators whose presentation of movement results in pictures. The black effort to cross Jordan is observed and interpreted most frequently by white male narrators—in several instances by white adolescents like young Bayard Sartoris, Charles Mallison, and Quentin Compson—who differ in their attitudes and behavior toward black people, but who share in common the traditions of the South, know how black people came to be there, know the conventions that have developed as a result of their presence and the treatment that they have received. Some of

5. Thomas Jefferson, *Notes on the State of Virginia* (New York: Harper, Row, 1964), 132–36.

them know, as Robert Penn Warren says, that "the 'nigger' is a creation of the white man," a social creation, possibly the inevitable result of an enforced set of social assumptions and an enforced etiquette that govern the behavior of the creation and its creators.[6] Some narrators know that the etiquette masks the reality of black persons.

John Sartoris's son Bayard, who is the narrator in *The Unvanquished*, knows these things and in that novel, which is in part the story of his initiation into adulthood, they provide a context for his presentation of black movement. The tensions that they create in him contribute to the meanings of the pictures that are produced as a result of the movement of black characters in the novel. Ringo, the son of two of his father's slaves, and he have been reared together, and they compete, and share their experiences. Bayard knows that Ringo, at least until the emancipation, was his father's property. He knows the concept of nigger and how that concept is enforced. Often he watches Ringo and thinks of what he is while he listens to what he says. He knows that Louvenia, Ringo's grandmother, is a nigger but that culturally and in terms of her loyalties, she is a white person who rejects her grandson Loosh's desire to be free. Bayard knows that his movement is different from Ringo's because Ringo is a nigger. He knows also that his father, who is away fighting in the war to keep Ringo a slave, respects Uncle Buck and Uncle Buddy Mac-Caslin whose attitudes toward race and slavery are unconventional. Bayard says, "Father said they were ahead of their time; he said they not only possessed, but put into practice, ideas about social relationships that maybe fifty years after they both were dead people would have a name for."[7] Bayard knew the commonly accepted mythology about black people, the complex of ideas and images, which summarized politely

6. Robert Penn Warren, "Faulkner: The South, the Negro, and Time," 259.
7. William Faulkner, *The Unvanquished*, 54.

231

mean they are different from us. The deputy sheriff in "Pantaloon in Black" summarizes the mythology less politely when he says, "They ain't human." Bayard, in spite of his closeness to Ringo—or perhaps because of the closeness—accepts some of the mythology.

Evidence of this acceptance is given on an occasion when Bayard and Ringo have been told something by Loosh that they do not know and do not wish to believe. Bayard responds to Loosh, but after his response he thinks, "But I was just talking too, I knew that, because niggers know, they know things; it would have to be something louder, much louder, than words to do any good."[8] Bayard thinks of Ringo as having this "nigger" capacity for knowing and of his being "nigger" in other ways, although he knows that Ringo is intellectually competent and does some things better than he can do them. The tension that is the result of the conflict produced by the simultaneous demands of his intelligence, his knowledge, and his feelings results in a series of pictures, photographs of black movement, and in his initiation into adulthood and the role that he must play as a particular man in a particular place.

Although Faulkner's narrators vary in the quality of their individual humanity, as Bayard and the deputy sheriff in "Pantaloon" do, they have in common an awareness of their region's history and customs, intelligence, and feelings. A narrator's presentation and interpretation of black motion are dependent upon these commonly held things and upon individual differences. The narrator's intelligence, his factual knowledge, and his feelings (which are frequently in conflict) are brought into play as he interprets black movement. His assessment of black motion that is rendered pictorially is determined when he considers who and what black people are

8. *Ibid.*, 7.

and by how he resolves mental conflicts which are caused by the differences between his knowledge and his feelings. Through the interaction of these the reader learns, not only the details of the black effort to cross Jordan, but the effect of that effort on the white narrator or observer as well. The effect upon a participant-observer, for example, is seen in "Dry September" in the behavior of McLendon, who has been a principal actor in the lynching of Will Mayes and has observed Mayes's movements, most of which the reader has not seen. When McLendon went home late in the evening he "half struck, half flung" his wife across a chair when she expressed concern about him, and he is seen at the end of the story naked, sweating and panting "with his body pressed against the dusty screen."[9] McLendon does not say how Will Mayes's movements affected him, but his behavior or the picture of his hot naked body sweating in the moonlight shows the effect. His abuse of his wife suggests that his participation in Will Mayes's death was not done to protect white womanhood. He may not know why he helped to destroy him, but his nakedness suggests that the rationalizations that he has used in the past to justify his behavior toward black people will no longer satisfy him.

Faulkner's narrators present the details of the movement of black characters in such a way that pictures are formed. When a narrator interacts with a black character, or observes or causes that character to act, the character's movement which the narrator controls forms pictures. The pictures may show that the movement (the behavior) of the black character is different from the images and concepts of behavior that are stored in the narrator's mind. When the movement does not approximate the narrator's expectations, he may seek to account for what he finds surprising or distasteful in it. When

9. William Faulkner, "Dry September," in *Collected Stories*, 182–83.

this occurs, it is evidence that the narrator's intelligence, his knowledge, and those things that make him what he is may be in conflict with his feelings. Resolution of that conflict may result in his beginning to question or to change his opinions or he may resolve it by finding a rationalization that is sufficiently satisfying to allow him to go on believing as experience has trained him to. He may of course not be affected by the movement of the character. Whether the narrator understands or fails to understand the movement, whether his response to it shows that he recognizes error in his own thinking or not, the reader is made aware of what Faulkner wants to show of, in, or through it.

It is true that the reader of Faulkner's fiction becomes aware of the significance of black movement through the effect of his use of many narrative devices. Perhaps the most important device for this purpose is the complex process of making pictures through which he says more perhaps than is said in his expository prose or dialogue. Frequently expository statements about black people are made much clearer through picture sequences that precede or follow them. For example, the understanding of Quentin Compson's statement in *The Sound and the Fury*—"a nigger is not a person so much as a form of behaviour; a sort of obverse reflection of the white people he lives among"[10]—is probably given a clearer meaning by a picture that has remained in Quentin's mind that appears later in the text. This picture is the product of black motion. Its subject behaves in a particular way because of the people around him and by what they expect him to do. The picture is of an old black man who stands beside a railroad crossing with his mule at Christmas time and asks white persons who pass for gifts. Quentin remembers the last

10. William Faulkner, *The Sound and the Fury* (New York: Vintage Books, 1946), 105.

234

time he saw him: "the train began to move. I leaned out the window, into the cold air, looking back. He stood there beside the gaunt rabbit of a mule, the two of them shabby and motionless and unimpatient. The train swung around the curve, the engine puffing with short, heavy blasts, and they passed smoothly from sight that way, with that quality about them of timeless patience, of static serenity."[11] Through the movement that is held in it, the picture makes Quentin's definition of nigger clearer. When the movement of black characters is delineated in pictures, it embodies and gives concreteness and vital range to ideas.

The pictures that are formed in an episode may be single or in sequence. Pictures that are formed in a sequence may appear one after another, without a considerable lapse of time, or they may be fragmented or interrupted by blocks of dialogue or exposition that take the reader's attention away from the movement from time to time. These interruptions arrest motion and frame the pictures within a sequence. The arrangement of the details that make a picture is often accumulative, and a sequence which begins with a single figure or two figures, as the sequence progresses, may become a montage or collage in which several pictures are fused. The interrupted series of pictures of the former slaves in *The Unvanquished* ends at the river and shows the confusion and desperate pathos of the slaves who have reached this crucial point in their journey and who see the bridge they wish to cross destroyed. Many of them plunge into the river and try to swim across or to cling to the wagons and buggies and horses that are already in the water. The narrator and his family are in the river in the center of this scene and their wagon is separated from their horses. The motives of the people who wish to cross the river are varied and to an extent

11. *Ibid.*, 106.

they are competing one against the other. The animals and the people are out of control, and animal terror and human terror are seen beside each other. Image is built on image. The movements of the people and the animals and the vehicles are conflicting: one general effect is of montage. Essentially the scene at the river is violent, a context in which the problems of the former slaves are shown, through the details of the pictures, to be inextricably mixed with those of former masters, soldiers, and others.

Blocks of dialogue or exposition frame or separate pictures, segmenting and unifying the movement in a particular episode. For example, in "Shall Not Perish," the black servant is seen, and his movement is presented in pictures by the boy who is the narrator. The boy and his mother are country people who lost a brother and son in the Second World War and come to Jefferson to share Major de Spain's grief when his son is killed in that war. They are dressed in their Sunday clothes and their shoes are shined for the occasion. The boy's response to the movement of Major de Spain's black servant frames the picture of the servant's movement. The framed passage reads, "And then it never mattered whether our shoes were shined at all or not: the whites of the monkey nigger's eyes for just a second when he opened the door for us, the white of his coat for just a second at the end of the hall before it was gone too, his feet not making any more noise than a cat's leaving us to find the right door by ourselves, if we could. And we did."[12] The servant's movement in space is ordered pictorially. His eyes, his uniform, and the quietness of his motion are presented and emphasized. He is described impressionistically in minstrel terms—a monkey nigger—and his movement is presented in the fixed space of a hallway. A picture is made and framed by the statements "And then it

12. William Faulkner, "Shall Not Perish," in *Collected Stories*, 106.

never mattered whether our shoes were shined at all or not," and "And we did."

Faulkner says in the 1956 *Paris Review* interview with Jean Stein that "life is motion" and that "the aim of every artist is to arrest motion, which is life, by artificial means and hold it fixed" so that it can be examined.[13] In the pictures of black movement, motion is sometimes arrested by the contrast of motion and stasis. Sometimes it is arrested by putting it in a fixed dance-like pattern such as that which is evident in section two of "Pantaloon in Black" and the centaur episode in "Centaur in Brass" that ends with Tom-Tom and Turl sitting on the bed of the ditch talking. The contrast of black motion and stasis is illustrated in the picture in *Intruder in the Dust* that the narrator Charles Mallison and his uncle, Gavin Stevens, observe as they drive to the site of the Gowrie grave. From the moving car they see a black man, a plow, and a mule framed in a landscape of sky, trees, and plowed ground, fixed in space. The man is plowing and is in motion; but from the faster moving car, he appears to be stopped in space and time and to be given a semblance of the kind of endurance that Faulkner gains through the use of Keats's urn in other stories.

Arrested motion is sometimes achieved through Faulkner's use of words such as motionless, immobile, soundless, and substanceless. Sometimes obstacles stop motion. Clytie stops Rosa Coldfield on the stair by touching her—black flesh touching white flesh. The dry ditch bed stops Tom-Tom and Turl's fall. The pictures of the man, the plow, and the mule; of Tom-Tom and Turl seated on the dry ditch bottom; and of Clytie compress lives into single moments and hold them fixed, so that they may be examined.

13. James B. Meriwether and Michael Millgate (eds.), *Lion in the Garden: Interviews with William Faulkner, 1926–1962* (Lincoln and London: University of Nebraska Press, 1980), 253.

Blacks in Motion

One of the images of the black man is of him running. Often this is a comic image. When obstacles interrupt a running black man as Tomey's Turl is interrupted in "Was," a feeling of force and speed is built and testimony of the individual's strength is given in the picturing of the arrested motion. Tomey's Turl has so much force and speed that running into Uncle Buck does not stop him. "He never even bobbled; he knocked Uncle Buck down and then caught him before he fell without even stopping, snatched him up under one arm, still running, and carried him along for about ten feet, saying, 'Look out of here, old Buck. Look out of here, old Buck,' before he threw him away and went on."[14] Tomey's Turl's running is at best only interrupted, but the expectation of stasis when he runs over Uncle Buck is sufficient to fix the moment, to give the content of the picture clarity and meaning.

Perspective is also gained by incongruity in this picture, as it is in many of Faulkner's pictures of arrested black motion. Tomey's Turl is Uncle Buck's slave, his half brother, and his nephew. It is not proper for a slave to treat his master as he does Uncle Buck. It is equally incongruous that Miss Emily Grierson should live alone in her house attended by a black man servant who when he is last seen leaving her house is making a gesture perhaps to protect her reputation. The comparisons of blacks and mules are incongruous as is the comparison of a black head to a cannon ball.

Pictures of blacks in motion often present and interpret the mythology of the stereotype which is part of the folklore of the South. Many of the examples of the incongruous come out of this folklore. In the episode above Uncle Buck remembers too late "that he had forgotten what even a little child should have known: not ever to stand right in front of or right behind a nigger when you scare him; but always to stand to

14. William Faulkner, "Was," in *Go Down, Moses* (New York: Random House, 1942), 19.

one side of him."[15] Images of niggers and mules, of niggers with razors, of niggers and light-skinned women, and of crap games are taken from the mythology of the stereotype. In this mythology the eyes and the heads of black persons are subjects for comedy, particularly when the eyes show fear and the head resembles a cannon ball.

Humor and violence are often mixed when comedy of this sort is used. Tomey's Turl's throwing Uncle Buck away is violent, although the only damage that he receives in his fall is the breaking of a bottle of whiskey that he carries in his back pocket. There is comedy in the crap game when Rider plays the nigger to persuade the watchman to permit him to join the game. He says, "'Dass awright, boss-man . . . Ah aint drunk. Ah jest cant wawk straight fer dis yar money weighin me down.'" This picture of Rider playing the fool, being the Pantaloon, is followed by one in which he joins the gamblers while still smiling "at the face of the white man." In the next picture he has grasped the white man's wrist and exposed the crooked dice while his face is "still fixed in the rigid and deadened smiling." In the last picture in the sequence, he kills the white man expertly with his razor "so that not even the first jet of blood touched his hand or arm."[16] His smile is fixed (assumed for a purpose) when Rider begins to clown; as the pictures move in sequence the smile is still fixed, and it is rigid and deadened. The comic and the violent are joined in these pictures. Frequently the pictures at the beginning of a sequence depend upon the mythology of the stereotype; but as the pictures in the sequence change, they transform the movement associated with the stereotype to reveal the true humanity of the person whose action is pictured.

Another example of the conjunction of humor and violence that is essentially a comic portrayal of black movement is use-

15. *Ibid*.
16. William Faulkner, "Pantaloon in Black," in *Go Down, Moses*, 152–54.

ful for an understanding of how these two are mixed to picture the black journey. "A Bear Hunt" is not about hunting bear but about Old Man Ash (or Uncle Ash) hunting Luke "Butch" Provine, who with two other members of the Provine Gang disrupted a picnic at a black church twenty years before the events that are related in this story. For the fun of it, these men rode up on horses "with drawn pistols and freshly lit cigars; and taking the Negro men one by one, held the burning cigar ends to the popular celluloid collars of the day, leaving each victim's neck ringed with an abrupt and faint and painless ring of carbon."[17] The main points of the story are why and how Uncle Ash gets his revenge. Uncle Ash at this time is a servant to Major de Spain and is with him at the hunting camp that is near an Indian mound and a small tribe of Indians who illegally make and sell whiskey.

When the story begins, Luke Provine, who is a guest at the camp, has had hiccups for several days, has tried many folk remedies to rid himself of them, and is nearly exhausted and painfully uncomfortable. Ratliff, who narrates the story, and the other guests of Major de Spain have been unable to sleep several nights because of the noise of Provine's hiccups. Ratliff and the others have teased Provine, but they have also tried to help him. It is Ratliff who suggests to Provine that he go up to the Indian mound and ask John Basket to cure him. He tells him, "'Them Indians knows all sorts of dodges that white doctors aint hyeard about yet. . . . Old Basket would be glad to cure them hiccups for you.'"[18]

Old Man Ash hears the suggestion that Ratliff gives Provine and when he knows that Provine is going to take it, leaves the camp ahead of him and goes up to the mound and tells the Indians that a new revenue agent was coming there that night, "'but dat he warn't much en dat all dey had to do was

17. William Faulkner, "A Bear Hunt," in *Collected Stories*, 65.
18. *Ibid.*, 71–72.

240

to give um a good skeer.'"[19] In this way he gains his revenge for the insult that was given him twenty years before.

The Indians caught Provine on his way up to the mound, took his gun and lantern, and took him to the top of the mound while speaking their tribal language and piling up wood for a fire. Then they tied Provine loosely, put him on the piled wood, and set fire to it, having behaved in every way as if they intended to burn him alive. He escaped, of course, without being burned and was so frightened that he lost his hiccups. When he gets back to camp, he attacks Ratliff and hurts him painfully.

The comedy of this story depends largely upon violence. The burning of the celluloid collars, the scare that Provine is given, and Ratliff's beating are violent acts. The picture of Uncle Ash's movement is built gradually until he is questioned about his part in Provine's visit to the Indians. He has been cautious not to come out of the character of the nigger servant, but when Ratliff asks him what he knows about the events up at the mound and threatens to tell his employer that he was involved in them, he replies "'I ain't skeered for him to know.'" This reply comes after his movements (typical activity for a black servant at a hunting camp) have been described: "he set there, rubbing that ere rifle with his hand. He was kind of looking down, like he was thinking. Not like he was trying to decide whether to tell me or not, but like he was remembering something from a long time back."[20] Violence and humor are joined in this story to picture Old Man Ash.

Rider in "Pantaloon in Black" and Tom-Tom and Turl in "Centaur in Brass" illustrate the complexity of Faulkner's treatment of black movement and several of the aspects of picture-making. Although the narrators of these two stories

19. *Ibid.*, 78.
20. *Ibid.*, 79.

perform their functions in rather different ways and are quite different from each other in their relationship to their materials, they present the movement of these characters in such ways that the metaphor, going to cross Jordan, is illuminated. The deputy sheriff who narrates the second part of "Pantaloon in Black" fails to understand Rider's behavior and the ironic tragedy and triumph of his life's journey. His social attitudes and convictions are not affected by them, and he appears to be almost without sensibility. This failure and lack, a lack of tension between his heart and head, are useful narrative devices that increase the reader's awareness of the meaning of the pictures. He has been close to the events that he narrates and the irony of his failing to understand them or to understand Rider's essential humanity characterizes him as a particular kind of person and emphasizes what the real Rider is.

The narrator in "Centaur in Brass" tells a story that he has heard. It may be a story that he has learned or pieced together from several sources. He did not observe or take part in the events when they were happening, but he knows the people who took part in them, and he is himself, like them, a representative member of their community in attitude and values. He is a more sensitive narrator than the deputy. Evidence of this is seen in his ambivalent tendency to laugh at Tom-Tom and Turl while at the same time he recognizes Flem Snopes's dishonesty and that Flem is outwitted by them. It is clear too from his telling that Tom-Tom and Turl are human and intelligent and that he respects them.

The black movement in part two of "Pantaloon in Black" and in part four of "Centaur in Brass," which the two rather different narrators are responsible for, results in the making of pictures that illustrate the full range and significance of the black journey. Through the movement in these stories, individual quests are explored and the general character of the movement of a people toward Jordan is described.

Rider is a young man who has deliberately given up a carefree life of pleasure to live a disciplined orderly life with a woman that he loves. He has chosen Lucas Beauchamp as a model; he has lighted the fire on his hearth and begun, with confidence in his strength and intelligence, a journey that is interrupted when six months after their marriage his wife dies. His grief for her, which is deeply felt but not conventionally expressed, causes conflict between his family and him and with the white community. While he grieves he begins to ask questions about life and death and about what is just and fair, and these lead to his death. Because he has lost his wife, he feels no need to be cautious or careful or restrained; and he says to his uncle, who has raised him and wants him to come home, "'Ah'm snakebit and de pizen cant hawm me.'" The pain and enlightenment, the snakebite, that his grief has brought him have made him aware of the vulnerability of man and skeptical that God helps. Because of his new awareness he tells his aunt, "'Efn He God, Ah dont needs to tole Him. Efn He God, He aweady know hit. Awright. Hyar Ah is. Leff Him come down hyar and do me some good.'" He leaves his aunt to go and gamble in the crap game that is run by the white night-watchman at the saw mill where he worked and where he knows the game is crooked and has many times before his wife's death knowingly allowed himself to be cheated. Although he permits himself to be cheated again on this occasion, he exposes the night watchman's use of crooked dice when he cheats another black player. He expressed his concern for the other players by saying "'Ah kin pass wid missouts. But dese hyar yuther boys——.'"[21] When Rider exposes the dishonesty, the watchman draws his pistol and Rider kills him with a razor before he is able to shoot.

The deputy sheriff who has assisted in arresting Rider tells

21. William Faulkner, "Pantaloon in Black," 150–53.

his wife about Rider's recent behavior in the second part of "Pantaloon in Black" while she prepares his dinner. Although she is the audience, the reader's attention is directed to the deputy's account as if his wife were not there. He presents the narrative as an example that will prove that what he believes about niggers is true. He prefaces his account of Rider's movement with a statement of this belief. "'Them damn niggers,'" he says. "'I swear to godfrey, it's a wonder we have as little trouble with them as we do. Because why? Because they aint human.'"[22] After this statement he describes Rider's behavior after he was apprehended and placed in the bull pen with the chain gang where he was kept until he was taken out of the cell to be lynched by the family of the man he killed.

At the end of the deputy sheriff's account and just before Rider is taken out of jail by the family of the dead man, the Birdsong boys, Rider says, "'Hit look lack Ah just cant quit thinking. Look lack Ah just cant quit.'"[23] This observation shows how the metaphor going to cross Jordan is illustrated in his life, and that he becomes for the deputy sheriff (who does not understand that he is human), the jailer, and the Birdsong boys a kind of scapegoat. Although the reader is not told what he thinks or why he laughs and cries at the end of the story, he may laugh at himself because of the terrible innocence that caused him to think that he could make the journey. He may laugh because both God and man appear to have conspired against him; and he may weep for mankind.

In the last two paragraphs of "Pantaloon in Black" there is a sequence of six pictures, framed and ordered as the movements of a dance are. The sequence can be called the dance of the pantaloon. In sixteenth-century Italian comedy the pantaloon was an old man who was the butt of the clown's

22. *Ibid.*, 154.
23. *Ibid.*, 153.

jokes. The situation in this story resembles that form of comedy, and it also resembles the relationship of the interlocutor and the end man in the minstrel show. The deputy is the clown and Rider is the pantaloon; the deputy does, by defining Rider as not human, make him the butt of a crude joke. The joke, however, backfires, and in this story it is the clown who is proved not to be human.

The pictures include Rider's (the pantaloon's) movements, his aunt, the chain gang, and Ketcham the jailer. The forming of the pictures, or the dance movements, begins when Rider and his aunt are locked in the bull pen with the chain gang. Rider begins and leads the dance and forms the first picture in the sequence when he lifts and holds a steel prison cot above his head "like a baby" and yells to his aunt who is "squinched in a corner" that he is not going to hurt her. The chain gang moves in the dance as he leads to avoid being hit when the cot is thrown. The second movement of the dance begins, and the second picture is made when Rider pulls the door that is made of steel bars out of the wall and walks out of the cell "toting the door over his head like it was a gauze window-screen and hollering, 'It's awright. Ah aint tryin to git away.'"[24]

The next four movements of the dance that form the remaining four pictures are led by Ketcham the jailer, who kicks the convicts and hits them with his gun until they rush Rider and form the third picture. In the fourth picture the pattern of the dance changes as Rider grabs the convicts as they come in and flings them across the room, "like they was rag dolls"—still saying that he is not trying to get out. In the fifth movement Rider is pulled down and under the mass of convicts, and the deputy sheriff describes that picture as "a big mass of nigger heads and arms and legs boiling around on

24. *Ibid.*, 158.

245

the floor." As the men boil around, "'every now and then a nigger would come flying out and go sailing through the air across the room, spraddled out like a flying squirrel and with his eyes sticking out like car headlights.'" In the last movement of the dance the picture becomes a kind of collage. Rider is underneath the "boiling" mass of convicts and Ketcham walks into the pile and peels the convicts away until he is visible, "'laying there under the pile of them, laughing, with tears as big as glass marbles running across his face and down past his ears and making a kind of popping sound on the floor like somebody dropping bird eggs, laughing and laughing'"and as he says in his last speech, thinking.[25]

The narrator begins this sequence of pictures realistically, but his diction changes as he moves from picture to picture, and when he speaks of "a mass of nigger heads boiling on the floor" the changed diction and the style of the pictures is dream-like and nightmarish. Men are peeled away like cabbage leaves and the pantaloon, the black traditional end man or butt of the clown's joke (the scapegoat), is revealed laughing, crying marble-sized tears, and thinking. Although the first pictures are essentially realistic, they, like the entire sequence, are marked by the exaggeration of what is humanly possible, and they cease to be realistic when Rider is pulled to the floor. The details of the last two pictures are surreal. Their conflict and violence, the opposing movements—a kind of counterpoint—and their use of the surreal contain elements that represent the essence of montage.

At the end of the story it is clear—and this is significant—that the meaning of Rider's name is changed. The name Rider was given him by his friends when he was a successful night prowler like Turl and was a tribute to his sexual competence. At the end of the story he has transcended his suffering and is

25. *Ibid.*, 159.

246

a rider; because he understands his world, has demonstrated that he is human, and while thinking and weeping can laugh at the joke fate is playing on him. Rider's quest is interrupted by his wife's death, but the interruption is a means of showing what the journey of life may be. Although her death ends his conscious quest, it is a means of revealing his quality. His movement after his wife's death gives his life meaning by showing his continuing desire to fulfill himself. His understanding of life, his physical strength, his concern for others, pictured in the context of the chase that follows his quest, illustrate the process of crossing Jordan, particularly when the deputy sheriff has said that he is not human.

Part four of "Centaur in Brass" shows how Tom-Tom and Turl who are day and night firemen at the city waterplant outwit Flem Snopes, the plant superintendent and their boss. Flem Snopes is stealing brass fixtures from the machinery in the plant in order to sell them, and forcing the firemen to help him steal by encouraging their distrust of each other and threatening that they will lose their jobs if they do not do what he wishes. Tom-Tom, who is sixty and a giant of a man who is married to a young wife, takes the brass and stores it in his barn. Snopes tries to force Turl to find the brass that he tells him Tom-Tom has hidden on his farm. When Turl goes out to Tom-Tom's farm he meets his wife and begins an affair with her. This affair is kept secret until Tom-Tom's wife falls suddenly ill and, because she thinks that she is going to die, confesses her sin to her husband. Tom-Tom makes plans to catch and punish Turl when he comes again to visit his wife. The outcome of their encounter is described in this section of the story.

The sequence of pictures that is formed after Turl is caught has, as "Pantaloon in Black" does, the characteristics of a dance that begins as slap-stick comedy and develops from that into patterns that are surrealistic. The movements of the two men are executed with precision and with a variety of patterns and rhythms that are comparable to those elements in a dance. Tom-Tom gets on the cot disguised as his wife, and Turl creeps into the room and touches him. When Turl discovers the trap and turns to run away Tom-Tom, with a butcher's knife in one of his hands, leaps with surprising agility astride Turl's shoulders and grasps him firmly around the neck with his other hand. The two are joined and Turl runs from the house into a cleared space and then into the woods where he attempts by bumping himself and Tom-Tom into trees to get Tom-Tom off his back. Tom-Tom's movements complement Turl's in their contrast of purpose and intensity; and the two men, in spite of being joined physically, who are in opposition in mood and movement, are joined in desperation as they fall into the ditch where their dance ends.

The narrator organizes the movement of the section as if it were a tall tale. His way of telling the story indicates that he is aware of the conventions that govern black and white relationships in his community; and through his narrative technique and the content of the story, it is apparent that he regards Tom-Tom and Turl as niggers toward whom white people must behave in a certain way. His attitude toward them is ambivalent; for while he laughs at black people and expects them to observe a particular etiquette, he does know that they are human and that Tom-Tom and Turl are morally superior to Flem Snopes. That they have used their intelligence to outwit him is a remarkable feat. Flem's reputation for shrewdness and successfully taking advantage of Ratliff, who is both a morally decent and a clever man, is established early in the story. The narrator realizes that Tom-Tom and Turl win in the contest with him without breaking the conventions of racial etiquette and he recognizes their intelligence and the significance of their victory.

The picture of Tom-Tom—who is sixty years old and weighs

two hundred pounds, wearing over his clothes one of his wife's nightgowns and lying on a cot with a butcher's knife beside him waiting for Turl, the young, handsome night prowler, who creeps across the porch to where the cot is and touches him and says "Honeybunch, papa's done arrived"—is minstrel comedy and is intended by the narrator to produce laughter. This beginning is important in the structure of meaning that is revealed in the completed movement. As other pictures are formed, this picture and the additional ones must take their meaning from the total context of the story. Consideration must be given to who the narrator is, who Flem Snopes is, and who Tom-Tom and Turl are. Given the context of the events in the story, what appears to be true in the first picture of the movement is explained or transformed in its meaning by the movements that follow.

Turl's touching Tom-Tom is followed by a sequence of pictures that explore and redefine the situation that is presented in the first picture. Tom-Tom clutches his knife and leaps astride Turl's shoulders, as Turl discovers his error and tries to escape by moving from the porch to the ground running full stride. Tom-Tom, while holding Turl's neck with one hand, has lifted his other hand high above his head and grasps the menacing knife in it. Joined in this way, they make "a strange and furious beast with two heads and a single pair of legs" that may cause laughter, but it is different from the minstrel comedy of the first picture. The forming of the beast with two heads suggests that the antagonists are not only joined but that they are mutually dependent, which is what they discover at the end of the sequence. This suggestion of mutual dependence is clearer as Turl runs in the moonlight from the clearing into the woods and trees and there tries desperately to rake Tom-Tom off his back by bumping into trees. When he bumps into a tree, both of them are hurt. When he runs out of the woods, Tom-Tom sees a ditch that

249

they are headed for and screams to make Turl aware of it, trying at the same time to change Turl's direction by twisting his head as he might that of a runaway horse. At this point each man is concerned about his own safety, and they each experience a new and common terror that pushes aside their original purposes. Turl says that he did not respond to Tom-Tom's warning, that his "'feets never even slowed up. They run far as from here to that door yonder out into nekkid air before us ever begun to fall. And they was still clawing that moonlight when me and Tom-Tom hit the bottom.'"[26] The moonlight, the gaping ditch, and Turl's legs moving surrealistically in air are not minstrel comedy.

The movement which began as comedy ends with the two men sprawled disentangled on a dry ditch bed talking with the air knocked out of them by the fall, and Tom-Tom's knife is dropped and forgotten. Their movement has culminated in awareness and understanding of what has happened to them and of the extent to which they were not free to prevent it. The narrator suggests that Tom-Tom does not injure Turl "because there is a sanctuary beyond despair for any beast which has dared all, which even its mortal enemy respects," but he undercuts this humanistic truism by adding, "or maybe it was just nigger nature." He concludes the paragraph with a statement of the outcome of the conversation between the two men, saying "Anyway, it was perfectly plain to both of them as they sat there, perhaps panting a little while they talked, that Tom-Tom's home had been outraged, not by Turl, but by Flem Snopes; that Turl's life and limbs had been endangered, not by Tom-Tom, but by Flem Snopes."[27] The narrator understands this too.

What Tom-Tom wants, the focus of his quest, is suggested in what he had after working for forty years as a fireman. His

26. William Faulkner, "Centaur in Brass," in *Collected Stories*, 165.
27. *Ibid*.

salary has increased from twelve to sixty dollars a month. He has a cabin, a little land, a mule and wagon, a gold watch and chain, and his third wife, whom he takes to church on Sunday and "guards like a Turk." The things that he has suggest that he wants and has worked for respect, a measure of security, and for pleasure. They suggest that he has pride and wants dignity that comes with manhood. The events of the story suggest the difficulty and the constraints that have characterized his quest. They suggest also that he understands the nature of the world that he lives in and that he has come as far as he has on his journey in spite of obstacles. Turl's journey may have been primarily that of the night prowler, but that has provided him the status that he has. He is aware of his youth and that his quest is not focused. As the two men discover that Flem Snopes is responsible for their conflict, they also discover how to outwit him. They demonstrate in doing this the human will engaged in the effort to fulfill itself or the effort to cross Jordan.

"Pantaloon in Black" and "Centaur in Brass," like most of Faulkner's stories that are mentioned in this essay, place the movement of black characters in a context in a particular world in time and space and portray them as individuals making the journey of life. The presentational method employed in these stories often creates the illusion that time has stopped and that the movement of the characters is caught and exists in pictures as if it were painted. Through these pictures the reader sees the individuals in these stories moving to cross Jordan. That metaphor describes the purpose that engages the individual character in a story, and it symbolizes the direction of the movement of the majority of Faulkner's black characters.

The Myriad Heart:
The Evolution of the Faulkner Hero

JAMES B. CAROTHERS

A chronological study of the Faulkner canon reveals not only the fundamental consistencies of subject matter, theme, technique, and style we expect to find in the work of a major author, and the peculiar consistency inherent in Faulkner's deliberate repetition of fictional setting in Yoknapatawpha County, Mississippi, and his recurrent use of the very particular characters who populate his fictional world, but also a striking and radical transformation. It is a long journey through literary space and authorial time from the irony, pessimism, and despair of Faulkner's early work to the affirmative rhetoric and comic resolution of his later books and public statements. To read Faulkner's work with attention is to discover literally thousands of repetitions and thousands of differences, for Faulkner, refusing to be bound by what he had previously written or published, regularly availed himself of his prerogative to repeat or alter character, incident, tone, and emphasis as the immediate creative exigency required. What are we to make of this phenomenon? To what extent, and in what ways, to cite one of the most important, difficult, and controversial instances of repetition and difference, is Quentin Compson of *The Sound and the Fury* the "same" character as the Quentin Compson of *Absalom, Absalom!*, or the Quentin of any of the other works, published and unpublished, in which Faulkner employed a character by that name? How far is the Snopes trilogy a unified work? Is Faulkner describing the same Jefferson in *Light in August* and *Intruder in the Dust*? Is he describing the same Memphis in *Sanctuary* as in *The Reivers*?

To come to terms with the totality of Faulkner's achievement, to understand and appreciate his life's work, it is necessary to ask such questions, and to develop a satisfactory method for answering them. The great paradox of the Faulkner canon—the simultaneous autonomy and interdependence of his stories and novels—admits of resolution when it is understood that not only do Faulkner's repetitions form patterns, but his differences-in-repetition form patterns as well. To read individual Faulkner works responsibly, with a view to apprehending the nature of his entire *oeuvre*, requires an openness to the hypothesis that what Faulkner changes from one fiction to the next is as important as what remains the same. A study of the central characters of Faulkner's fiction, taking individual works in the order of their publication, supplemented by what we know or may surmise about the sometimes rather different order of their composition, shows that the essential consistency of Faulkner's work is of a special and limited kind, the consistency imparted by a *developing* genius.

To apply what I shall call the developmental method to the subject of the Faulkner hero, it is first necessary to define the problem that the method seeks to solve, and to show how the developmental method differs from and supplements or corrects what may be described as the three major methods of Faulkner criticism. Next, it is appropriate to stipulate a definition of heroism, and to apply that definition to a variety of Faulkner's principal characters, to see how far the evolution of the Faulkner hero follows a pattern. This pattern, this consistency-within-difference, may then be compared with a recent product of a set of critical assumptions opposed to those

253

of the developmental method. We may then conclude with some suggestions as to how the developmental method might be fruitfully applied to aspects of Faulkner's fiction beyond the heroic.

Textual scholarship, in the strictest sense, is concerned with establishing the definitive text of a work of literature, that version of a poem, play, story, or novel which most closely approximates the author's "final intention." The controlling assumption of such scholarship is that there is, ideally, a "best text," a text that can be approached, if not always achieved, by rigorous application of bibliographical methods. Thus, when two editions of a text differ from one another, it is the critic's task to discover the specific differences, and to determine the extent of the author's responsibility for and approval of those changes. Shakespeare's *First Folio*, for example, presents a large number of such textual problems, and Charlton Hinman, in his effort to produce a "best text" of the *Folio*, made extensive use of his collating machine, a device that permits rapid alteration of the images of two different texts upon a single screen. Identical portions of the two texts appear as a single image; portions that differ appear as a blur. The textual scholar, having located the differences, then considers other information regarding the two texts, to determine priority and preference.

The interpretive critic proceeds analogously. Assuming that there is a discoverable meaning, a "best reading" of a particular literary work, the critic analyzes whatever information is available to produce a coherent reading of that work. The task of the Faulkner critic has most often been to discover and describe the essential unity of the individual work of fiction: reconciling the four points of view of *The Sound and the Fury*, the three plots of *Light in August*, the two time settings of *Absalom, Absalom!*, the contrapuntal narratives of *The Wild Palms*, and the seemingly disparate stories of *Go Down,*

Moses, to name some of the most familiar. This is, in itself, a formidable task, for Faulkner is among the most complex and demanding of modern authors, but the results of this enterprise have been highly rewarding, for we now have available to us several excellent extended treatments of individual Faulkner novels, and three distinguished general treatments of the entire Faulkner canon by critics who have concentrated their attention on the search for the unities of the individual text.[1] When these studies are read in conjunction with the invaluable and rigorous bibliographical studies and briefer critical treatments—particularly the successive volumes of the Faulkner Concordance Project and the summer issues of *The Mississippi Quarterly*—and when these studies are read in light of the vast and often seemingly contradictory materials of the biography, it seems possible that we may come to know Faulkner's works better than we can know those of any other American author.

But the attempt to discover the unities of the entire Faulkner canon has proved more difficult, and has yielded somewhat less satisfactory results, for there are hazards in the practice of treating the entire Faulkner canon as a single text, and in the practice of viewing individual Faulkner works as successive versions of a single text. These practices are based in the questionable assumption that every instance of obvious repetition in Faulkner—repetition of a character such as

1. The distinguished general treatments are, of course, Cleanth Brooks's *William Faulkner: The Yoknapatawpha Country* (New Haven and London: Yale University Press, 1963); Michael Millgate's *The Achievement of William Faulkner* (New York, Random House, 1966); and Olga W. Vickery's *The Novels of William Faulkner: A Critical Interpretation* (Baton Rouge: Louisiana State University Press, 1964). The best studies of individual novels are André Bleikasten's *Faulkner's "As I Lay Dying"* (Bloomington and London: Indiana University Press, 1973); the same author's *The Most Splendid Failure: Faulkner's "The Sound and the Fury"* (Bloomington and London: Indiana University Press, 1976); François Pitavy's *Faulkner's "Light in August"* (Bloomington and London: Indiana University Press, 1973); and Thomas L. McHaney's *William Faulkner's "The Wild Palms": A Study* (Jackson: University Press of Mississippi, 1975).

Quentin Compson, of an event such as the sale of the spotted ponies, of a place such as Jefferson, of a situation such as the conflict between fathers and sons, or of a theme such as the Southern heritage—is genetically related to its predecessors and successors in hierarchical relation. Often, then, two or more versions of a single element in Faulkner's work are assumed to represent some sort of improvement or some sort of deterioration on the author's part. At times, the later versions are assumed to be superior, and many anthologists have accordingly followed Malcolm Cowley's practice of reprinting excerpts from Faulkner's novels rather than the earlier magazine short story versions of the corresponding material. Other critics have preferred earlier versions to later ones, choosing to reprint units from *Go Down, Moses* rather than from *Big Woods*. This preferential selection of texts is by no means peculiar to Faulkner scholarship; we do the same thing when we choose to study the earlier versions of *The Prelude* or *Tender Is the Night* or the later versions of the poems of Whitman and Yeats.

The process of comparing Faulkner's works wih a view to demonstrating unity has yielded provocative analyses of many particular and limited aspects of Faulkner's subjects and themes, of his aesthetic, of his craft, and of his characters, but it has also yielded far too many instances of misreading and special pleading, for there are numerous discrepancies and contradictions among Faulkner's works and even, occasionally, within a single work. In assessing these discrepancies and contradictions, three distinct practices have been followed. The first practice, followed by critics who assume the primacy and autonomy of the individual text, is to treat the discrepancies and contradictions between texts as irrelevant. If Quentin Compson commits suicide at the age of nineteen in *The Sound and the Fury* because of his inability to accept his sister's dishonor and because of his inability to resolve his guilt over his own incestuous desires for her, and if there is, nevertheless, no mention of Quentin Compson's sister in *Absalom, Absalom!*, and if Quentin is "resurrected" as the twenty-four year-old narrator of "That Evening Sun," such inconsistencies, as Huck Finn tells us, "ain't no matter."

A second critical practice is to assume that there is, or ought to be, a hard core of narrative fact embedded in the Faulkner saga, and that close reading will reveal the deep structural connections among Faulkner's works. Thus we have the argument that since *The Sound and the Fury* describes Quentin's incestuous desires for Caddy, and since the Quentin Compson of *Absalom, Absalom!* is obviously the same character, we may legitimately infer that Quentin's fascination in the latter novel with the Sutpen story derives from his interest in the incestuous aspects of the relationships among the children of Thomas Sutpen. In this sort of reading, then, the later text not only modifies and enriches the earlier, it is seen to depend on the earlier in significant ways.

The third general practice of Faulkner criticism is to assume that a single design informs all of Faulkner's work, or at least all of his best work. Whether this design is found in the matter of Jefferson, Yoknapatawpha, in Faulkner's repeated treatments of particular characters and families, in some aspect of his aesthetic or his presumed philosophy, or in his consecutive treatments of such themes and subjects as time, Southern history, race relations, or the community, the critics have mined particular works for evidence consistent with this design, dismissing or derogating entire works or elements of particular works that are demonstrably inconsistent with this design. Thus, insofar as Faulkner's work has been read developmentally, it has often been to express the wish that Faulkner had broken his pencil in 1942.

By careful selection of evidence, it is possible to produce useful results for any of these three kinds of reading, but to

257

do so as an exclusive method, I submit, is to ignore one of the central patterns of Faulkner's life's work, and to misread many of his particular works. It was not for nothing that Faulkner returned again and again to Quentin Compson, but neither was it accidental that he omitted mention of Caddy in *Absalom, Absalom!* The *Sound and the Fury* is no more betrayed or diminished by *The Reivers* than *Hamlet* is betrayed or diminished by *The Tempest.* There is certainly a design or a combination of designs within an individual Faulkner text, there are designs formed by the relations among successive texts, and there may even be a design or a combination of designs within the entire canon, but it is best to approach the latter design as a dynamic one.

Faulkner himself provided much of the impetus for what might be called the teleological reading, especially in two important and often-quoted comments on his own work. In a 1944 letter to Malcolm Cowley, he wrote: "As regards any specific book, I'm trying primarily to tell a story, in the most effective way I can think of, the most moving, the most exhaustive. But I think even that is incidental to what I am trying to do, taking my output (the course of it) as a whole. I am telling the same story over and over, which is myself and the world."[2] The second major statement on this issue, which has come to be quoted about as often as any of Faulkner's pronouncements, with the certain exception of the Nobel Prize address and the possible exception of the prefatory note to the Modern Library edition of *Sanctuary*, appeared in Faulkner's 1956 interview with Jean Stein:

> With *Soldiers' Pay* I found out writing was fun. But I found out after that not only each book had to have a design but the whole output or sum of an artist's work had to have a design. With *Soldiers' Pay* and *Mosquitoes* I wrote for the sake of writing because

2. *The Faulkner–Cowley File: Letters and Memories, 1944–1962* (New York: Viking Press, 1966), 14.

it was fun. Beginning with *Sartoris* I discovered that my own little postage stamp of native soil was worth writing about and that I would never live long enough to exhaust it, and by sublimating the actual into apocryphal I would have complete liberty to use whatever talent I might have to the absolute top. It opened up a gold mine of other peoples, so I created a cosmos of my own. I can move these people around like God, not only in space but in time too.[3]

Both of these statements must be read and applied with qualifications, particularly since Faulkner shows in both of them that he retained always a sense of the importance of the individual story. But to identify and describe, to analyze and evaluate the story Faulkner said he told over and over and the design that is assumed to inform his work has been among the primary aims of the first fifty years of Faulkner criticism. Indeed, the successive monuments of Faulkner criticism and the blur of footprints leading up to and away from these monuments have usually claimed to identify either the broad outlines or the clear particulars of Faulkner's design. George Marion O'Donnell's articulation of the Sartoris–Snopes conflict, Malcolm Cowley's exposition of Faulkner's "legend of the South," Richard P. Adams's description of Faulkner's aesthetic, and John T. Irwin's analysis of the paradigm of doubling and incest[4]—each of these studies has assumed, or sought to prove, that there is a single discoverable design in the Faulkner canon, a perfect Platonic form, if you will, that is reflected imperfectly in each of its myriad avatars in Faulkner's work. What I want to argue, by contrast, is that there are many Faulkner designs, that the designs are dynamic

3. *Lion in the Garden: Interviews with William Faulkner 1926–1962*, James B. Meriwether and Michael Millgate, eds. (New York: Random House, 1968), 255.

4. George Marion O'Donnell, "Faulkner's Mythology," *Kenyon Review*, 1 (1939), 33–47; Malcolm Cowley, "Introduction," *The Portable Faulkner* (New York: Viking Press, 1946); Richard P. Adams, *Faulkner: Myth and Motion* (Princeton: Princeton University Press, 1968); and John T. Irwin, *Doubling and Incest/Repetition and Revenge: A Speculative Reading of Faulkner* (Baltimore and London: Johns Hopkins University Press, 1975).

rather than static, that they may be inferred only after a careful analysis of individual texts and of the entire canon, and that any of these designs, including the one I shall attempt to describe, may well be as much a creation of the critic as of Faulkner's sustained and conscious intention.

Faulkner's fiction, then, proceeds according to a design that encompasses two kinds of change, two kinds of discrepancies and contradictions. One is the simple alteration of narrative fact, which occurs when Miss Quentin escapes from the Compson household by climbing down a pear tree in *The Sound and the Fury* and by climbing down a rainpipe in the Compson appendix. It may be observed when characters' names are changed, as when Surratt becomes Ratliff, or when Ernest Cotton of "The Hound" becomes Mink Snopes in *The Hamlet*, and it may be observed when a character's age is altered, as is done for Boon Hogganbeck between *Go Down, Moses* and *The Reivers*. Like Old Het in "Mule in the Yard," some of Faulkner's characters "would have to be around a hundred and at least triplets"[5] to accomplish all the things ascribed to them. The second kind of change is more general and more complex, and it involves the highest issues of narrative purpose, for Faulkner's attitude toward himself and the world and the methods and substance through which he manifested those attitudes in his works changed profoundly over the years.

To demonstrate changes of both kinds, with a view to discovering the designs which subsume them, then, let us focus on the nature of the hero in Faulkner's fiction. To do so I wish to avoid the questionable practice of selecting a single Faulkner character as heroic exemplar, and the even more questionable practice of applying a single Faulkner statement on

5. William Faulkner, *Collected Stories* (New York: Random House, 1950), 249.

the subject to the entire range of his works. Rather, I should like to stipulate a definition of the hero which comes neither from Faulkner's fiction nor from his commentary on that fiction, but instead from the broader context of Western literature in general. This definition is not a description of "the Faulkner hero," but constitutes an attempt to provide a standard by which the ostensibly heroic among Faulkner's characters may be judged.

A hero, then, is an individual who is uniquely capable of acting decisively, possessing in appropriate combination strength, courage, intelligence, and virtue, and who, given the opportunity, so acts, at significant personal risk, to create, preserve, or restore a harmonious and benevolent order to that community, based in a clearly defined system of values, of which the hero is, or becomes, the acknowledged champion. This is, to be sure, a complex and demanding standard, and, if it may be true that no Faulkner character meets this standard in every particular, it is also true that there are differences among the ways the potential heroes fail, and it may be useful to acknowledge and specify the difficulties of achieving the heroic state before making positive application of the heroic standard to Faulkner's characters.

A hero is, first of all, an *individual*. Since the hero must act in splendid isolation, we ought not to identify as heroic the cooperative enterprise of the creators of order in the prose sections of *Requiem for a Nun*, the preservers of order in *The Town*, who defend Jefferson from Byron Snopes's demented children, or the restorers of order in *Intruder in the Dust*, who identify the murderer of Vinson Gowrie and save Lucas Beauchamp from lynching. However much they may otherwise conform to the definition, such characters are not individually heroic, though they are certainly admirable. If we note that each of these examples of cooperative action occurs in Faulkner's later fiction, we may begin to see that there was a change in Faulkner's attitude toward the sustaining community itself.

A hero must be capable of acting decisively, and must do so. It is not heroic simply to desire to act decisively, as do Bayard Sartoris in *Sartoris*, Quentin Compson in *The Sound and the Fury*, Gail Hightower in *Light in August*, or the young man in "Carcassonne" who yearns to perform something *"bold and tragical and austere."*[6] Neither is it heroic merely to attempt decisive action, as when Horace Benbow endeavors to rescue Temple Drake and Lee Goodwin in *Sanctuary*, when Hawkshaw makes a brief and futile gesture to save Will Mayes in "Dry September," when the Corporal and his fellow mutineers attempt to end the war in *A Fable*, or even, in a comic mode, when Boon Hogganbeck vainly struggles to push the Winton Flyer by main strength through the mud of Hell Creek Bottom. Faulkner's early fiction characteristically involves characters who are unable to attempt decisive action, and much of his later fiction presents characters whose actions are ineffectual gestures.

The hero's action must be undertaken at personal risk. If there is no risk, the consequence may appear trivial, as when Ratliff thwarts the political ambitions of Clarence Snopes in *The Mansion* without confronting him publicly. For the Faulkner characters themselves, the exemplary hero is often a warrior, such as the "Carolina Bayard" of honored memory in *Sartoris* who loses his life in a glorious and absurd attempt to liberate some anchovies from the Yankees, or Gail Hightower I, revered by his grandson for his Civil War exploits. But for the contemporary Faulkner protagonists, as for Faulkner himself, the heroic opportunity of battle is often denied. When an opportunity does offer for a Faulkner protagonist to

6. *Ibid.*, 899.

262

act at physical risk, as it does for Quentin Compson in his confrontation with Dalton Ames, for Gowan Stevens in *Sanctuary*, or for Gavin Stevens in *The Town*, the result is, often, a failure of courage or of strength.

Since the hero's action must also *create harmonious order where none has existed, preserve such order when it is threatened, or restore such order when it has been abrogated*, those who act in simple conformity to the prevailing dictates of the established order are, at best, fulfilling their natural obligations and, at worst, viciously respectable. Gavin Stevens's behavior in arranging for the burial of Samuel Worsham Beauchamp in *Go Down, Moses* is of the first type, while the work of the ladies who arrange the marriage of Drusilla Hawk and John Sartoris in *The Unvanquished* is of the second. Those who act to create or maintain a demonstrably malevolent order, such as Jason Compson, Thomas Sutpen, and L. Q. C. McCaslin, and those who seek to destroy the order of the community where it already exists, as do Ab Snopes, Max Harriss of "Knight's Gambit," and Butch Lovemaiden, are not only anti-heroic, but also, as Ratliff might put it, "actively" villainous.

Yet another distinction must be noted for those characters who are capable of action, and who undertake actions involving a high degree of personal risk, but who act only to satisfy some immediate personal need, rather than to contribute to the well-being of the larger community. Young Bayard Sartoris of *Sartoris*, for example, undertakes a dangerous sequence of activities involving horses, automobiles, and airplanes, but he does so to rid himself of the guilt he feels over his brother's death, or to fulfill his Sartoris destiny, rather than to establish and maintain peace within his family and his community. Rider, in *Go Down, Moses*, performs a number of Herculean feats of strength, and he finally loses his life in a brave but foolhardy attempt to assuage his grief over his wife's death, but his behavior is incomprehensible to those who observe it. The problem for the moral individual is to make personal desire consonant with communal needs. When the individual satisfies his own appetites in opposition to the community, or at the expense of the community, the result is not only selfish, but often also catastrophic for the individual and for the community as well.

Similarly, however, *the community itself must be based on a harmonious and sustaining order.* When the community is debased, corrupted, or depraved, as is the case in *Mosquitoes, Sanctuary,* and *The Hamlet* among the novels, or "Red Leaves," "Mountain Victory," or "Golden Land" among the short stories, it cannot be saved by a hero; it can only be perpetuated by despots and tyrants like Mrs. Maurier, Popeye, Eustace Graham, Will Varner, Moketubbe, Vatch, and Ira Ewing. There are, of course, individuals among Faulkner's protagonists who endeavor, by taking extreme action, to reform or redeem an entire community. Bayard Sartoris in *The Unvanquished,* the Corporal in *A Fable,* and, arguably, Eula Varner Snopes in *The Town* are among those who take the ultimate risk.

There are, then, a good many reasons why so many of Faulkner's characters fail to act heroically, and why so few of them conform to the stipulated definition of heroism in most or all of its particulars. Faulkner's central characters, protagonists though they may be, are seldom heroic. Yet the heroic theme sounds repeatedly throughout the course of Faulkner's fiction, and if it is true that Faulkner's characters seldom achieve the heroic standard, it is also true that they fail for different reasons at different times. Each of Faulkner's protagonists faces the existential question, Shall I live?, and each faces the ethical question, How shall I live? Each answers these questions differently, within the detailed complex of character and circumstance. Throughout Faulkner's fiction the standard by which individual action is judged remains constant. The nature of the situation in which individual morality is tested remains constant. Superficially, at least, even the individuals who are tested remain constant, insofar as they are given the same name and the same background from one work to the next. What changes are the results of the test.

The burden of Faulkner's early fiction is to show that decisive action is possible only for the vicious, and that individuals of good will and good intentions are unable to act, or their attempts at action will be ineffectual, or they will be destroyed in the attempt to act. Thus the protagonists of the early fiction are either denied the heroic opportunity, or when presented with it they fail to act or fail to act decisively. For the most part, the best that they can do is to remove themselves from the community in which they have failed, often because that community itself seems unworthy of or antagonistic to the heroic commitment. The characteristic method of Faulkner's novels through *Light in August* is to diffuse or fragment the capacity and opportunity for heroic action among several major characters. The result is an ironic pessimism, for which Faulkner found an appropriate technical method in the limited first-person point of view. The usual state of the protagonist in this early fiction is that of the pathetic Juliet Bunden in the story "Adolescence": "At last she, too, was frankly crying because everything seemed so transient and pointless, so futile; that every effort, every impulse she had toward the attainment of happiness was thwarted by blind circumstance, that even trying to break away from the family she hated was frustrated by something within herself. Even dying couldn't help her: death being nothing but that state those left behind are cast into."[7] Lest one consider that

7. *Uncollected Stories of William Faulkner*, Joseph Blotner, ed. (New York: Random House, 1979), 472.

Juliet Bunden's feeling of helplessness, like Quentin Compson's, which it resembles and anticipates, is a peculiarly adolescent attitude, compare the similar sentiments expressed
by Rector Mahon in *Soldiers' Pay*: "As I grow older, Mr.
Jones, I become more firmly convinced that we learn nothing
whatever which can ever help us or be of any particular bene-
fit to us, even."[8]

The basic situation of *Soldiers' Pay* (1926) points up the
theme of pessimism and futility. The central fact of the novel
is that Donald Mahon is dying. Each of the other characters
in the novel reacts to this fact with a different degree of understanding and each takes a different and ineffectual action.
Margaret Powers and Joe Gilligan offer a timid sympathy for
Donald and his father. Gilligan reads to Donald and Margaret
eventually even marries him, but neither can do anything to
alter the inevitable, and both contribute to the Rector's willful ignorance of his son's condition. Cecily Saunders reacts
with horror, turning from Mahon to Januarius Jones and
George Farr. Emmy seeks solace in self-pity and tears. Young
Robert Saunders reacts with morbid curiosity. Januarius Jones
occupies himself with irony and sexual conquest. Lesser representatives of the community, such as Aunt Callie Nelson
and her son, Mrs. Worthington, and Mrs. Burney, offer only
fear, resentment, and condescension to the Mahons. Margaret Powers, the single character in the novel possessed of
sufficient intelligence, sympathy, and energy to undertake
the task of creating a new order, finally declines Joe Gilligan's
offer of love, fearing that she is, literally, a *femme fatale*.

In Faulkner's second novel, *Mosquitoes* (1927), Mrs. Maurier struggles vainly and pathetically to create, maintain, and
restore decorous relations among the bizarre assortment of
characters who make up her yachting party, but virtually all

8. William Faulkner, *Soldiers' Pay* (New York: Boni & Liveright, 1926), 69.

of these resist her impulses toward "civilization." The vulnerability of Mrs. Maurier's pretense to order is demonstrated early on when her nephew, Gus Robyn, dismantles a piece of the ship's machinery to secure a stem for a pipe he is making. The steering gear is thus rendered inoperative, and the yacht drifts pointlessly and goes aground. The men in the party, particularly Dawson Fairchild and Julius Kauffman, individually and collectively resist Mrs. Maurier's inanity and her grapefruit, and seek refuge in alcohol, irony, and aestheticism. Ernest Talliaferro rushes nervously from one opposing faction to the other, earning the contempt of both. The potential lovers, David West and Patricia Robyn, follow their impulse to break away from the meaningless activities aboard the yacht, but, unable to cope with the forces of Louisiana nature in general and the savage mosquitoes in particular, they return, defeated, to the adult gathering. Only the sculptor, Gordon, manages to maintain a modicum of dignity and achievement, but he does so by refusing to succumb to the silliness of his travelling companions, and by objectifying his loathing of Mrs. Maurier in a sculpture. *Mosquitoes*, more than any of Faulkner's other novels, shows the debilitating effects of an engagement with words to the exclusion of action.

Sartoris (1929) deals more explicitly and more extensively with the heroic question than either of the two previous novels. The Sartoris men, from the Carolina Bayard and Colonel John Sartoris to the twin grandsons Bayard and John, are capable of action and are drawn instinctively to it, but the characteristic Sartoris action is a grandiose gesture which is either ineffectual or self-destructive. The younger Bayard is given the opportunity to achieve peaceful order with Narcissa, but he quickly reverts to the frenzied and inarticulate motion that leads to his death. At the opposite extreme is Horace Benbow, sensitive and articulate, but unable to act with purpose

267

or with consequence. The most nearly heroic character in *Sartoris* is Miss Jenny Du Pre. She understands the vainglorious weakness of the Sartoris men, and she seeks to maintain the family through all of its adversity. But Miss Jenny is unable to effect decisive change; Old Bayard flouts her will by allowing Old Man Falls to treat the growth on his face, and her effort to restrain young Bayard's fast driving is thwarted when Old Bayard is killed.

The Sound and the Fury (1929) is, among other things, one of Faulkner's most trenchant expositions of the theme of the failed hero. The idiot Benjy is simply incapable of understanding, articulation, or effective action. A quintessential victim, first of heredity and finally of environment, he can only bellow his grief and rage. Quentin Compson is capable of decisive action only in regard to himself. His suicide represents his absolute inability to change the world to conform to his image of purity, or to live with the consequences of a fallen world. Jason Compson maintains a kind of order within his family's household, but he does so at the expense of all morality and simple humanity. Even Jason is thwarted at last by the girl Quentin, who removes herself from the family as her namesake had done by suicide, as her grandfather had retreated into alcoholism and her grandmother into hypochondria. Caddy, as far as circumstances allow her, acts from motives of love and generosity, but these lead her to disgrace and banishment. Dilsey, too, acts affirmatively within her limits, but she can accomplish little beyond maintaining the conditions of material endurance, and she is physically helpless before the brutality of Jason.

As in the Compson family, so in the Bundren family of *As I Lay Dying* (1930), the possibilities of genuine achievement and renewal are sharply divided among the family members, and radically limited by the deficiencies and selfishness of each. Cash Bundren acts, but often clumsily and ineffectually, and he is immobilized by the grotesque cement cast on his broken leg. Darl Bundren, sensitive and introverted, resorts to the dire expedient of firing the barn where his mother's coffin lies, and is taken away to the insane asylum. Jewel, the most active and the most physically heroic of the Bundrens, proves his courage by taming the wild horse and by retrieving Addie's coffin from the flood and from the burning barn, but he is consumed by inarticulate rage and helpless before the manipulations of Anse. Dewey Dell is too obsessed with her unwanted pregnancy to contribute meaningfully to the family's welfare. Vardaman is simply too young to understand the situation, as attested by his most memorable actions, chopping up the catfish and boring holes in his mother's coffin so she can breathe. Anse Bundren himself is passive, cowardly, and selfish. Though the novel ends on a note of apparent affirmation—the family finally manages to get Addie buried in Jefferson and Anse acquires new teeth, a phonograph, and a new wife—the suggestions of restored order emphasize the irony of Faulkner's mock-epic treatment of the Bundren odyssey.[9]

Sanctuary (1931) presents the most melodramatic and, arguably, the most pessimistic of Faulkner's investigations of the possibilities of heroic action in the modern world. Corruption is everywhere, from the unspeakable violation and murder of the Old Frenchman's place to the equally degrading and equally murderous Memphis tenderloin and to the patent miscarriage of justice in Jefferson, where the legal

9. André Bleikasten points out that Darl Bundren is "one of those wounded heroes (literally or figuratively) who appear so often in Faulkner's early novels" and he notes that Jewel Bundren "has the brutal simplicity of the epic hero" (*Faulkner's "As I Lay Dying,"* 90, 92). Judith Bryant Wittenberg sees Cash Bundren as the redemptive figure in the novel; see *Faulkner: The Transfiguration of Biography* (Lincoln and London: University of Nebraska Press, 1979), 106–111.

lynching of Lee Goodwin is superseded by an illegal one. The dominant characters of *Sanctuary* work for selfish and corrupt ends. Those, like Popeye, Red, Clarence Snopes, and Eustace Graham, who are capable of decisive action do so only to destroy and degrade. A few of the characters are well-meaning, but they are capable only of murmuring with Tommy, "Durn them fellers," or of frantic ineffectual gestures such as Horace Benbow's futile attempts to rescue Temple and save Lee Goodwin. Though many critics have persisted in seeing Temple herself as the source of evil in the novel, it must be remarked that Temple's famous "affinity for evil" is no greater than or different from that of her fellow characters, or of the respectable society that sustains them.

In *Light in August* (1932), however, Faulkner turns away from a world in which the major characters either acquiesce passively to the evil in the world or actively enter into it themselves. Principally through his depiction of Lena Grove, Byron Bunch, and Gail Hightower, Faulkner in this novel demonstrates both the possibilities and the difficulties of effective moral action. Lena Grove not only endures, she also manages to act decisively, within a limited sphere, and she renews or creates the capacity for love in many of the people whom she encounters. Her effect on Byron Bunch is the most pronounced. Byron, for love of Lena, moves from an initial position of isolation and denial to a position of loving commitment. Hightower, too, principally through his experience with Lena and Byron, is brought, at least temporarily, out of the state of moral catatonia in which he has so long existed. His attempt to provide an alibi for Joe Christmas, though it is too little and though it comes too late, is nevertheless a signal indication of his decision to re-enter humanity. Joe Christmas, whether he is treated as a naturalistic victim, a melodramatic villain, a Christian martyr, or a tragic anti-hero, remains to remind us of the earlier and later Faulkner characters who, unable to act positively, become murderous or self-destructive.

The principal characters of *Pylon* (1935) live outside of and in opposition to the values of the established community to which they are forced to turn for economic subsistence, but that community, as it is represented in New Valois, is a grossly commercial and debased one. Within their peculiar *ménage* Roger and Laverne Schumann and Jack Holmes seek to establish and maintain their own community, with its own code of honor. They are heroic insofar as they act at extreme risk, the risk of social ostracism and the risk of death. Their strange compound of courage and honor, functioning in belligerent opposition to the dictates of conventional morality, fascinates the unnamed reporter. Like Gail Hightower, the reporter attempts to enter humanity, helping Roger Schumann to secure a second airplane and giving money to the little boy, but neither of these actions succeed, in their purpose, for Roger is killed in the second aircraft, and the money is scorned by Roger's father, who believes that Laverne has earned it through prostitution.

In *Absalom, Absalom!* (1936) Thomas Sutpen acts decisively, and he attempts to act in accordance with the values of the community, as far as he understands them, but he ignores the moral imperative of love and thus destroys the order he had hoped to create. Charles Bon attempts to act decisively by marrying Judith, but in flouting the communal taboo against incest and especially the taboo against miscegenation, he makes inevitable his own murder. Henry Sutpen, unable to bring about a reconciliation between his father and his brother, murders Charles and retreats from the world. Judith Sutpen, like so many of Faulkner's other women characters, has an instinct and will to love and harmony, but she is unable to prevail against the furious contention among the rigid and vainglorious men who surround her. Miss Rosa Coldfield,

271

seeking to avenge her sister, heralds Thomas Sutpen's de-
monic fame to succeeding generations. Clytie, first like Dilsey and finally like Darl Bundren, maintains what she can of
the Sutpen household but finally fires the house and dies.
Quentin Compson is admirable to the extent that he seeks to
analyze and articulate the Sutpen story, and to the extent that
he makes the perilous journey to Sutpen's Hundred to encounter Henry Sutpen, but he is denied the opportunity to
participate significantly and, in the end, he seems unable or
unwilling to accept the consquences of the story he has told.

Bayard Sartoris, in *The Unvanquished* (1938), acts decisively, at personal risk, to restore order to his community. By
facing Redmond unarmed rather than taking the conventional
murderous revenge of his father's killer, Bayard provides a
specific corrective to the selfish ambitions of Drusilla and to
the unquestioning traditionalism of Ringo, Professor Wilkins,
and George Wyatt. This episode in "An Odor of Verbena"
represents a clear and final stage in Bayard's development
from the boy who shot at the Yankee and hid behind his
grandmother's skirts in "Ambuscade" through the young man
who avenged his grandmother's death by hunting down and
killing Grumby in "Vendée." Bayard also differs significantly
from the other protagonists Faulkner had created up to this
point in his career in that he functions as the narrator of his
own story, recounting the events from a distant and mature
perspective. Bayard is thus a more comprehensive and affirmative character than Quentin Compson of either *The
Sound and the Fury* or *Absalom, Absalom!* and he is also a
more nearly heroic character than Old Bayard of *Sartoris*,
nominally the same character, who lacks the intelligence, the
sophistication, and the moral perspective of his later avatar.
In *The Unvanquished*, as he did on so many other occasions,
Faulkner looked back to a character he had developed previ-

ously, providing in the process an entirely new assessment of that character, with new additional substance.[10]

In the counterpointed stories of *The Wild Palms* (1939) Faulkner developed a structural manifestation of the theme of responsible action. Harry Wilbourne and Charlotte Rittenmeyer violate the standards of the community, first by choosing adulterous love over tedious respectability and finally by risking the criminal abortion that leads to the death of both Charlotte and her unborn child. The tall convict, by contrast, rejects opportunity to re-enter the community by accepting the risk of love, choosing instead to return to the safety of the prison. Between grief and nothing, Harry chooses grief. The tall convict, faced with an analogous choice, takes nothing, though in surviving the flood and delivering the baby he shows himself capable of significant action, and in the process demonstrates many of the attributes traditionally associated with the hero.

The Hamlet (1940) in many respects seems to constitute a reversion on Faulkner's part to his earlier world view, for the novel is often as pessimistic and despairing as *Sanctuary*. Flem Snopes acts decisively, but from rapacious self-interest. The community of Frenchman's Bend is debased. Ratliff, who offers himself as the champion of the right, is ultimately defeated, for he too is a victim of the pride and greed that taint nearly all of the major characters. By winning Eula in romantic combat with her other suitors, Hoake McCarron acts decisively, but he is unable to accept the consequences of his action and lights out for Texas. Will Varner and Jody attempt to thwart Flem, but, like Ratliff, they are ultimately beaten at

10. See, for example, Mary M. Dunlap's analysis of Gavin Stevens, "William Faulkner's 'Knight's Gambit' and Gavin Stevens," *Mississippi Quarterly*, 23 (Summer, 1970), 223–40, and Estella Schoenberg's *Old Tales and Talking: Quentin Compson in William Faulkner's "Absalom, Absalom!" and Related Works* (Jackson: University Press of Mississippi, 1977).

their own game. Ab Snopes and Mink Snopes, in their roles as barnburner and murderer respectively, are prototypical anti-heroes, who act decisively by destroying the settled order of the community. Flem's triumph in Frenchman's Bend is complete, his success in Jefferson is foretold, and there is no clear-cut anticipation of the successful opposition he would eventually encounter in *The Town* and *The Mansion*.[11]

In *Go Down, Moses* (1942), another novel derived significantly from short story materials, Ike McCaslin acts decisively in a moral effort, but he does so in a negative fashion, repudiating his family and relinquishing his property. Sam Fathers, though he acts to instruct Ike, remains solitary. Major de Spain, Walter Ewell, Ash, and the others of the hunting camp constitute a kind of community, but it is a community of the greenwood, which serves only as their temporary means of escape from the quotidian world of Jefferson. In *Go Down, Moses*, those who act do so on instinct, without reflection or conscious will, as the dog Lion attacks Old Ben, and as Boon Hogganbeck risks his own life to save the dog whom he loves. In the "Delta Autumn" section, Ike, now grown old, talks hopefully of meeting the threat of the Second World War, but his words are belied by his behavior in his encounter with the woman at the hunting camp. The verities of the human heart, of which so much has been made in discussions of "The Bear," seem to be developed and sustained only in the diminishing context of the wilderness. They are not, at least for Isaac McCaslin, transferable to the civilized community.

If *Light in August* marks the beginning of the second stage of Faulkner's attitude toward the possibility of effective moral action, *Intruder in the Dust* (1948) marks the beginning of a

11. In insisting on the autonomy of the three volumes of the Snopes trilogy, I differ from the two most extended studies of the trilogy that have so far appeared: Warren Beck, *Man in Motion: Faulkner's Trilogy* (Madison: University of Wisconsin Press, 1961) and James Gray Watson, *The Snopes Dilemma: Faulkner's Trilogy* (Coral Gables: University of Miami Press, 1968).

third stage. In this novel, and in all the novels which follow it, Faulkner develops a situation in which his central character attempts to act positively, and achieves some significant results. Following the instructions of Lucas Beauchamp, Chick Mallison, Aleck Sander, and Miss Eunice Habersham act to restore order to the community. They discover the truth about the Gowrie murder, of which Lucas has been falsely accused, and Miss Habersham repels a subsequent threat to the communal order by preventing the lynching of Lucas. The roles of these three characters are thus differentiated from that of Gavin Stevens, whose essential function is to talk, articulating the mixture of bigotry and good will in the Jefferson community. Justice, Faulkner seems to be saying, is possible, but it is by no means inevitable, and it is achieved, in this instance, only as a result of extraordinary concerted action. The contrast between *Intruder in the Dust* and earlier Faulkner fictions dealing with similar themes and situations is profound. Consider the cooperative effort to save Lucas in contrast to Horace Benbow's lonely and unsuccessful effort to save Lee Goodwin in *Sanctuary*, or Gail Hightower's brief and pathetic gesture on behalf of Joe Christmas in *Light in August*, or Hawkshaw's tentative struggle on behalf of Will Mayes in "Dry September." Those who maintain that Faulkner invariably preferred the past to the present, it seems to me, ignore the evidence of *Intruder* and of Gavin Stevens's declaration of his own improvement in the title story of *Knight's Gambit*.

Requiem for a Nun (1951), like *The Unvanquished*, shows Faulkner returning to a character he had developed in a previous novel, with strikingly different results. Nancy Mannigoe has acted decisively, at risk, with the motive of preserving order in the family which she serves. The means of her action, however, are such that she dooms herself, even though she contributes to the redemption of Temple Drake Stevens.

Gavin Stevens defends Nancy, as Horace Benbow had attempted to save Lee Goodwin, and Gavin, unlike Horace, at
least manages to complete the salvation of Temple. In the
prose interchapters of the novel Faulkner again availed himself of the contrapuntal technique, describing the creation of
communal order in "THE COURTHOUSE (A Name for the
City)" and the preservation of communal order in "THE JAIL
(Nor Even Yet Quite Relinquish————)."

A *Fable* (1954) constitutes Faulkner's most extended and
explicit treatment of the theme of individual action. The mutiny against the war represents the ultimate risk and the final
sacrifice for all who join it. Faulkner's approval of the mutiny,
regardless of its effects, is explained in part by a statement he
made at Charlottesville: "I think that man's free will functions
against a Greek background of fate, that he has the free will
to choose and the courage, the fortitude to die for his choice,
is my conception of man, is why I believe that man will endure. That fate—sometimes fate lets him alone. But he can
never depend on that. But he has always the right to free will
and we hope the courage to die for his choice."[12] The Corporal and those who join with him have the grandest ambitions:
to stop the war and to reestablish the peace, first through
mutiny and finally through martyrdom. Like Gail Hightower,
Harry, the English groom, relinquishes his isolation and enters into humanity.

In *The Town* (1957) Flem Snopes continues to act selfishly
and usually effectively, though he is now opposed by Gavin
Stevens, Ratliff, and Chick Mallison. Gavin works for a vir-
tuous and harmonious order at the expense of his own appetites, but he is incapable of acting effectively on his own behalf or on behalf of the community, try though he may. Unlike

12. *Faulkner in the University: Class Conferences at the University of Virginia,
1957–1958*, Frederick L. Gwynn and Joseph L. Blotner, eds. (Charlottesville: University of Virginia Press, 1959), 38–39.

Gavin, Ratliff knows that Flem has been bitten by the bug of respectability, and may, therefore, be successfully opposed on occasion. But it is Eula, more than any of the other characters, who acts to restore some semblance of order to the community whose standards of behavior she herself has violated. Her suicide, whether or not it is the result of boredom, constitutes a self-sacrifice of expiation and redemption, for her death pays the wages of her sin with Manfred de Spain and frees Linda from Flem.

The Mansion (1959) is, as Faulkner said, the final chapter of a work conceived and begun in 1925, but it is brought to a very different conclusion from that Faulkner had envisioned at earlier points in his career. Flem's destruction, immediately by Mink Snopes, arguably by his own self-destruction, and also as a result of the machinations of Linda, has been questioned by critics who believe it to be a contrivance, based on the questionable assumption that Snopesism will destroy itself. But *The Mansion* also reflects a deeper view. As Faulkner explained,

> the impulse to eradicate Snopes is in my opinion so strong that it selects its champions when the crisis comes. When the battle comes it always produces a Roland. It doesn't mean that they will get rid of Snopes or the impulse which produces Snopes, but always there's something in man that don't like Snopes and objects to Snopes and if necessary will step in to keep Snopes from doing some irreparable harm. Whatever it is that keeps us still trying to paint the pictures, to make the music, to write the books—there's a great deal of pressure not to do that, because certainly the artist has no place in nature and almost no place at all in our American culture and economy, but yet people still try to write books, still try to paint pictures. They still go to a lot of trouble to produce the music, and a few people will always go to hear the music. . . . It's a slow process but yet it apparently goes on. That we will even outlast atom and hydrogen bombs—I don't know right now how we will do it but my bet is we will.[13]

13. *Ibid.*, 34.

Faulkner had expressed similar views much earlier—for example, in Ike McCaslin's optimistic prediction of the destruction of Hitler in "Delta Autumn"—and he demonstrated this
belief in *Intruder in the Dust, Requiem for a Nun,* and *A
Fable,* as well as in *The Town* and *The Mansion.* In the latter
novel Ratliff, Gavin, and Chick again act in concert, with occasional success. Linda and Mink act independently and de-
structively, but at the end of the novel Snopesism is van-
quished, order is restored, and the values of a benevolent
community are reaffirmed.

The Reivers (1962) shows a variety of characters who act
decisively, with an interest in the community. Lucius, as the
agent of Everbe Corinthia's reform, is the most obvious example. The emphasis in *The Reivers* is on cooperation, on
honor among thieves. The final resolution depends not only
on Lucius, but also on Boon Hogganbeck, Miss Reba, Sam
Caldwell, Uncle Parsham Hood, Mr. Poleymus, and most especially on that shrewdly intelligent trickster, Ned William
McCaslin. Those who act selfishly and against the interests of
the community, such as Otis, Butch Lovemaiden, and even
McWillie, are immediately opposed and finally overcome.
Order is restored, horses and automobiles are returned to
their rightful owners, and Everbe Corinthia is saved from
shame and accepted into the generating community. Lucius
Priest, taught to "live with it," acknowledges his own
transgressions and assumes the role of the Ancient Mariner,
telling his story to his own grandchildren.

What patterns, then, can be observed in Faulkner's repeated investigations of the heroic problem? As I have suggested, there seem to me to be three distinct stages. The
first, which includes the novels from *Soldiers' Pay* through
Sanctuary, posits a world in which heroic action is precluded
by the weakness of individuals, the corruption of the community, or a combination of both. The second stage, which

includes the novels from *Light in August* through *Go Down, Moses*, features a number of individual characters who are capable, at least occasionally, of making the heroic attempt, on behalf of a community which is at least partially worthy of the risk, though the gestures are frequently unsuccessful, and though the community may not be initially pure or finally redeemed. In the third stage, which includes the novels from *Intruder in the Dust* through *The Reivers*, Faulkner presents situations in which his protagonists, usually acting in concert rather than in isolation, act consciously and often effectively to oppose evil and to create, preserve, or restore a benevolent communal order. This pattern of Faulkner's development is by no means as clear, simplistic, or inevitable as this bald outline might seem to suggest. There are elements of comedy and affirmation in his earliest fiction, there are elements of tragedy and despair in his later fiction, and the novels of the middle period are individually and serially so compounded of a mixture of these elements that one is tempted to resort to the expedient of calling them "transitional." Nevertheless, I think the pattern of Faulkner's evolution is a clear one, following a movement from situations of paralysis and despair for his early protagonists, through situations of heroic gesture in the middle period, to situations of cooperative action in the novels of the last phase. Faulkner's attitude toward the community itself undergoes a similar change; from the deeply satiric attitude toward Charlestown in *Soldiers' Pay*, toward New Orleans in *Mosquitoes*, and toward Jefferson and Memphis in *Sanctuary*, he moved to the thoroughly mixed community of Jefferson in *Light in August* and the other novels of the middle phase, to an essentially benevolent community in the last novels.

Faulkner always was, as George Marion O'Donnell asserted in 1939, a traditional moralist, in the best sense. He was not, however, always an optimist. But if we consider the possibility that he judged his own characters by the same standard he used to judge his writing contemporaries and his own works—that the best are those who attempt the impossible and fail gloriously—if we reapply the heroic standard that I have described, we should see, I believe, that Faulkner's protagonists move through a wide variety of possibilities along any of the moral lines we may choose to draw. The advantage of the developmental method is that it enables us to perform the initial and difficult task of reading Faulkner's individual fictions with care and, at the same time, to undertake the larger task of describing, analyzing, and evaluating the entire range of his achievement, coming to terms with the thousands of links, large and small, in the intricate chain of his works.

Alternative critical methods seem to me to be limited. Their chief limitation is in their quest for abstract absolutes, for the perfect Platonic Faulkner. This sort of endeavor has yielded some provocative results, but these results seem to me to limit and reduce our capacity for understanding and appreciating the splendid individualities of Faulkner's fiction. Let me take a controversial example from recent criticism. In the essential structure of Faulkner's work, John T. Irwin writes, "the struggle between the father and the son in the incest complex is played out again and again in a series of spatial and temporal repetitions, a series of substitutive doublings and reversals in which generation in time becomes a self-perpetuating cycle of revenge on a substitute, the passing on from Father to son of a fated repetition as a positive or negative inheritance."[14] This structure, Irwin admits, "exists in no single Faulkner novel nor in the sum total of those novels; it exists, rather, in the space that the novels create *in between* themselves by their interaction. The analysis of one

14. Irwin, *Doubling and Incest/Repetition and Revenge*, 157.

novel will not reveal it, nor will it be revealed by an analysis
of all the novels in a process of simple addition, for since the
structure is created by means of an interplay between texts,
it must be approached through a critical process that, like the
solving of a simultaneous equation, oscillates between two or
more tests at once."[15] The key to the critical oscillation, as
Irwin describes it, is Quentin Compson in *The Sound and the
Fury* and *Absalom, Absalom!* Irwin's demonstration is at least
partially attractive for, if Faulkner's art is a sequence of arrested motions, the constituent elements of each arrested
motion form a *tableau*, and it is possible to isolate just the
sort of pattern that Irwin identifies. If we examine Irwin's
paradigm developmentally, however, if we search for the differences among the *tableaux* as well as for the similarities,
then we can see that even within the Oedipal situation there
are patterns of difference as well as patterns of sameness. Irwin's analysis, for example, could be used to explain a number
of aspects of "Knight's Gambit," particularly the relations
among Max Harriss, Melisandre Harriss, Captain Gualdres,
and Gavin Stevens, but one should also note that Faulkner's
sympathy and approbation have shifted from the youthful
brother-avenger to the mature father-figure. The paradigm
can also be observed with a difference in *Light in August*,
where the seducer Lucas Burch is simply dismissed, while
the avenger, Byron Bunch, satisfies himself with the beloved
rather than with revenge, with the full approval of the father-
figure, Gail Hightower. The same paradigm is treated in
comic fashion in *The Town*, where the seducer, Manfred de
Spain, and the seduced, Eula Varner Snopes, as well as the
supposedly wronged father-figure, Flem Snopes, seem to
conspire in amiable cuckoldry against the ethical avenger,
Gavin Stevens. And in *The Reivers*, Lucius Priest's revenge

15. *Ibid.*, 157–58.

on the corrupting Otis helps to redeem Everbe Corinthia and effect her matrimonial reconciliation with Boon Hogganbeck. There are even, I think, illuminating differences between the paradigm as it is rendered in *The Sound and the Fury* and *Absalom, Absalom!*, for, by omitting allusions to Caddy and to Quentin's suicide in the latter novel, Faulkner suggests a conclusion for Quentin that is something less than the despairing absolute.

The developmental method, I believe, can be applied as a descriptive and analytical tool to many other kinds of Faulknerian repetition: to his attitude towards his women characters, or to his attitude toward the possibility of racial justice, to his treatment of the Civil War or of World War I, or to his use of the narrator as protagonist. I do not mean to hold to a doctrine of Faulknerian progress, to maintain that the novels of his later phase are "better" in either the aesthetic or moral sense than his earlier works, but I do believe that studying Faulkner developmentally will yield rich specific evidence of the many changes that take place in his fiction, whether we are disposed to approve of them or not.

The functions of the artist, as Faulkner understood them, are, after all, essentially identical to the functions of the hero, as defined here. The artist's perennial first duty is to create, drawing on the resources of his intelligence, his imagination, and his heart, a harmonious order, by means of which the individual reader may survive in peace and dignity. The artist also preserves evidence of such order as may have existed in the past, whether it is the order of the wilderness or of the Sartoris courage. And finally the artist defends the meaningful order of the present when it is threatened, by Sutpen or by Snopes, and he seeks through his art to restore a disordered community by presenting models for personal and communal action.

Faulkner, throughout his fiction, sought to preserve the

images of peace and harmony that are worthy of preservation,— though he often did so by presenting their negatives in human conduct, the tragic and pathetic failures as well as the occasional and partial successes. His fictions, and the characters who give them life, are not monuments to individual pride and vanity, grotesque marble effigies of the tomb. They are, rather, the bold and tragical and austere performances that represent the best that has been said and thought because they embody the best that has been done in our fiction. They are the rich and sustaining achievement of his myriad heart.

Faulkner in Time

ELLEN DOUGLAS

For years then I forgot you, I put you down,
ingratitude is the necessary curse
of making things new. . . .

Your high figures float
again across my mind and all your past
fills my walled garden with your honey breath
wherein I move, a mote.
John Berryman
The Dream Songs, 312

When Professor Harrington asked me to take part in the conference on Faulkner this year, my immediate response—particularly to a man who knows a great deal more about Faulkner's work than I do—was that I am not a scholar or a critic
and, therefore, perhaps not qualified for his faculty. I am a
writer of novels. As soon as I said that I was a writer, not a
critic, however, I thought of something else: almost everyone
who cares about the arts is interested in *process*, in how a
writer, an artist, becomes what he is and does what he does;
and although I am not an authority on Faulkner, I am qualified to talk about process in myself. The connection between
Faulkner and what I know about writing books is that not
only to me, but, I believe, to every Southern writer of my
generation, those of us who were young in the nineteen thirties and nineteen forties, Faulkner has loomed at one time or

284

another as a huge part of the process of learning to write; that he contributed largely to how we became what we are and do what we do. His work has affected me in different ways at different times. Not only did the work—his vision of the world—change in his later years, but my needs and capacity to put his work to use changed too.

I decided that I might try to analyze these changes, to call back, if I could, what it was like for me, as an adolescent and young adult, a beginning writer, growing up in the South in Mississippi and Louisiana during the depression and war years, to read Faulkner for the first time; to talk about the powerful spell he cast upon us all; to recall also the point at which his work was no longer relevant to me and to ask questions about why that came to be true—What happened to the spell? To his work?—and finally to say something about my rereading this year of the major works after our long separation.

It is difficult, but not, I think, impossible to shovel away the sediment laid down by forty years of reading, writing, and experiencing the world and go back to one's early adolescence, the Eden of one's adult reading—to re-imagine first the child, then the emerging adult.

First, the child: I had read obsessively, uncritically from my seventh year. I believe that a child reads as he runs and swims, because he can, with compulsive joy in the act, in growing, acquiring skills. I remember that by the end of the first few weeks of a school year I would have read through all my textbooks and would be frantic for more books, more texts, more stories, more printed words. I remember a curious habit I had, when called on in class to read aloud, of reading to myself a paragraph ahead, simply because I couldn't talk as fast as I wanted to read. I remember an almost unconscious immersion in language, sensation, emotion, make-believe—the *story*. I remember sitting down, plunging into a book, hearing nothing, aware of no one for hours at a time.

I remember, too, the kinds of books I liked best: Fairy stories to begin with—Anderson and Grimm; then the adventures and travail of heroic children and princes and outlaws—Elsie Dinsmore, Oliver Twist, Robin Hood; and a little later, savage tales of the jungle, Gothic ones of ruined houses, tortured heroes and heroines—Edgar Rice Burroughs and Poe. Sometimes—often—I would be trapped in the house of one of my grandparents whose library was—in my terms—disgracefully limited. To feed my habit, I would read Foxe's *Book of Martyrs* or all four volumes of *The Rise of the Dutch Republic.*

Reading was like playing. I plunged into it and was wholly taken up with the make-believe. In short, it was very close to being a function of the unconscious. But, just as, from the tree where I was hiding from a pack of savage head hunters, I heard and finally responded to the call to supper, so I roused reluctantly from my reading and took a bath or did my homework or went off to Sunday School with my sisters. That is, without difficulty or even thought, I separated the make-believe from the real world.

It goes without saying that I was always writing too. I suppose I wrote my first poems at the age of seven or eight. They were based on ballad form or on the hymns I sang every Sunday in church. I wrote plays for my sisters and friends to act and stories that I read aloud to my mother. Like reading, like play, this too happened mostly at the unconscious level. Never mind parsing sentences, organizing paragraphs, or learning to "speak the king's English," as my mother put it. Inside my head the language box was humming like a powerful transformer, pouring dreams and fantasies into the forms and language furnished me by Poe and Burroughs and Dr. Watt.

Then, in adolescence, something happened to the language- and myth- and make-believe-smitten child. It happened abruptly, immediately, and specifically in relation to two things I read, things so disparate that they serve to illustrate not only the kind of change I am talking about, but also the relation of the emerging adolescent to the world of literature. As a child, of course, I had not read "literature." I had absorbed myth, adventure. I had no tools to make even the most rudimentary literary judgments. I was at the very beginning of becoming a human being.

At fifteen I read one day Milton's "On His Blindness." I suppose I must have had to read it for a high school English class—along with "Thanatopsis" and "The Legend of Sleepy Hollow" and *As You Like It* and Gray's "Elegy," none of which moved me deeply at the time. They couldn't compare with *John Carter, Warlord of Mars*. But the Milton sonnet hit me like a ton of brick. I don't know why. I sometimes think it may have been because my mother was deaf and I lived every day a witness to her stoicism and resourcefulness. But I don't remember thinking of her at the time. What I thought was Milton was a *man*. He was blind. This marvelous poem is about what it is really like in the real world to be blind. It is about human fate. Tarzan and John Carter and "For-the-love-of-God, Montresor," the Little Mermaid, and Robin Hood receded into the mists of childhood.

Not long afterwards I read what is probably a fairly lightweight book—I don't know. I haven't seen it again in the intervening forty-odd years—a memoir by a leftist American journalist, Vincent Sheean, called, I think, *Personal History*. (Was it a Book-of-the-Month Club selection? I remember at the same time the appearance on our book shelves of *Kristin Lavransdatter*, and I can't believe my mother bought either out of genuine interest.) In any case I read it and the same insight moved me: This man is writing about the struggles of real people in the real world, about the real effects on their lives of political and economic systems. *So that's what writers do!* welled up like a shout, broke over my horizon like the rising sun. Books, the books that I love above all else to spend my time with, are the great tools for understanding one's life and the lives of other people.

It was not long after this, after I had consciously made this first adult discovery, that I wrote my first "real" story and that I read my first book by Faulkner. My story, I remember, although I had not yet read Faulkner, had a sublime disregard for probability that would have done him proud. It was about an old black man whose place in the world is defined by his mystical, almost magical ability to predict the rises and falls of the river and who, when his prediction proves wrong, walks into the flood and drowns himself, singing the while, "Ole Man River, He don't say nothin. . . ."

Now, as I begin to talk about how the first reading of Faulkner affected me, you should put out of your minds two orders of thinking and feeling: first, what the scholar and critic, the teacher, looks for when he is reading, and second, what the general reader looks for. Beginning writers are not beginning critics and they are not beginning general readers. The critic and teacher look for ways to fit a writer into his tradition, ways to locate and analyze him for the student. They identify trends and map literary landscapes. The general reader looks first for entertainment, then (if the writer is lucky) for aesthetic pleasure and stirred emotion, finally, for insight into the human condition. But obsessively, selfishly, single-mindedly, again, almost unconsciously, the beginning writer *uses* other writers—just as I unconsciously used hymns and fairy stories, *imitated* them. He says, "What's in it for me?"

He may not even ask that question, but he absorbs and uses, must use, other writers to become himself, to find his own window in the house of fiction, his own focus and frame for the world of his art, to learn to hear his own voice. He

precariously clings, at the beginning, like a small new leaf to
the top of a supporting tree whose branches are the giants of
modern literature and whose roots reach back to Homer and
Vergil and the Old Testament prophets. He must read to hear
the voices of his tradition and to find where he belongs in it,
where he may be fortunate enough to move it and to contribute to it. He reads to learn the great questions. His reading
gives him his language and his grasp of form. It gives him
something else as well: It contributes, along with his own experience of the world to his unique ordering of his experience, to his moral and ethical vision.

How fortunate and at the same time how overwhelming,
indeed, almost paralyzing for a young Southern writer, sixteen years old in 1938, to lay her hand on a book by William
Faulkner, the man whose voice was that very moment in the
act of shaping the modern perception of the world she lived
in. Doubly, triply fortunate and overwhelming. In every way
I felt the joyous sensation of *coming home*. Here were my
outlaws, my heroic children, my heroines riding—oh, joy!—
into battle with their lovers, my good witches and bad
witches, even a jungle! And here, simultaneously, was the
adult world I had begun to grope toward, not as it had been
for Milton in seventeenth-century England or Sheean in New
York or in Russia, but *here, now*, the very streets, the very
houses, the very people by whom I was surrounded. And all
in a language more seductive, more powerful than any Edgar
Rice Burroughs ever dreamed of.

The book was *The Unvanquished*, published early that
same year. I am not sure now who directed me to it, but I
think that out of my own random reading I directed myself.
I did not get it from a library. I went out and bought it. At the
time Faulkner would never have been mentioned in a high
school literature course in a small town in the South. We were
taught, not the people who were making American litera-

289

ture—Hemingway or Fitzgerald or Dos Passos—but those who had once made it and were thoroughly and safely dead— Hawthorne and Irving and Longfellow and William Cullen Bryant.

In any case, I bought *The Unvanquished* and read it and I remember how peculiarly it suited my needs. Put together from half a dozen or so stories which had been separately published in magazines, it was not in any finished, structured sense of the word, a novel at all. In terms of Faulkner's highest standards it was a pot boiler. But that did not trouble me. It was accessible to my uneducated adolescent mind. It was romantic and sentimental. It was about the world I sprang from, and it dealt with the questions that loom all through Faulkner's work and that I would soon begin to address myself to. That is, under the treacle I lapped up so readily were the moral issues that Faulkner had from the beginning heroically addressed: the temptation to violence, the nature of heroism, the indissoluble marriage of love and hate between white and black, the pernicious nature of respectability, the obligations of the individual to society—and everything laid out in that rolling, hypnotic, irresistible language. Like the glittering lure that the young and reckless bass snaps at without thought, the stories, to begin with, caught my eye. The hooks caught me.

The following winter, as a freshman in college, I read *Light in August*. I had read the first book as scarcely more than a child. I read the second as the adult world began to open out before me. Here was no potboiler, but a novel whose power seemed to me unquestionable. It moved me from where I was to some place else. Again, I go back and try to shovel away the intervening layers of experience and remember what it was like to be what I then was—seventeen, an upper middle class Southern girl from an unusually pious radically sheltering family, a freshman in one of those colleges for young ladies in Virginia, struggling frantically, almost hyster- ically to escape the rigid world in which I was expected to function happily.

At first thought, it seems to me now that the unbending character, the terrible suffering, the crucifixion of Joe Christ- mas would have been so utterly foreign to me that I would have been unable to grasp their significance. The monstrous McEachern, the insane Hightower, the sex-obsessed Joanna Burden—what had these people to do with me? No one had ever struck me with anything heavier than a fragile china- berry tree switch. I thought *whore* was pronounced *wore* be- cause I had only seen it, not heard it spoken. And then I remember that at sixteen and seventeen I was not so shel- tered as my parents might have wished and believed me to be. I was observant and I listened. I knew well enough that a black man had been lynched the year we moved into the little central Louisiana town where we lived. I had seen the hungry faces of beggars at the kitchen door, the ragged tenant farmers riding into town on Saturdays in their wagons. I was already in love. I knew how important sex would be to me. And more. I could take these characters in, not only in their relation to the real world I knew, but in relation to the world of myth and fairy tale from which I was emerging. And it is true, too, that I had learned from my first day in Sunday School that moral meanings, ethical meanings were a reality in that sheltered, rigid Presbyterian world.

And what spun like a tornado into my life, all indissolubly one—language, form, and story—was the product of one man's moral vision, moral obsession. Faulkner, I saw, wrestled titanically with that threatening, fascinating, com- plex, confusing world into which I had begun a puny struggle to make my way. He was obsessed with what it was at that moment essential for me to be obsessed with. The questions that every writer must in some fashion face, he faced in terms

291

of the world that I looked out at from my window in the dormitory at Randolph Macon Women's College, asking: What does it all mean? How can I write about it until I understand what it all means?

I did not know then that what I have called "process"—the process of making something—is the way the artist *finds out* what he means, that what he means is the work of art. But I have only to check my preoccupation with Faulkner against my other preoccupations at the time (I had begun to read Conrad and Dostoievsky) to recognize that in every case it was the problem of the moral order of the world that obsessed *me*.

Again, in *Light in August*, I hit upon the book which, at that age, in terms of my own situation, was most useful to me. Not *Sanctuary*, to which I might easily have gone, since it was already in the Modern Library and which, I might add, had a scandalous reputation particularly attractive to the sheltered young college freshman from the devout Presbyterian household. And not the others of his great books which might have presented to my unsophisticated mind even larger difficulties in form—*Absalom, Absalom!* or *As I Lay Dying* or *The Sound and the Fury*. *Light in August* gave me immediately the kind of experience that I could take in and squirrel away.

There was, first, of course, the terrible dilemma of the white black man or the black white man who was crucified on the cross of racial hatred. And then, equally immediate to me, there was the role of the Protestant church in the moral life of the South—McEachern's cold vindictive Calvinism, Doc Hines's insane religious perversion of sexuality, Gail Hightower's equally insane perversion of the pulpit to the glorification of the past. These issues—What does one do about being white (or black)? What does one do about being a Presbyterian (or an atheist)? What does one do about the

Civil War? Hate it or fall back into it?—were the issues I had at that time to take account of.

Then there were other things that I began to observe, again almost unconsciously, about art, about writing. There was the careful and convincing development of the story, so that the reader moves along always thinking, And next? What happens next? There was the balanced counterpoint of the tragic story of Joe Christmas with the comic one of Lena and Byron, stories so disparate, yet so artfully joined, the marvelous plotting that joins these two to the story of Gail Hightower. There was the richness of specific detail, the glory of the language. And yet almost nothing was sentimental. All was solid and powerful and fully imagined. And the characters themselves, in part because the form was accessible, were more accessible to me than, for example, I could possibly have found Benjy in the opening monologue of *The Sound and the Fury* or Quentin as he is presented in *Absalom, Abaslom!* or any of the characters in *As I Lay Dying*. *Light in August* gave me, too, concretely, realistically, at a time when I needed to learn to think in specifics, the appearance and behavior of real people, people on a human scale (Lena and Byron), to counterbalance the monstrous incarnations of Doc Hines and McEachern.

I have three more things to say about Faulkner's power over my imagination then. I went on reading. The summer after *Light in August* I probably read *Pylon* and *The Wild Palms*. By 1944 I had read *Absalom, Absalom!*, *As I Lay Dying*, *Sanctuary*, and the stories in *These Thirteen*, and I had tried and failed twice to work my way through *The Sound and the Fury*.

First, I was continuing to learn from him things about my craft that would stand me in good stead. I could test the speech of his characters against the speech of the people in my region, as I heard it, and begin to develop my ear. I saw in the real world the landscape that he so powerfully imagined in his books, and I tested it against my own imaginings of that landscape. I learned about moving a story along through using, successively, different points of view as glasses through which to see the action. I began to learn how to withhold information and maintain suspense—as I saw him do it both convincingly and unconvincingly.

Second, his language exercised a power over me that was almost hypnotic. Like all young writers who fall under the spell of a master, I imitated his style, not because I tried to, but because I couldn't help it. For a time I saw, as it were, with his eyes. Particularly, I absorbed, and I hope finally turned to my own uses, a power of evoking with passion the specific in the natural and the human world. Listen to this from *Old Man*. (The convict has just rescued the pregnant woman from a tree and is trying to control a frail skiff in the middle of a flood):

> . . . he crouched, his teeth bared in his blood-caked and swollen face, his lungs bursting, flailing at the water while the trees stooped hugely down at him. The skiff struck, spun, struck again; the woman half lay in the bow, clutching the gunwales, as if she were trying to crouch behind her own pregnancy; he banged now not at the water but at the living sapblooded wood with the paddle, his desire now not to go anywhere, reach any destination, but just to keep the skiff from beating itself to fragments against the tree trunks. Then something exploded, this time against the back of his head, and stooping trees and dizzy water, the woman's face and all, fled together and vanished in bright soundless flash and glare.
>
> An hour later the skiff came slowly up an old logging road and so out of the bottom, the forest, and into (or onto) a cottonfield— a gray and limitless desolation now free of turmoil, broken only by a thin line of telephone poles like a wading millipede. The woman was now paddling, steadily and deliberately, with that curious lethargic care, while the convict squatted, his head between his knees, trying to stanch the fresh and apparently inexhaustible flow of blood from his nose with handfuls of water. The

woman ceased paddling, the skiff drifted on, slowing, while she looked about. "We're done out," she said.

The convict raised his head and also looked about. "Out where?"

"I thought you might know."

"I don't even know where I used to be."[1]

How could a young writer not try to do as well as this? I *should* have been overwhelmed. I should have imitated Faulkner. *It's the way one learns to write.* But at the same time I was beginning to learn from his lapses to try to avoid the sentimental, to look with skepticism at overstatement everywhere I found it.

Third, I was beginning to know what a phenomenon Faulkner was. Although almost everything of his was out of print, although he was regarded with scorn by most of the current literary establishment, a network, almost a secret society of people in the South *knew* what he was—the American writer of the twentieth century who was laboring most heroically, most largely to understand and present the human predicament in our time, who had grappled with the history and tragedy and comedy of his own country and his own people, who dared, as he put it, to fail as largely as he could. How could I not make my obeisance to that passionate and incorruptible ambition?

I see him now. I was at the University of Mississippi in the early 1940s and I *did* see him crossing the square in Oxford, small, self-contained, the arrogant handsome head held high, the eyes clear and sharp, the mouth secretive, the disciplined body, as I sometimes thought, too small, too fragile to contain the whirlwind of his genius. He wanted to say it all.

And then something happened. I began to feel, not drawn to, but repelled by the hypnotically repetitive, overblown,

1. William Faulkner, *The Wild Palms* (New York: Random House, 1939), 152–53.

latinate language. I began to question as gratuitous the obscurities in some of the work. I began to feel insulted by what came to seem to me his cavalier disregard of the reader's intelligence. Never mind, he seemed to say, never mind if I said one thing on page 12 and another on page 312. Never mind if I contradict myself. You haven't sense enough anyhow to remember by page 312 what I wrote on 12. And besides, I haven't the time or the patience to check it out. And the sentimentality, the romanticism of my adolescence was being tempered, radically altered by the beginnings of maturity. I read with impatience and irritation as well as with pleasure and awe *Go Down, Moses* and *The Hamlet*. I skipped *Knight's Gambit*. I did not finish *Intruder in the Dust*. I read *Requiem for a Nun* and was horrified by the bombast, the weaknesses in motivation, the groaning of the plot. That was it. The bond, the spell snapped. I read no more.

During those 25 or more years when I no longer read Faulkner, I used to say to myself that perhaps I experienced that revulsion from his work because he was a threat to me as a writer, because he had so powerfully imagined the world that I, perforce, being also a Southerner, a Mississippian, felt constrained to imagine, that I would never be able to say anything of my own about it, would always be in thrall to *his* imaginings. But I did not think of myself as "Faulknerian." I did not *really* think that that was what had happened.

What did happen? One thing that happened, I feel sure, is precisely the kind of thing that happens when you fall out of love. The magical spell, for whatever reason, is broken. You seem to awake, to open your eyes. In a way, the beloved becomes *himself* instead of a construct of your own imagination. So Faulkner became himself and I looked at him with the cold, and perhaps equally prejudiced, eye of the ex-lover, even though that cold eye did not in fact concern itself much with the past works. I still knew they were just as good as I had believed them to be, as the lover knows that those magic nights of love were indeed magic, no matter that he cannot return to them.

More important, though, and less fanciful, is another suggestion. From my point of view as writer first, before I am reader, something else happened. Faulkner was no longer useful to me. His work bored me, in part, not because it was intrinsically boring so much as because I had my attention on other writers who either continued to be useful or who became useful in the same terms that Faulkner was useful to begin with: Warren, for a while; Mann, Joyce Cary, strange books like *The Notebooks of Malte Laurids Brigge*, monumental works like Campbell's *The Masks of God* and Malraux's *The Metamorphosis of the Gods*. I was through with Faulkner.

But at the same time something was happening to Faulkner's work as well as to my perception of it. More and more, during those years, it seems to me, he wrote glosses on his own works, books that said, "After all, I didn't quite mean what I wrote earlier. We're a lot better than I said we were. Let's change the past—*my* past, the past I have created." A curious characteristic of Faulkner's vision of the world that one notes again and again in his books is the static quality of his images. Listen, for example, to this description from *Absalom, Absalom!* of the first appearance of Thomas Sutpen in Jefferson: "there the stranger was, halfway across the square on a big hardridden roan horse, man and beast looking as if they had been created out of thin air and set down in the bright summer sabbath sunshine."[2] Or this from *Sanctuary*: "They appeared to come from nowhere, to emerge in mid-stride out of nothingness, fully dressed, in the middle of the street, running."[3] His images are framed, frozen, seeming al-

2. William Faulkner, *Absalom, Absalom!* (New York: Random House, 1936), 32.

ways to *appear*, to *disappear*. He invents verbs like "abrupt"—
a character *abrupts* onto the scene. And was it Quentin who
said, "I am not is I was"? In short, I am the past materialized.
I am already dead.

Jean-Paul Sartre in his penetrating essay on time in Faulkner spoke of the "abrupting" of the nonexistent future into
the present in Faulkner's work. He pointed out that in Faulkner's metaphysic, "the present is irrational in its essence; it is
an event, monstrous and incomprehensible, which comes
upon us like a thief—comes upon us and disappears. Beyond
this present, there is nothing, since the future does not exist.
One present, emerging from the unknown, drives out another present. It is like a sum that we compute again and
again." But "the past can be named and described. Up to a
certain point it can be fixed by concepts or intuitively
grasped." And the outline of the past "is hard, clear and immutable. The indefinable and elusive present is helpless before it; it is full of holes through which past things, fixed,
motionless and silent, invade it." Again, "at every point the
consciousness of the hero 'falls into the past' and rises once
more to fall again."[4] This is Faulkner's organic metaphor for
the predicament of the South. The idiot Benjy, for example,
who cannot conceive of a future, to whom all past exists simultaneously, is doomed to fall forever through a delusive
present, clutching at a past, as the South has seemed to be
trapped by its misunderstood past, helpless in a delusive
present. In short, the handling of the subject arises out of the
metaphysic of the author.

Reading Faulkner again these past months, I have found
that this characteristic of his vision of reality has loomed

3. William Faulkner, *Sanctuary* (New York: Random House, 1931), 288.

4. Jean-Paul Sartre, "Time in Faulkner: *The Sound and the Fury*," in *William Faulkner: Three Decades of Criticism*, ed. Frederick J. Hoffman and Olga W. Vick-ery (New York: Harcourt, Brace & World, Inc., 1960), 226–28.

larger and larger for me, and I have come to connect it with what began to happen to his work in the late 1930s and 1940s, why what he wrote seemed to me more and more unreadable—parodic. Thinking again of my adolescence, I see him abrupting into my life, a superhuman presence, seizing a moment, emerging full stride into the present to tell me of the terrible, delusive nature of that frozen Southern past.

Can it be, as it now seems to me, that he became the prisoner of his own metaphysic of time? That he fell increasingly into a past, already delusive, created by him and therefore his to change, the past of his beloved and hated South? This is what I mean when I say that in the later years he began to write glosses on his own work. The tension between that love and hatred for the South, for the world, for the human race, which he had sustained in his most powerful and terrifying work, became unendurable. He, too, fell back into the past of his own work and began to reinterpret it so that it would be less intolerable to him. For example, let me quote here two Faulknerian versions of the significance of the human capacity to endure which will illustrate what I mean. The first is from *Pylon*.

> " . . . and the cab went faster; presently the street straightened and became the ribbonstraight road running across the terraqueous plain, and now the illusion began, the sense of being suspended in a small airtight glass box clinging by two puny fingers of light in the silent and rushing immensity of space. By looking back he could still see the city, the glare of it, no further away; if he were moving, regardless at what terrific speed and in what loneliness, so was it, paralleling him. Symbolic and encompassing it outlay all gasolinespanned distances and all clock- or sun-stipulated destinations. It would be there—the eternal smell of the coffee the sugar the hemp sweating slow iron plates above the forked deliberate brown water and lost lost lost all ultimate blue of latitude and horizon; the hot rain gutterfull plaiting the eaten heads of shrimp; the ten thousand inescapable mornings wherein ten thousand swinging airplanes stippleprop the soft scrofulous soaring of sweating brick and ten thousand pairs of

splayed brown hired Leonorafeet tigerbarred by jaloused armistice with the invincible sun: the thin black coffee, the myriad fish stewed in a myriad oil—tomorrow and tomorrow and tomorrow; not only not to hope, not even to wait: just to endure."[5]

The second, the gloss, is from the Nobel Prize Address.

I decline to accept the end of man. It is easy enough to say that man is immortal simply because he will endure: that when the last ding-dong of doom has clanged and faded from the last worthless rock hanging tideless in the last red and dying evening, that even then there will still be one more sound: that of his puny inexhaustible voice, still talking. I refuse to accept this. I believe that man will not merely endure. He will prevail. He is immortal, not because he alone among creatures has an inexhaustible voice, but because he has a soul, a spirit capable of compassion and sacrifice and endurance. The poet's, the writer's, duty is to write about these things. It is his privilege to help man endure by lifting his heart, by reminding him of the courage and honor and hope and pride and compassion and pity and sacrifice which have been the glory of his past. The poet's voice need not merely be the record of man, it can be one of the props, the pillars to help him endure and prevail.

The contrast between these two passages is not only a contrast between the glorious language of the first and the overblown, sentimental language of the second, it is a contrast between austerity and clarity in moral stance and self-indulgence and confusion. The first puts itself clearly and directly into relationship with Shakespeare—"And all our yesterdays will light the way to dusty death"—and gives us an austere vision of the tragedy of human fate.

The second is meant to transform our view of Faulkner's work, his tragic vision, but it succeeds only in confusing me. Man is not immortal because he has an inexhaustible voice? Why should he be, any more than birds are immortal because they sing? Man *is* immortal because he has a soul? Is this not a tautology? Man is immortal because he is immortal? He will

5. William Faulkner, *Pylon* (New York: Random House, 1935), 283–84.

prevail because he is noble? Is there anything in the long and tragic history of the human race or in Faulkner's own greatest work that will support such a contention? And what is this duty and privilege of the poet's that Faulkner speaks of? At his best, *he* reminds us of man's cruelty and hatred and obsession and madness and greed and whining self-pity. This "endure and prevail"? In every one of his greatest books characters, good and bad, die bitter and meaningless deaths or are thwarted by circumstances or by their own weakness or destroyed by human inhumanity. Rare indeed is the Faulkner character who prevails for more than an illusory moment.

But in the long run it does not matter that in his later years Faulkner could not bring his past, his present, under the kind of furious control that is everywhere evident in his great work. It does not matter that he changed his mind, that the tension slacked. The work is there, indestructible and grand. No gloss of his or of mine or of anyone's can destroy or alter its value or the nobility of the lifetime of dedication that produced it.

Contributors

LOUIS DANIEL BRODSKY, poet and businessman from Farm-ington, Missouri, has had poems in *Harper's*, *Texas Quar-terly*, *The American Scholar*, and *The Anthology of Magazine Verse for 1979*, and has published eight books of verse. He is co-author of "Faulkner's 'L'Apres-Midi d'un Faune': The Evo-lution of a Poem" in *Studies in Bibliography* and a book, *The William Faulkner Collection of Louis Daniel Brodsky: A De-scriptive Catalogue*. The Department of Archives and Special Collections of the University's John Davis Williams Library exhibited portions of his collection during the 1980 Faulkner and Yoknapatawpha Conference.

PANTHEA REID BROUGHTON is the author of *William Faulk-ner: The Abstract and the Actual*; co-author of *Literature*; and editor of *Walker Percy: Stratagems for Being*. She has also published numerous articles about Faulkner and others, and for the past several years has reviewed Faulkner scholarship in *American Literary Scholarship*. She is an associate profes-sor of English at Louisiana State University.

JAMES B. CAROTHERS wrote his dissertation on Faulkner at the University of Virginia in 1970. His teaching interests are modern American fiction, American humor, fiction writing, and baseball in American literature. He is currently finishing a book on William Faulkner entitled *The Myriad Heart*. He is Associate Professor of English at the University of Kansas.

ELLEN DOUGLAS (a pseudonym for Josephine Haxton) is a na-tive Mississippian and an alumna of the University of Missis-sippi. Her first novel, *A Family's Affairs*, was selected by the

303

Contributors

New York *Times* as one of the five best novels of 1962. Her novel *Apostles of Light* was nominated for a National Book Award in 1973. Her most recent novel, *The Rock Cried Out*, was an alternate selection of the Book-of-the-Month Club in the fall of 1979. She lives in Greenville, Mississippi, and is writer-in-residence at the University of Mississippi during the fall semester and at Northeast Louisiana University in Monroe during the spring semester each year.

ROBERT W. HAMBLIN wrote his dissertation on William Faulkner at the University of Mississippi under the direction of John Pilkington, Distinguished Professor of English. Professor Hamblin has published articles on Faulkner in *The Southern Review* and *Studies in Bibliography*. He is co-editor of *Selections from the William Faulkner Collection of Louis Daniel Brodsky: A Descriptive Catalogue*. He is Professor of English at Southeast Missouri State University.

CHARLES H. NILON is the author of one of the earliest examinations of Faulkner's depiction of his black characters, *Faulkner and the Negro*. He is also author of *Bibliography of English Language and Literature*. He is secretary of the American Literature Section of the Modern Language Association of America and a professor of English at the University of Colorado.

FRANÇOIS L. PITAVY, Associate Professor in American Studies at the University of Dijon, France, is the author of articles appearing in both American and French journals. His study of *Light in August* was published by Indiana University Press in 1973. Translator of *Absalom, Absalom!* and *Pylon*, Professor Pitavy is, along with André Bleikasten, in charge of the continuation of the French edition of Faulkner in the Gallimard Pléiade series.